ReHab

jovis

Fabrizio Paone, Angelo Sampieri (eds.)

ReHab

Living
Inhabitants
Houses

jovis

Foreword

ReHab is a book about housing containing twelve essays on topics ranging from the history of ideas to jurisprudence, from urban planning to the arts. Two visual essays focus on ceramic and wood models. Living, inhabitants, and houses are the three sections of the book. Living is the term used to indicate expressed or attributed meanings of the relationship between residents and houses; inhabitants are considered to be the individuals who use or own houses and their classification; houses are the material objects, homes, used in everyday parlance and in technical processes. Living, inhabitants, and houses can in turn be related to three adjectives: real, imaginary, and symbolic. By real we do not simply mean the physical, material being of the houses and inhabitants, but rather that which reacts to our research studies and provides feedback. By imaginary we mean the collective mental representations of living and houses, found in literature and ways of living, where the social link in the construction of the living imagery is visible (family memories, expectations about the future, representations in time and down through generations, return and reintegration with the original house). The symbolic aspect establishes continuity and discontinuity with the imagery level, delving deep and leading to new meanings. Tackling such general and ostensibly nuanced subjects perhaps involves a certain degree of imprudence. And yet it upsets us to think that we cannot inhabit (the earth, a new house, etc.) or that we cannot desire to inhabit, at least not in the reassuring ways we would like to think. It has led to a hiatus in the discourse on housing; it has prompted recent studies and literature to primarily focus on specific aspects of living and houses (e.g., extreme poverty, immigration, and cohousing) in ways that do not allow us to pinpoint the importance of specificities within a broader framework. In this book, we propose to redefine these frameworks, without fearing to include different disciplinary fields and literature.

Liv

ing

Living

Surprisingly enough, it was only in the mid-nineteenth century that the term "housing", together with the term "urbanisation", rose to the surface of the discourse in European languages. Up to that point, usage and tradition had embraced the issue of dwellings in the city and countryside, indicating a tacit presence. It was then that the "housing question" burst onto the scene, a term coined by the first author who made it possible, Friedrich Engels. The housing question is not related to all houses; it focuses in particular on workers' houses, low-cost and public housing; their shortage, insalubrity, and cost contribute to establishing the guidelines of a social theory concerning the relationships between classes within the production process and the distribution of surplus value. It rapidly became a question affecting all classes (white- collar workers, managers, soldiers, the clergy, etc.), enslaving workers to their job so as to gain ownership of a house, i.e., a long-lasting bond with their workplace and a single affiliation. Engels' approach led to an international concept of housing policies. However, the housing question was disputed; it was part of the framework of a very controversial European mindset, corresponding politically to a scenario of restoration after the revolutions in 1848 and the expansive affirmation of nation states. Regarding housing policies, on one hand, there is a search for maximum efficient public intervention, supported by socialism, and on the other hand, there is a search for minimum efficient intervention by states, interpreted by liberalism.

Meanwhile "living" seems like an everyday word, present in all European languages. The verbal use of the term does not produce murkiness or misunderstandings; it puts forward an action that has something to do with being, with routinely residing. Its proximity is often cited with the verb *habere*, with regards to which living appears to express a sort of possessive paroxysm. When scientific knowledge became a form of collectively validated knowledge, it is at that point that positivism and progressivism emerged and reconfigured the housing field, both as a general historical interpretation of living, and as a proposal to use "housing" within new scientific doctrines of society and politics. Living as an essentially biological problem (statement by Le Corbusier, openly reassuming the nineteenth-century enunciation of the problem) brings to the fore the debt that modern living owes to positivist culture, in particular evolutionism. The reference is in particular to E. Viollet-Le-Duc (1875), *Histoire de l'habitation humaine: depuis les temps préhistoriques jusqu'à nos jours*, Hetzel, Paris, Eng. trans. (1876) *The Habitations of Man in All Ages*, Osgood and co., Boston; and to C. Garnier, A. Ammann (1892), *L'habitation humaine*, Hachette, Paris. Living and forms of habitation correspond and are historically determined. They are arranged in a linear sequence, from the ancient to the modern, from their elemental version to their most complex and varied. The evolutionist idea of housing therefore leads directly to great aporias. This raises several questions: how can we incorporate the forms which evolved independently from the main line of development of the European and Western house (the Japanese house, in particular, the shapes of the dwellings of Native Americans, the Arab house, and many others, in all regions of the world, including Europe)? How can we assess these different houses using a single system of nomination and values? A symmetrical problem appears at the other end of the spectrum: how can we recognise systems of belonging and local rights, based on criteria such as the climate, customs, cultures, and languages, without falling into the trap of absolute relativism?

It is within the idea of living as an evolutionary act that the logical-discursive structures of the archetype and the origin are consolidated. In his book *Essay sur l'Architecture*, Duchesne: Paris, 1753, Paris, Abbot Laugier uses the archetype of the *Primitive Hut* to highlight three interwoven terms: the origin of architecture, the origin of houses, and the meaning of living. Two archetypes are considered in opposition to one another, the *cave* and the *tent*, also thanks to the contribution by Quatremére de Quincey (*Dictionnaire d'Architecture* in: Encyclopédie Metodique, Panckouke: Paris, 1788–1825, 3 vols., partially republished as *Dictionnaire historique d'Architecture comprenant dans son plan les notions historiques, descriptives, archeologiques, biographiques, theoriques, didactiques et pratiques de cet art*, Librairie d'Arieu le Clérc: Paris, 1832, 2 vols.). The three archetypes, the cave, the tent, and the hut, reflect three generative actions. The hut appears to come from the act of shaping materials, assembling them into objects subject to the rules of the art of construction and susceptible to express the idea of perfection. The cave illuminates an action of living that considers man as one who lives in ways similar to those adopted by other animals, selecting and transforming cavities capable of protecting his vital functions when he is most vulnerable, i.e., asleep, sick, or defenceless against the elements, the cold, and high temperatures. The tent expresses the need for movement, migration, the ability to take along the bare necessities that constitute a habitation.

The attempt to codify living within a strict and tendentially univocal conceptual framework took place in the 1920's and 30's thanks to the concept of the *Functional City*. This construct is the core reasoning of a cognitive theory of the city, architecture, and planning, collectively developed by Cornelis van Eesteren and the CIAM (Congrès Internationaux d'Architecture Moderne) held before the Second World War. The four functions of the body of the city (dwelling, work, transportation, recreation) are nourished by reciprocal relationships and become independent variables of the human condition. An effort was made to veer towards living as a mathematical function rather than a biological function, subject to biopolitical regulations by nation states. It's no accident that Otto Neurath— economist, sociologist, and neo-positivist philosopher, member of the Circle of Vienna, privileged interlocutor for the ambitions of functionalist theorists—was on the steamer *Patris II* en route to Athens to celebrate the 1933 CIAM dedicated to the Functional City. Establishing living as a function does not signal the negation of nineteenth-century and bourgeois living (which it nevertheless opposes aesthetically and programmatically); rather, it completes the collective research on housing that began in Europe in the nineteenth century.

However, the meanings of living tend to remain jointly present, rather than cancelling each other out. Two important anthropological pauses help to illustrate the sequence in the production of texts and discontinuities in the rhetorics of living: the two great wars in the twentieth century. They confirm the epochal loss of the important status European states enjoyed in the world's political, economic, and military order. In 1914, there was a sudden lull in the intense, international, problem-solving publications about housing, destined to develop the technical project required for Fordist-Taylorist production. At the same time, the *Lebensraum* concept as the dynamic and expansive relationship between space and population was no longer able to extend the possibility of living on Earth, but on the contrary reinforced the desire for power of all nation states, a process that generated a permanent state of war. The key issue involved conceptually rethinking the role of technology in the transformations of the human societies, and its ambivalence for human wellbeing. Unsurprisingly, in the decades that followed, the metaphors of the "machine" and the "organism" were increasingly used when referring to society, production, and the city. Houses became unusual and optimised "machines for living in", or the more reassuring "housing organisms". The second pause was just as crucial, albeit different, as the first. The theory of living as function and the development of the positive myth of technology were unable to survive the second catastrophic event coming so soon on the heels of the first. The nation states' desire for power, together with public expenditure in the military sector, scientific knowledge, and technical weapons, had reached a point when certain things were possible: the victory of the players at war, the annihilation of the enemy, and even absolute destruction.

The Universal Declaration of Human Rights (UDHR), proclaimed by the United Nations General Assembly on 10 December 1948, is important to understand how living can be included in a new beginning of rights, established by experts from different cultural backgrounds. There are two reasons why the Declaration, translated into 500 languages, is particularly interesting for us: the first is the continued presence of a functionalist approach, ranging from the theoretical features of architecture and modern urban planning to a broader and shared theory of civilisation. The second reason is the enduring difficulty to define housing, which does not appear in the Declaration by itself, like other constructs including freedom, movement, labour, ownership, education, and leisure. The Declaration seems to stop just before affirming the general right to have a house that fits the definition (local or universal?) of minimum standards. Instead, housing is placed in the short list of basic social services, as specified in article 25, point 1: "Everyone has the right to a standard of living adequate for the health and well-being of himself and of his family, including food, clothing, housing and medical care and necessary social services, and the right to security in the event of unemployment, sickness, disability, widowhood, old age and other lack of livelihood in circumstances beyond his control."

In the early fifties, Martin Heidegger presented his dense intervention *Bauen, Wohnen, Denken (Building, Dwelling, Thinking)* to an audience of architects during the conference *Mensch und Raum (Man and Space)*. His essay published after the conference was to become the most quoted text in the decades that followed (in: O. Bartning, *Mensch und Raum*, herausgegeben im Auftrag des Magistrats der Stadt Darmstadt und des Komitees Darmstädter Gespräch 1951, Neue Darmstädter Verlagsanstalt: Darmstadt, 1952, now in: M. Heidegger, *Vorträge und Aufsätze*, Verlag Günther Neske: Pfullingen, 1954). To the extent that living expresses a belonging, it touches on several roots of our being. Living is possibly starting with a position that belongs to ontology and not to the technical development relating to housing (estimate of needs, quantities, costs, entrepreneurial organisation, availability of a bank loan). We can imagine standing next to Cézanne when he talks to Gasquet and says that peasants don't know what landscape is; they don't see it, but they look at the land to assess whether or not it can be cultivated. We can imagine Heidegger listening and agreeing. He would like to do what the peasants do: ruminate on places by instinct until he sees a built habitation emerge between the ground and the sky. We intellectually and artificially recreate the meaning of a spontaneous living. Rather than leading to a season of order for our houses and cities, Heidegger's text instead triggered intellectual experimentation and authorial expressive adventures within a tumultuous theoretical framework.

The essays presented by ReHab focus on the importance of what happened in the first three decades after the war, especially in England. The English situation was crucial to not only dismiss previous theories (which nevertheless survived, but were broken down into big thematic blocks), but also share the commercial and political action produced on a global scale by the United States. The radical nature of the housing and urban policies that were implemented, especially New Towns and the Greater London Plan, represent a sort of catharsis compared to the urban and territorial imbalances that England had allowed to develop during the advent of the industrial era. Towards the end of the 1940s, it was clear that a new situation of international influence had been launched regarding events within each individual state, the latter's development models, and housing policies. The subject was basically downgraded in the visions of communist countries after putting aside the visionary explorations of the early twenties in the USSR, especially the house-communes in which the advent of New Man would have ushered in New Living, and after having quenched the unrepeatable parenthesis of Red Vienna (1919–1933). Relations of production and the functioning of the economy are considered priority issues compared to housing; the private sphere is declared to be antithetical compared to political participation. So, in essence, there is no housing problem because housing goods cannot be treated separately. Housing conditions are established after first having tackled the rationalisation of industrial production, agricultural labour, internal and external empowerment of the state apparatus, and military investments. On the other hand, the states aligned in the joint declaration of liberalism, democracy, and capitalism, enthusiastically produce houses. They also focus on credit policies for segments of the population that must be made to maintain their productive performance and honour their electoral consensus by making ownership of real estate the family's objective. Northern European and Scandinavian social democracies, especially Sweden, The Netherlands, and Denmark, are the countries where new, experimental housing solutions have been tested the most. Housing policies are part of an organic system of welfare measures provided by the state. This European configuration began to show signs of wear and tear in 1973–1974 during the first international oil crisis, testifying to the collective doubt regarding the development model that had been pursued up to that point. The configuration breaks down completely in the 1980s, followed by the worldwide victory of neoliberalism, the multiplication of the international movement of goods, persons, and data, and the overall increase of the effects produced by the anthropisation of the planet.

Living is an evocative concept that can add a positive aura to objects, components, and home automation technologies. New economies that have arisen thanks to globalisation and the increase in design efficiency generated by technical innovations have produced a greater number of houses compared to what was possible in the past. However, the democratisation of this asset has not produced housing equality. Exclusion from adequate housing has increased everywhere compared to previous decades, as the words slums, favelas, bidonvilles, nomad camps, and other names remind us. Housing homologation has assumed forms of selective trivialisation: all over the world there are rooms or houses with electricity and beds and bathroom facilities that are all the same size. A sort of technology-based minimum domesticity that has become universal, while safety has become a satisfactory parameter regarding the possibility to inhabit. Letting the market establish the rules reflects the real, silent, regularly repeated capitalist miracle: establishing the price. Generally speaking, this has reiterated existing preferences and the standardisation of the worldwide presentation of domestic interiors, which is becoming increasingly important in terms of pre-adherence to a sale or to encourage a viewing visit. The freedom provided by free time, smart working, sports, mobility ensured by better education, and the pursuit of job opportunities has led far beyond the rhetoric of living as belonging, in favour of the pleasant appeal of finite accommodation. Hopefully, this will turn into the dream of living with a lighter footstep on the Earth, without the myths of conquering frontiers, without having to affirm or defend the relationship between space and population. Living will thus be achieved through diffuse intelligence in the contextual and affective adherence to individual places, regions, and cities where, instead of establishing a new homogeneous habitat, a topological space will be rendered interpretable thanks to the presence of niches that seem to express areas of self-regulation, where we could even think about living.

This is Tomorrow, one of the exhibition posters, and the catalogue

Sebastiano Roveroni

This is Tomorrow 1956. The Future Is Already Underway

The exhibition *This is Tomorrow* was inaugurated at the Whitechapel Art Gallery on 8 January 1956; the focus of the exhibition was to investigate the near future from an aesthetic and existential point of view. It was set up in one room, divided into exposition modules, each entrusted to a group of artists, architects, or intellectuals. The exhibition was an instant success; almost a thousand visitors a day saw it during its thirty-day run.

One of the visitors was a yet unknown twenty-six-year-old, James G. Ballard. "In 1956, the year that I published my first short story, I visited a remarkable exhibition at the Whitechapel Art Gallery, *This is Tomorrow*. Recently I told Nicholas Serota, director of the Tate and a former director of the Whitechapel, that I thought *This is Tomorrow* was the most important event in the visual arts in Britain until the opening of Tate Modern, and he did not disagree.Among its many achievements, *This is Tomorrow* is generally thought of as the birthplace of pop art. A dozen teams, involving an architect, a painter and sculptor, each designed and built an installation that would embody their vision of the future. The participants included the artist Richard Hamilton, who displayed his collage *Just what is it that makes today's homes so different, so appealing?*, in my judgement the greatest ever work of pop art. Another of the teams brought together the sculptor Eduardo Paolozzi and the architects Peter and Alison Smithson, who constructed a basic unit of human habitation in what would be left of the world after nuclear war. Their terminal hut, as I thought of it, stood on a patch of sand, on which were laid out the basic implements that modern man would need to survive: a power tool, a bicycle wheel and a pistol. The overall effect of *This is Tomorrow* was a revelation to me, and a vote of confidence, in effect, in my choice of science fiction. The Whitechapel exhibition, and especially the Hamilton and Paolozzi exhibit, created a huge stir in the British art world. The artists most in favour with the Arts Council, the British

This is Tomorrow 1956

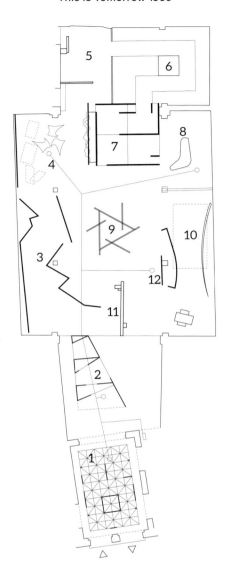

The exhibition plan, 1956
Group 1: Theo Crosby, William Turnbull, Germano Facetti, Edward Wright; Group 2: Richard Hamilton, John McHale, John Voelcker; Group 3: J.D.H. Catleugh, James Hull, Leslie Thornton; Group 4: Anthony Jackson, Sarah Jackson, Emilio Scanavino; Group 5: John Ernest, Anthony Hill, Denis Williams; Group 6: Eduardo Paolozzi, Alison and Peter Smithson, Nigel Henderson; Group 7: Victor Pasmore, Erno Goldfinger, Helen Phillips; Group 8: James Stirling, Michael Pine, Richard Matthews; Group 9: Mary Martin, John Weeks, Kenneth Martin; Group 10: Robert Adams, Frank Newby, Peter Carter, Colin St. John Wilson; Group 11: Adrian Heath, John Weeks; Group 12: Lawrence Alloway, Geoffrey Holroyd, Toni del Renzio

Council and the academic critics of the day were Henry Moore, Barbara Hepworth, John Piper, and Graham Sutherland, who together formed a closed fine art world largely preoccupied with formalist experiment. The light of everyday reality never shone into the aseptic whiteness of their studio-bound imaginations.

This is Tomorrow opened all the doors and windows onto the street. The show leaned a little on Hollywood and American science fiction; Hamilton had got hold of Robby the Robot from the film *Forbidden Planet*. But for the first time the visitor to the Whitechapel saw the response of imaginations tuned to the visual culture of the street, to advertising, road signs, films and popular magazines, to the design of packaging and consumer goods, an entire universe that we moved through in our everyday lives but which rarely appeared in the approved fine art of the day. Hamilton's *Just what is it…?* was a convincing vision of the future that lay ahead—the muscleman husband and his stripper wife in their suburban home, the consumer goods, such as the tin of ham, regarded as ornaments in their own right, the notion of the home as a prime selling point and sales aid for the consumer society. We are what we sell and buy. In Paolozzi's display, the power tool laid on the post-nuclear sand was not just a portable device for drilling holes but a symbolic object with almost magical properties. If the future was to be built of anything, it would be from a set of building blocks provided by consumerism. An advertisement for a new cake mix contained the codes that defined a mother's relationship to her children, imitated all over our planet.

This is Tomorrow convinced me that science fiction was far closer to reality than the conventional realist novel of the day, whether the angry young men with their grudges and grouses, or novelists such as Anthony Powell and C.P. Snow. Above all, science fiction had a huge vitality that had bled away from the modernist novel. It was a visionary engine that created a new future with every revolution, a hot rod accelerating away from the reader, propelled by an exotic literary fuel as rich and dangerous as anything that drove the surrealists".[1]

1   J.G. Ballard, *Miracles of Life. Shanghai to Shepperton. An Autobiography*, Fourth Estate: London, 2008.

An exhibition

Bryan Robertson began to direct the Whitechapel Art Gallery[2] in 1952; this young art critic became very influential in England thanks to the exhibitions he organised at the Whitechapel Gallery. The idea for the exhibition *This is Tomorrow* developed after an intense exchange between numerous players and fine-tuned to focus on issues deemed urgent by members of the Independent Group[3]: architects, critics, painters, sculptors, writers of the younger generation, including Reyner Banham, Richard Hamilton, Eduardo Paolozzi, John McHale, Lawrence Alloway, James Stirling, and Alison and Peter Smithson, who usually met at the Institute of Contemporary Arts in London. After Banham resigned as President, in order to concentrate on his doctoral dissertation at the Courtauld Institute of Art, *This is Tomorrow* was the group's last public initiative.[4]

The exhibition layout was very simple: twelve sections were organised inside the gallery, each assigned to a group of artists, architects, engineers, designers, musicians, writers, and critics. Each group was responsible for providing the works, organising the set-up, and designing the poster of their section. The goal was to obtain maximum expressive pluralism within the framework of a common approach, on a budget that was to be as low as possible.

Ballard's comments, cited above, emphasise the importance of the issues proposed by the young, restless researchers, convinced that they belonged to a new generation, not only

2   The Whitechapel Gallery, in the London Borough of Tower Hamlets, was founded in 1901; it was one of the first public galleries in London to organise temporary art exhibitions. In 1938, it was the first to exhibit Picasso's *Guernica*. After the success of *This is Tomorrow,* it organised the first British one-man shows for Jackson Pollock in 1958 (police were summoned to control the crowds queuing in) and Rothko in 1961, as well as the collective *The New Generation* in 1964 (David Hockney, Brian Ferry, and others).

3   D. Robbins (ed.), *The Independent Group: Postwar Britain and The Aesthetics of Plenty*, MIT Press: Cambridge (MA), 1990; A. Massey, *The Independent Group: Modernism and Mass Culture in Britain, 1945–59*, Manchester University: Manchester, 1995.

4   The common topics and researches among members of the group continued freely between 1955 and 1962, without formal meetings or events promoted with the acronym of the IG.

owing to their date of birth. Post-war conditions and ensuing reconstruction were reshaping international relations, leading to an unusual period in the history of civilisation. The first acknowledgment of this state of affairs is something we could call a relationship with reality, first and foremost human and social reality, in search of a new realism (or neorealism). This begs a question regarding what expressive mediums—transversal compared to traditional fields of knowledge and disciplines—were used to try and critically represent a new reality. It determined a certain fluidity between literary and artistic genres, part of an attempt to combine new aesthetic and existential materials. In the pages of the *Architectural Review*, Banham described *This is Tomorrow* as "an invitation to smash all boundaries between the arts, to treat them all as modes of communicating experience from person to persons (...) modes that could embrace all the available channels of human perception".[5]

The exhibition put across the idea that in the future there would be an upheaval, compared to what British and European citizens were used to. It conveyed the idea that the future was very near and that this new state of affairs had already potentially penetrated the present—something most people were not aware of.

Change, modernity, housing

All this has an enormous impact on housing, on the profound and superficial meanings of living. Richard Hamilton's collage entitled *Just what is it that makes today's homes so different, so appealing?* is emblematic. The work displays a modern sitting room and an urban exterior filled with adverts. The bodybuilder in the scene is holding a huge lollipop in his hand. The woman next to him is wearing almost nothing and has a lampshade on her head. Domestic appliances, especially electrical appliances, are strewn around the room: a tape

5   R. Banham, "This Is Tomorrow", *Architectural Review*, vol. 120, n. 716, September 1956, p. 187.

Just what is it that makes today's homes so different, so appealing,
Group 2 (R. Hamilton, J. McHale, J. Voelcker), R. Hamilton, collage, 1956

recorder, a television, a vacuum cleaner, and a can of tinned ham. An attractive, glittery city is visible outside the window at the rear of the room. Hamilton's collage is not a direct critique of the fledgling consumer society. Instead, it is an attempt to iconically predict the domestic future invaded by the global communication and production logic portrayed outside the window; compared to this logic, nineteenth-century bourgeois interiors will be powerless to resist, neither aesthetically or commercially, and the interiors will lose their decorative neutrality. At the same time, the restlessness of the generation of the Independent Group signals, with a certain existential urgency, that the tension towards modernity and modernisms will no longer be represented by the formal purism with which it had tried to become established in the thirties. Nor will technique be considered in an innocent and fideistic manner, preaching a linear time in which mechanisation would take command and guarantee new collective rationality.

"Doubts or criticisms, depending on the point of view, would quickly arrive, initially fuelled by all those nomad objects that Reyner Banham (Nikolaus Pevsner's very young pupil) used to reconstruct history, considering on an equal footing the Belvedere in the Vatican Museums and the dream cars—Pontiac or Cadillac—imported in very small numbers into England, brusquely disrupting the image of a country still obsessed with the nineteenth century. What can I say? Nothing extraordinary, nothing more than what, during that same period, Nigel Henderson depicts in his photographs, capturing the first neon signs dotted along the streets of London; nothing more than what is portrayed in works by Peter Blake or David Hockney: a new culture, disseminated by magazines, jazz, and comic strips, is now spreading, represented by amazing objects, inhabited by titanic stars like that of the Forbidden Planet, by helicopters with dragonfly bodies that architecture ignores, but which producers of vacuum cleaners already try to imitate, and by wireless radios or televisions. Sensual, mass-produced rather than standardised objects (with the evergreen, classic Volkswagen, launched on the market without a chrome-plated finish or accessories, representing its personified conviction) had one thing in common: they circumvented the tastes of architects, but above all they invaded homes that had already deliberately rejected the common styles of kitsch and deco. This was openly in contrast with the trend initiated by Le Corbusier—who had furnished the Pavillon de l'Esprit Nouveau with industrial furniture and equipment, lamps with factory-style switches and other "clean" objects—that was to lead to the collage in which Richard Hamilton tried hard to furnish a modern interior, literally bombing an anonymous, dull space with deliberately foreign objects. Two figures (a very muscular man with a racket, and a scantily dressed woman with a straw hat) dominate the scene between a tape recorder, a pot-bellied vacuum-cleaner, green plants and a switched-on television, towered over by a ceiling depicting the earth's globe, and a bedcover cut out of a marine landscape on a holiday. Beach, space, figures and objects blur in order to answer a question: Just What Is It That Makes Today's Home so Different, so Appealing? A question that urban planning in the fifties was careful not to consider. Nevertheless, the mobility of these things that upset the room without trying to transform it, these patterns that enlightened it, when the twenties had instead tried to sculpt it, certainly do not represent the only element of uncertainty that mass housing has to solve."[6]

Hamilton's collage was not the only place where domestic imagery was shocked and shaken. Robbie the Robot, capable of eliciting empathy and doing useful domestic chores, was the protagonist of the very successful sci-fi film *The Forbidden Planet* (1956) as well as the protagonist of the installation of Group 2 entitled *We are already living in the future*. The entrance to the installation was a blown-up, oversize photograph of the face of a man with arrows and words on it, inviting people to use their five senses in order to get the best out of their experience of the domestic interior. This perceptive ambiguity was placed next to mass media images and images of popular culture. The walls and floors of the installation referred to geometric art: the surfaces were divided into strips, rectangles, and black and white zigzag elements, representing an art with very strong iconic contents. The everyday objects portrayed in it include: a big bottle of Guinness beer, Marilyn Monroe with her skirt blown up by the wind, a jukebox, Robbie

6   B. Fortier, *Amate città*, Electa: Milan, 1995, p. 123.

the Robot holding a woman who has fainted (taken from the poster of the film), and *The Sunflowers* by Van Gogh, the best-selling reproduction sold in the bookshop of the National Gallery. Image value and use value replace one another, reciprocally activating each other.

The house, the domestic landscape, everyday and ordinary life are no longer "set apart" and separated from the world; they are jumbled by the huge shuffling that comes from the exterior. Bourgeois divisions, reflections of bourgeois living in big twentieth-century capitals (Paris, London, Berlin, Vienna) will survive as special cases, niche markets, or as objects of selective conservation. The marginality that took place in Europe broke onto the scene, and the new centrality of the international middle class was decisive in fuelling consumerism. At the same time, there was growing unease, replacing the division between technique and progressive myths. Man's technological innovations made him the narrative protagonist of his own potential destruction.

From the House of the Future to Patio and Pavilion

The installation by Group 6 (Nigel Henderson, Eduardo Paolozzi, and Alison and Peter Smithson) entitled *Patio and Pavilion* was very different. The group's installation used poor materials; the pavilion, built using leftover wood, was filled with debris and found objects, alluding to a precarious post-war situation. The idea of domestic life in the future is very different also to the one designed by the Smithson's a few months earlier for the annual *Ideal Home* show at the Kensington Olympia in London. In a completely different context, the *House of the Future* was placed inside a high-density urbanised area. The centre of the house was a patio, a garden around which the rooms were arranged. The living areas were not separated by immobile walls, and the shapes of the furnishings were fluid and futuristic. Everything was designed to optimise use and comfort. The *House of the Future* embodied the architectural concepts present in the first phase of the Smithson's work, characterised by trust in technology and in the design of future life.

27

House of the Future. Interior of one-bed town house with central patio garden,
A. and P. Smithson, 1956, *Daily Mail Ideal Home* exhibition
Patio and Pavilion installation, Group 6
(N. Henderson, E. Paolozzi, A. and P. Smithson), 1956, *This is Tomorrow* exhibition

Sebastiano Roveroni

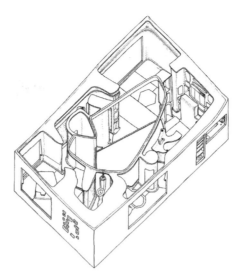

House of the Future, A. and P. Smithson, 1956, *Daily Mail Ideal Home* exhibition

Instead, the pavilion designed for the *This is Tomorrow* exhibition contains a sort of self-declaration relating to the modernist optimism and abstract geometric principles of the International Style. In the catalogue, the designers wrote that the pavilion represented the necessities of the human habitat. The first necessity was to eke out a piece of the world represented by a geometric figure (the patio). The second was an enclosed space (the pavilion). Both spaces are furnished with the symbols of everything man needs. Man appears to be the protagonist of the space; observers are reflected in the metal panels on the inside and thus take part in the set-up, as if it were the reflection of life inside the pavilion before the catastrophic event that put an end to it—life that can also be interpreted using the everyday objects scattered amongst the "ruins" inside the pavilion. The ideal end of the itinerary inside the pavilion is Nigel Henderson's collage entitled *Head of a Man,* depicting a human face created by superimposing photographs of deteriorated material surfaces. While the installation was being set up, Alison and Peter Smithson departed to attend the CIAM X in Dubrovnik.[7]

7   The tenth and last CIAM was held in Dubrovnik from 3 to 13 August 1956. Le Corbusier, Gropius, and Van Eesteren did not attend; an announcement was made regarding the end of the Congresses and the official foundation of Team X to promote the topics of open form and the participation of users.

The house as a work of art

The section curated by Group 8 (architects James Stirling and Michael Pine, artist Richard Matthews) presented several white, gypsum, honeycomb-shaped statues. The walls were covered with photographs of enlargements of organic structures and details of soap bubbles. The curved surfaces of the sculptures created a porous structure, similar to that of a sponge. The organic image of the house of the future was placed in search of a new biological concept of domestic life. The gypsum sculptures in the exhibition could turn into futuristic housing structures.

"Why clutter up your building with 'pieces' of sculpture when the architect can make his medium so exciting that the need for sculpture will be done away with and its very presence nullified? The painting is as obsolete as the picture rail. Architecture, one of the practical arts, has, along with the popular arts, deflated the position of painters, sculptors, the fine arts. The ego-maniac in the attic has at last starved himself to death. If the fine arts cannot recover the vitality of the research artists of the twenties (who through the magazines generated a vocabulary for the practical arts), then the artist must become a consultant, just as the engineer or quantity surveyor is to the architect, though their relationship to the specialist, e.g. industrial designer or furniture maker, would be more intimate for they would be directly concerned with conception. The artist feels the loss of vitality in the formal expressions of art and realizes that his work is more than the satisfaction of a personal and emotional requirement. The elements of painting and sculpture have already lost a sense of descriptive function or intentional indication of scale. They can be extended in size, shape, or role and in the process of interpretation, these are only determined by the superimposition of a finger, a human figure or a crowd. The single element extends by implication from the smallest constructed part, to architecture and to the whole environment without clear individual demarcation. A total sense of environment will only be brought about by people themselves wanting it.

Architects, painters, and sculptors can only help by developing together their means of expression to act as a stimulus to this end, and not by working in a formalist vacuum. This means of expression has already been increased in painting and sculpture through the breaking down of conventional form (elsewhere modern musicians are doing the same). This type of disruption is only about to take place in architecture—the wall at least is beginning to go. The next step will be with the volume of the building, which at present is based on structural geometry. Schwitters' ideal was a cathedral of wood filled with wheels—the static volume disrupted into a dynamic one by implication, for wheels are always revolving even when they are not being propelled. Finally, the total plastic expression (architecture, painting, sculpture) will be in the landscape with no fixed composition, but made up of people, volumes, components—in the way that trees, all different, all growing, all disrupted into each other, are brought together in an integrated dump".[8]

One of the reasons why this young, vibrant piece of writing is so interesting is the scale change regarding the way in which an anthropised environment and its special components are considered. It broke the box-shaped, objectual essence of the house and virtually launched studies that were to lead to the megastructure temptations of the following decades and the assembly of cells and spatial capsules in unusual total structures.

Collage Home

The remarkable success of the exhibition, and ultimately people's interest in it, depended on its compact and centrifugal ingredients. Compact because it was based on a strong approach involving like-minded ideas developed by the Independent Group, in an atmosphere that was clearly shared by a young generation that was about to turn thirty and was just emerging on the intellectual and professional stage. "We reject

8   T. Crosby and E. Wright (eds.), *This is tomorrow*, The Whitechapel Art Gallery, London, 9 August–9 September 1956, s.n.: London 1956, [Group 8, p. 74].

The *Bubble Sculpture* installation, Group 8 (R. Matthews, M. Pine, J. Stirling)

the notion that 'tomorrow' can be expressed through the presentation of rigid formal concepts. Tomorrow can only extend the range of the present body of visual experience. What is needed is not a definition of meaningful imagery but the development of our perceptive potentialities to accept and utilise the continual enrichment of visual material".[9]

The common issues reacted to: reconstruction; the unprecedented destructive potential of the war (rather than of weapons); the new economic and political international scenario; and the direct inapplicability of disciplinary modernity developed in the twenties and thirties. The successful libertarian and recursive approach of the exhibition ultimately revealed personal interpretations, but also a common nucleus of reflections on changes in our environment, something that captured visitors' imagination and affected the housing possibilities of future generations (our houses and the planet).[10]

One strong thematic issue, transversal to the sections, was the way in which we fill our houses. Without furniture, painted in dark colours, and with the superficial nineteenth-century objects of the revolution of the modern, they had revealed, before the war, a new abundance of light, air, and salubrity. Instead, they now began to fill up again with industrial objects (fridges, washing machines, hair dryers, toasters, etc.) and media objects (adverts, ephemeral magazines, electric lights, radio, television, recorders, etc.). Technology was injected into the house (heating, cooling, lifts, etc.). However, this new refilling was heteroclite and bulimic, open, and continuously evolving, not only in Hamilton's collage. The ensuing spatial condition was not a purist simplification, or synthesis of the arts, but one of copresence. Thus, the importance of the collage technique lies in restoring a new, emerging domestic spatiality.[11]

---

9   T. Crosby and E. Wright (eds.), *op. cit.* [Group 2, p. 30].
10   For a short visual tour of the exposition, cf. the footage of the cinema newsreel Pathé, now in: https://www.youtube.com/watch?v=UXvz55V54DI, accessed on 24 September 2021, also showing the contrast between the bewilderment of visitors and the installations.
11   L. Alloway (ed.), *Collages and Objects*, catalogue of an exhibition at the Institute of Contemporary Arts, London, 13 October–20 November 1954,

Visitors during the exhibition

The focus shifted from domestic design capable of infusing substantial aesthetic unity into the domestic institution (an objective pursued by architects, engineers, sculptors, painters, decorators, craftsmen as a synthesis of the arts) to the importance of what was everyday. The domestic scene conveyed by a substantially international civilising culture was not the customary culture linked to everyday objects and their transmigration between generations, but the new advertisement graphics introduced by the exponential enlargement of trade and adverts. This sparked a new, decisive phenomenon for British and European reconstruction inspired by "Americanisation". It's not surprising that the materials in Hamilton's collage are taken from the pages of American magazines. This prompted a strong synonymy between industrialisation, consumerism, the mass media, and Americanisation. It would, however, be more useful to interpret these phenomena from the point of view of their non-coincidence.

Another few years had to pass before this iconoclastic and generationally compact approach manifested its ability to make an epochal change in the music world, with the advent of pop music and the global record industry, the re-discovery of popular traditions on a global scale, the programmatic mix of "high" and "low" genres, the decisive commercial role exerted by the preferences of the middle classes, and, finally, the revived experimental debate regarding the legacy of the past.

Institute of Contemporary Arts: London, 1954. For a review of the collage technique, the genealogy and representations of domestic environments, cf. also M.M. Lamberti and M.G. Messina (eds.), *Collage/Collages dal Cubismo al New Dada*, Electa: Milan, 2007.

Conviction, L. Hellman, 1995

Michela Rosso

London 1972 (and its Surroundings). Modern Architecture Reviewed by History

In 1972, just after the Robin Hood Gardens housing estate (RHG) was inaugurated in the working-class district of Poplar in London, it was stormed by some of its inhabitants.[1] How can we interpret this only ostensibly enigmatic event? A review of its history reveals a rather swift end to the relevance of an event that appears to be the result of a twenty-year study of social housing which, for many people, is still a crucial reference for architectural culture in the second half of the twentieth century.[2]

Criticised from all sides, Alison Smithson pointed her finger at the political responsibilities for the episodes of vandalism and used strong language to describe its inhabitants.[3] Some time later, the scholar Jane Darke tried to explain the problems that arose in the RHG and other popular housing estates in England. Studying the methods and sources behind the projects, Darke declared that the architects' analyses were unsatisfactory, that the assumptions regarding future users and their aspirations were reductive and simplistic, and that the study of their needs was "generic, imprecise and stereotyped".[4]

1   Problems regarding crime, social unrest, and vandalism were the Smithson's main concerns, even before the estate had been completed. Cf. the documentary *The Smithsons on Housing*, BBC Two, 1970.
2   Cf. The Biennale of Venice, in collaboration with the Victoria and Albert Museum, *Robin Hood Gardens. A Ruin in Reverse*, 16th International Architecture Exhibition, Venice, 2018
3   Cf. A. Smithson, "The Violent Consumer or Waiting for the Goodies", *Architectural Design*, vol. 44, May 1974, pp. 274–278; P. Smithson, "Collective Design: Initiators and Successors", *Architectural Design*, vol. 43, October 1973, pp. 621–623.
4   J. Darke, "Architects and user requirements in public-sector housing: 1. Architects' assumptions about the users", *Environment and Planning B: Planning and Design,* vol. 11, n. 4, December 1984, pp. 389–433: 391.

P. Smithson, "Robin Hood Gardens, London E14",
Architectural Design, n. 42, September 1972, pp. 561–562, 571, 569

The early seventies were marked by a series of events which were as emblematic as they were unfortunate; although they did not directly involve architecture, the city, or the built environment, they were destined to profoundly influence the latter's history. The facts are well-known and have been commented and studied, involving nearly all the industrialised West.

The year was 1972: while the apartments and maisonettes in the RHG were gradually being filled by the families of the first assignees, a group of economists, entrepreneurs, and political leaders published a document entitled *The Limits to Growth*. It was in many ways prophetic, finally clarifying the anything but optimistic horizons of a growth which until then had been considered as a tendentially linear, seamless, and potentially unlimited process. A year afterwards, the oil embargo instated after the Yom Kippur War triggered an unprecedented energy crisis throughout Europe. In the meantime, the advent of the new decade saw the demise of the great masters of modern architecture—Le Corbusier, Gropius, and Mies—while in April of that year a decision was taken to use dynamite to demolish two of the thirty-three buildings in the Pruitt-Igoe public residential complex in Saint Louis, believed by many to be one of the symbols of modernist orthodoxy.[5] The problem of how to

5   "Happily, we can date the death of Modern Architecture to a precise moment in time. Unlike the legal death of a person, which is becoming a complex affair of brain waves versus heartbeats, Modern Architecture went out with a bang (...) Modern Architecture died in St Louis, Missouri on July 15, 1972 at 3.32 (or thereabouts) when the infamous Pruitt-Igoe scheme or rather several of its slab blocks were given the final *coup de grace* by dynamite. Previously it had been vandalised, mutilated and defaced by its black inhabitants, and although millions of dollars were pumped back, trying to keep it alive (fixing the broken elevators, repairing smashed windows, repainting), it was finally put out of its misery. Boom, boom, boom", in C. Jencks, *The Language of Post-Modern Architecture*, Academy: London, 1977 (1991 edition, p. 23). A picture of the now famously sad demolition appears, full page, at the beginning of part one, "The Death of Modern Architecture". The caption is meaningful: "Minoru Yamasaki, Pruitt-Igoe, St. Louis; 1952–55. Several slab blocks of this scheme were blown up in 1972 after they were continuously vandalised. The crime rate was higher than in other developments, and Oscar Newman attributed this, in his book *Defensible Space*, to the long corridors, anonymity, and lack of controlled semi-private space. Another factor: it was designed in a purist language at variance with the architectural codes of the inhabitants". Some years earlier the images of the demolition were used as illustrations in P. Blake, "The Folly of Modern Architecture", *The Atlantic Monthly*, n. 274, 1974, pp. 59–66. The sequence of the three successive shots is also present in P. Blake, *Form Follows Fiasco. Why Modern Architecture Hasn't Worked*, Little, Brown & Co.:

critically review the legacy of modern architecture emerged in all its urgency. Rediscussing the issue took place at different levels and in multiple venues: sectoral publications, schools, and exhibitions.[6] Scholars of the economy, society, and culture have provided excellent descriptions of the vigorous attack that was soon to be levied against the modern and the various ensuing forms of disengagement, neo-traditionalism, and revival.[7] The attack was accompanied by radical changes in the economy and social structure of the West: the decline of Fordism as the main production method; the dismantling of its regulatory system (the welfare state)[8]; the advent of a new focus on heritage.[9] But the roots of what was conventionally described as "postmodern" in literary critiques, even before it was expressed in architectural literature, lie in the previous decade: the events that took place in 1968 revealed numerous cracks in society and mass culture. The protests unmasked demands for individualism and local identity, to be juxtaposed against the cold, hermetic, impersonal rigidity of modernism and its alleged "symbolic poverty".[10]

Accordingly, the long decade of the seventies began in 1968, ostensibly a watershed year even for the history of architecture. On 16 May 1968, for example, there was a gas leak on the eighteenth floor of one of the towers of the Ronan Point residential estate in London; four people died and seventeen were injured. The incident was repeatedly cited in British books

New York, 1977, p. 155.

6   See, as an example, the catalogues of three emblematic American exhibitions that took place between 1975 and the end of the decade: *The Architecture of the École des Beaux Arts*, The Museum of Modern Art: New York, October 1975–January 1976; Venturi, S. Brown and Associates (eds.), *Signs of Life: Symbols in The American City*, Renwick Gallery National Collection of Fine Arts: Washington, D.C., 1976; A. Drexler (ed.), *Transformations in Modern Architecture*, The Museum of Modern Art: New York, February–April 1979.

7   Cf. A. Potts, "The New Right and Architectural Aesthetics", *History Workshop Journal,* n. 12, 1981, pp. 159–162.

8   Cf. D. Harvey, *The Condition of Postmodernity: An Enquiry into the Origins of Cultural Change*, Blackwell: Cambridge (MA), 1989; M. McLeod, "Architecture and Politics in the Reagan Era: from Postmodernism to Deconstructivism", *Assemblage,* n. 8, February 1989, pp. 23–60.

9   Cf. R. Hewison, *The Heritage Industry. Britain in A Climate of Decline,* Methuen: London, 1987.

10   Cf. M. Rustin, "Postmodernism and Antimodernism in Contemporary British Architecture", *Assemblage,* n. 8, February 1989, pp. 89–104.

about the history of architecture; it prompted dozens of satirical cartoons[11] and many believed it to be tangible proof of a growing divide between modern architecture and public opinion.[12] Users and their demands began to take centre stage, in both the institutional venues of the disciplinary debate and elsewhere.[13]

The history of the Robin Hood Gardens is part of this complex situation. The estate was completed at the start of a decade defined by many in Great Britain as gloomy, pessimistic, and violent.[14] It was in fact at the turn of the decade that the alleged quality of several emblematic housing initiatives became the focus of audits that were as detailed as they were embarrassing for those working in this field: the pioneering study on Le Corbusier's *Quartiers Moderners Frugès* in Pessac by the French architect and urban planner Philippe Boudon was published in December 1969, with a preface by the sociologist Henri Lefebvre. This was the first time a study highlighted the divide between an architect's initial goals and the end result of a canonical project of modernity.[15] In September 1970, the last of the eight special issues of *Architectural Review*, "Manplan", was dedicated to social housing. The column had been inaugurated in 1969 by Hubert de Cronin Hastings, the owner of Architectural Press and one of the most important editors of the journal; it published a self-critical review of the

11   For an amusing review of these materials, see: C. Knevitt, *From Pecksniff to the Prince of Wales. 150 years of Punch Architecture, Planning and Development 1841–1991*, Polymath: Streatley, 1990; C. Knevitt, *Monstrous Carbuncles: a Cartoon Guide to Architecture*, Lund Humphries-Faber-Castell: London, 1985.

12   Cf. V. Bignell, G. Peters, and C. Pym (eds.), *Catastrophic Failure*, Open University Press: Milton Keynes, 1977.

13   As an example, see the wide range of this kind of experience that characterised the seventies: from attempts to define the models of settlement configurations from the city to everyday spaces, by C. Alexander et al., *A Pattern Language. Towns, Buildings, Construction*, Oxford University Press: New York, 1977, to the participated design practices launched by G. De Carlo in Villaggio Matteotti in Terni from 1970 to 1975, and the successful essay by H. Fathy, *Construire avec le peuple, histoire d'un village d'Egypte, Gourna*, Sindbad: Paris, 1970.

14   Cf. E. Harwood and A. Powers, "From Downturn to Diversity. Revisiting the 1970s", *Twentieth Century Architecture*, n. 10, "The Seventies: Rediscovering a Lost Decade of British Architecture", 2012, pp. 8–35; G. Stamp, "Suburban Affinities", *ivi*, pp. 137–171.

15   P. Boudon, *Pessac de Le Corbusier*, Dunod: Paris, 1969.

Camelot Estate, Greater London Council, Department of Architecture & Civic Design,
London, 1960

contemporary architectural scene and built city and assigned the inhabitants and their needs a preeminent role.[16]

In the meantime, while the most important architectural journal in England sponsored a ruthless review of the state of the discipline—and risked becoming unpopular with its own readers—, the crisis of the paradigm seemed to be a fait accompli, so much so that it was reflected in the mass media. On 20 October 1970, an episode of the popular series Monty Python, entitled "The Architect's Sketch" was shown on BBC Two: the actor John Cleese held up a model of a twelve-storey apartment tower which in actual fact was a slaughterhouse to slaughter residents, while in the next scene, the architect interpreted by Eric Idle, illustrated a model of a multi-storey condominium collapsing in ruins and catching fire.[17] This more or less sarcastic or light-hearted irony used in Great Britain is in fact the way the country prefers to convey criticism and, in this case, use the crisis of the modern to express unusual ideas. The architect Louis Hellman was to declare that the disappointment many felt towards the Modern Movement, so perfectly expressed by the collapse of Ronan Point, was behind his choice to focus on architectural satire. In fact, during that period he created a column of architectural vignettes that are still being published by the weekly Architects' Journal.[18] Hellman was not only a shrewd witness of contemporary events, he was also directly involved in the profession; however, he never appeared to be a fanatic of the neo-Brutalism so dear to the two architects from Newcastle and other protagonists of the contemporary British architectural scene. In one of

16   "Housing, Manplan 8", The Architectural Review, vol. 148, n. 883, September 1970. In March 1969, the critic Reyner Banham, the editor Paul Barker, the geographer Peter Hall, and the architect Cedric Price published an essay in the journal New Society entitled "Non-Plan: An Experiment in Freedom", which they defined as "A precise and carefully observed experiment in non-planning". Six months later, Hubert de Cronin Hastings published his answer in the column "Manplan" in The Architectural Review. Cf. S. Parnell, "Manplan. The bravest moment in architectural planning", The Architectural Review, vol. 235, n. 1405, March 2014, pp. 100–101; V. Carullo, "Tony Ray-Jones and the Manplan Housing Survey", The Journal of Architecture, vol. 23, n. 1, January 2018, p. 168.

17   See "The Architect Sketch", https://www.youtube.com/watch?v=QfArEGCm7yM, accessed on 4 May 2022.

18   L. Hellman, "Something is Happening Here but You Don't Know What It Is", Twentieth Century Architecture, n. 10, "The Seventies: Rediscovering a Lost Decade of British Architecture", 2012, pp. 51–63: 51.

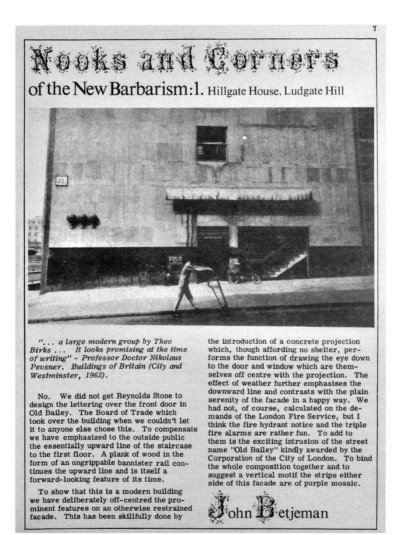

J. Betjeman, "Hillgate House, Ludgate Hill" (first article of the column
"Nooks and Corners of the New Barbarism", *Private Eye*, n. 246, 21 May 1971, p. 7)

his famous cartoons he depicts the Park Hill residential estate in Sheffield as a prison. Questioned on those years, he stated: "To me it smacked of a patronising architectural view of the plebs, 'they love their old slum streets so, I know, let's give them streets in the air and preserve high-rise at the same time. It is sure to please the man in-the-street-in-the-sky and preserve his way of life'".[19]

The catalogue of the documents that reveal the much-altered cultural climate at that time is extensive and one is spoilt for choice. The optimism of the swinging sixties gave way to widespread discontent. Several publications highlighted this trend between 1971 and 1974: on 21 May 1971, the first edition of the column "Nooks and Corners of the New Barbarism"[20] was published in the fortnightly satirical magazine of current affairs and politics, *Private Eye*; it was an unequivocal parodistic reference to the New Brutalism historicised for the first time by the critic Reyner Banham in December 1955 in the pages of *The Architectural Review*. However, the target of the scathing essays by John Betjeman—not trained as an architect, but since the thirties the author of witty, ironic autobiographical essays about architecture[21]—was the mediocrity of so many contemporary British buildings, Brutalist and otherwise. The following year, the Canadian architect Oscar Newman published *Defensible Space. People and Design in the Violent City*, establishing a direct relationship between architectural form, social degeneration, and crime.[22]

19   Conversation between the author and L. Hellman, August 2020.
20   From 1973 to the present day, the column "Nooks & Corners", initially an architectural series of the satirical fortnightly *Private Eye* founded in 1961, provided a hilarious diary of the most controversial architectural and urban planning events in Great Britain. Invented by John Betjeman (1906–84), and initially entitled "Nooks and Corners of the New Barbarism", the column was continued by his daughter Candida Lycett Green (1942–2014) and later by the architectural historian and critic Gavin Stamp (1948–2017) who since the early eighties has signed his stinging articles with the pseudonym 'Piloti'.
21   Cf. for example, J. Betjeman, *Ghastly Good Taste. Or, a Depressing Story of the Rise and Fall of English Architecture*, Chapman & Hall: London, 1933 [revised edition: London: Anthony Blond, 1970]; id., *First and Last Loves*, Murray: London, 1952.
22   O. Newman, *Defensible Space, Crime Prevention through Urban Design*, Macmillan: New York, 1972, published in Great Britain with the title *Defensible Space, People and Design in the Violent City*, Architectural Press: London, 1973.

Shortly afterwards Newman visited the by now infamous Aylesbury Estate. His visit is documented in the 1974 film *The Writing on the Wall* by John M. Mansfield, most of which was actually dedicated to the Pruitt-Igoe complex.[23] The doubts and criticisms raised in many quarters were confirmed by the analyses of more recent constructions, including the Robin Hood Gardens. In 1974, Scot Malcolm MacEwan, trained as a lawyer and editor of the *Riba Journal*, published his book *Crisis in Architecture*; in it he emphasised the historical misunderstanding that had characterised a period of modern architecture, a misunderstanding that the use of the term "Brutalist", in its realist sense of "rough", "crude", and "coarse",[24] had helped to exacerbate: the indifference of a class of professionals to the aspirations of the final users of said architecture. In line with these criticisms, two years later, the American architect Brent Brolin once again reflected on the Smithsons' contribution to modern architecture.[25] Brolin considered that the origin of the now glaring flaw in communications between architects and their public was the socio-cultural gap between designers and users, as well as the absence of common perception and experiences.[26] Likewise, even the elegant theoretical research undertaken by the Smithsons turned out to be a failed attempt at solving social problems simply by using form[27]; the two designers had developed what they called "form-language" (a glossary of forms they hoped users could immediately interpret),[28] and had identified elements such as the deck street,

23 See: O. Newman, "Oscar Writing on the Wall Horizon Documentary", https://www.youtube.com/watch?v=9KQP_BYuM6k, accessed on 4 May 2022.
24 Traits underlined as far back as the original text on the subject, R. Banham, "The New Brutalism", *The Architectural Review*, n. 118, December 1955, pp. 354–361: 357. "In the last resort what characterises the New Brutalism in architecture as in painting is precisely its brutality, its je-m'en-foutisme, its bloody-mindedness".
25 B.C. Brolin, *The Failure of Modern Architecture*, Studio Vista: London, 1976; in particular the chapter "The New Humanism", pp. 70–87.
26 "If the physical expression of the social pattern is to be understood by the designer and the user, there must be some common ground between them. The problem is that when the user is from a different culture or class than the architect, there are often fewer shared social experiences, and when designers refuse to look at how people actually live and instead establish their own patterns, the lack of common ground is assured", *ivi*, p. 73.
27 "The social aspect is used as a device to justify what is felt to be an innovative form in much the same way that the early modernists used new technical capabilities to justify their new forms", *ivi*, p. 79.
28 "The form-language sets up a dialogue between object and user. The object

ideally able to foster relations between individuals. In a mere fifteen years, the deck street was to inspire diametrically contrasting visions. While in 1962 Reyner Banham considered it somewhat romantically as "the real backbone of social communication", adding that "kids play, mums natter, teenagers smooth and squabble, dads hash over union matters and the pools"[29], in 1976 Brolin used statistics to show that only four per cent of residents used the decks to socialise.[30] As Hellman would note, the gap between theory and practice was reflected in the fracture in the British class system: "They may know what they like, but we know what they need".[31]

And while many authors, both in England and elsewhere, were engaged in deconstructing the myth of the Modern Movement, in 1973 Nicholas Taylor, editor of *The Architectural Review*, author of the radio series *The Island Now*, published *The Village in the City*,[32] extolling the virtues of small provincial towns, considered as the epitome of Englishness and the antidote to tower blocks and comprehensive redevelopments. Taylor writes: "Without a city wall (...) most of us in the industrialized city live in suburbs, and enjoy it; and for Englishmen in particular there's nothing new in this. Thanks to the encircling sea, which serves it in the office of a wall or as a moat defensive to a house, the pattern of settlements has for many centuries differed radically from that in the war-torn countries

suggests how it can be used, the user responds by using it well—the object improves; or it is used badly—the object is degraded, the dialogue ceases", in A. and P. Smithson, "Signs of Occupancy", *Architectural Design*, vol. 42, February 1972, pp. 91–97: 97.

29   In R. Banham, *Guide to Modern Architecture*, Architectural Press: London, 1962, p. 134.

30   B.C. Brolin, *op. cit.*, p. 71: "The street decks seemed like an ideal marriage of traditional ways of life and new architectural forms. Some six years after the residents had moved in, a social worker and resident in Park Hill took a random one-in-five sample survey of tenants to get their reactions to the project. The survey which was published in *The Architectural Review* in 1967, showed that, as a means of access, the decks were very successful (...) But the decks seem to have had little effect as generators of social activities compared to the streets they were supposed to have replaced. Only 4 per cent of the people 'remembered' that they could use the decks as a place in which to stand and talk with their friends".

31   Conversation between the author and L. Hellman, August 2020: "I remember the mantra at the GLC (Greater London Council) that 'They may know what they like, but we know what they need'".

32   N. Taylor, *The Village in the City*, Temple Smith: London, 1973.

of the Continent. Instead of a compact walled mass with formal piazzas and inevitable avenues, the typical English market town such as Lavenham or Chipping Campden has grown gradually as a rambling comfortable sprawl of cottages and workshops and farmyards, responding freely to the logic and local geography, local climate and local family life. There was in fact an instinctive rightness in the landscape of the English cottage long before anyone thought of calling it 'picturesque' or reproducing it for quaint effect".[33]

The almost plethoric list of contemporary documents can stop here; apart from determining the crisis of a dwelling model, they highlight the well-known diffidence of the British towards more radical expressions of modernity and their legendary commitment to national traditions.

While for several years there has been a contemporary renaissance of architectural modernism coupled with the museification in extremis of the RHG, [34] processes involving the privatisation and regeneration of numerous British housing projects have become widespread. While Park Hill in Sheffield (1957–60) and the Barbican (1955–82) and Balfron Tower (1965–67) in London[35] have been listed as Grade II buildings, traces of their original social and political significance have become weak and fragmented. Today, some of these sites are living 'a second life', revealing themselves to be ideal habitats for an emerging class of young professionals.[36] Brutalism, in turn, is experiencing a

33   *Ivi*, p. 7.
34   Cf. G. Ricci, "Imparare dai Robin Hood Gardens per la città che verrà", https://www.domusweb.it/it/speciali/domus-paper/2018/imparare-dai-robin-hood-gardens-per-la-citt-che-verr.html, accessed on 4 May 2022.
35   Park Hill was built by the Sheffield Corporation City Architect's Department headed by J.L. Womersley, based on a design by J. Lynn and I. Smith with F.E. Nicklin and J. Forrester; it was inaugurated in 1961 and declared a Grade II building in December 1998. Balfron Tower, built according to a design by Ernö Goldfinger, became formally part of the catalogue of national monuments in March 1996. The Barbican Centre, designed in 1955–1959 and built in 1962–1982, based on a project by Chamberlin, Powell and Bon for the Corporation of the City of London, was listed as a Grade II building in September 2001.
36   T. Burrows, "Balfron 2.0: how Goldfinger's utopian tower became luxury flats. The selloff of Erno Goldfinger's landmark building in Poplar is a central element of a new plan to transform London's East End", *The Guardian*, 19 September 2019, https://www.theguardian.com/cities/2019/sep/19/balfron-20-how-goldfingers-utopian-tower-became-luxury-flats, accessed on 4 May 2022.

new golden age in a cultural market increasingly greedy and eager to obtain images to be turned into models and new trends: this has led to the advent of numerous publications focusing on providing a purely aesthetic interpretation of this season of British and international architecture, much more complex and stratified than they wish to portray. [37]

37   Recent studies include: J. Gatley and S. King (eds.), *Brutalism Resurgent*, Routledge: Oxford, 2016; B. Calder, *Raw Concrete: The Beauty of Brutalism*, William Heinemann-Penguin/Random House: London, 2016; B. Highmore, *The Art of Brutalism*, Yale University Press: New Haven, 2017; D. Deschermeier - Wüstenrot Foundation (ed.), *Brutalism. Contribution to the international symposium in Berlin 2012*, Park Books: Zurich, 2017; C. van Uffelen, *Massive, Expressive, Sculptural: Brutalism now and then*, Braun Publishing AG: Salenstein, 2017; J. Grindrod, *How to Love Brutalism*, Batsford: London 2018.

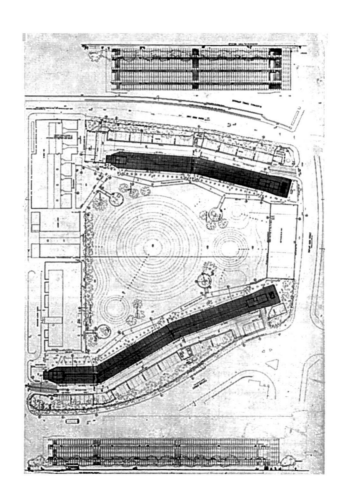

Robin Hood Gardens, site plan and street facades
(A. and P. Smithson, "Gentle Cultural Accommodation", in B.B. Taylor (ed.), "Team 10+20",
L'Architecture d'Aujourd'Hui, n. 177, January/February 1975, p. 6)

The Robin Hood Gardens.
Model or Failure?

A disputed destiny

The Robin Hood Gardens public housing complex (from now on RHG), designed and built in East London between 1966 and 1972, was commissioned by the London County Council, later the Greater London Council (1965–1966). Designed by the famous duo of British architects, Alison and Peter Smithson, from 2007 to 2017 it was the focus of a lively debate between two opposing factions: those in favour of demolition and those who preferred conservation.[1] Today we know how that conflict ended: for those who maintained that the RHG had to be eliminated from the skyline of the British capital, the decision to demolish the complex to make way for an ambitious urban redevelopment plan was only implemented in August 2017; on the other hand, when demolition was underway, the initiative by the Victoria and Albert Museum to acquire an entire 'maisonette' and display it at the Venice Biennale in 2018—before making it part of its own permanent collection—tangibly embodies the reasons proposed by those who, over the years, had fought to save the complex designed by the Smithsons. But how did this conflict start?

From the second half of the eighties, after the last docks were abandoned, the borough of Tower Hamlets launched a series of urban regeneration policies in a neighbourhood still chiefly occupied by the working classes. Driven by deregulation, the borough council decided to open this market to private

1   This contribution is based on the doctoral research by A. Ronzino: *Unpacking Robin Hood Gardens. The troubled history of a British public housing project (1952) 1963–1972 (2018)*, supervised by professors M. Rosso and P.A. Croset. The research traces the RHG project from its conception to its early years by systematically organising and studying archival material (Harvard University; London Metropolitan Archives, Tower Hamlets Archives in London), and the descriptions provided by the architects in their publications and ensuing critiques ten years after its completion.

investors, who quickly turned the Isle of Dogs district into a business centre rivalling the City. In the early years of the twenty-first century, the Greater London Authority and the London Borough of Tower Hamlets—owners and administrators of the land where the RHG was located—started to discuss how to develop the plot. In a very short space of time, the regeneration plan—the Blackwall Reach Development Frame-work—was drafted in August 2007 and formally submitted to the authority; it envisaged the demolition of existing buildings to make way for 1,575 new apartments and proposed to leave social housing unaltered, but offered new public spaces, services, and better housing standards. One of the documents provided by the Borough included a Certificate of Immunity from Listing (COI) for the residential complex; if approved by the ministry, it would have prevented the RHG to be listed as a protected building, making it possible to radically transform the area in the future. The COI is a legally binding public document which, if granted by the Secretary of State—after assessment by English Heritage—makes it impossible—for five years after its issuance—for the building in question to be listed amongst the ones to be protected, thereby granting the owners permis-sion to act freely without restrictions or constraints.[2]

In the meantime, the Twentieth Century Society—a registered UK charity (founded in 1979 as the Thirties Society, a name it maintained until 1992) campaigning to study and protect twentieth-century English buildings—became alarmed at news of the proposed demolition. It asked English Heritage to reject the request for immunity and instead list the RHG as a Grade II building.[3] From early 2007 to May 2009—when the COI was finally granted—, disagreement over the fate of the complex became a hot topic for English Heritage, the institution en-trusted with its assessment. After a long debate, the recom-mendations of the consultants committee, in favour of

2   English Heritage, formerly Historic England, is a charity that manages cultural heritage in England. Founded in 1983 as the Historic Building and Monuments Commission for England, it advises the government regarding protection and conservation and works for the Ministry for Digital, Culture, Media and Sports.
3   Grade II protection, a high level of protection in the English regulation, is assigned to buildings of special interest which, once listed, cannot be modified or altered, much less demolished.

conservation, were ignored by the board of trustees; the latter essentially believed that the complex was stylistically and historiographically an obsolete project, neither innovative nor influential enough to warrant protection.

In parallel to the institutional process, the specialist English magazine *Building Design* became the main platform for a public debate regarding the fate of the residential complex. In February 2008, the magazine—directed by Amanda Baillieu—launched a campaign in favour of its protection; she gathered stories and opinions in order to persuade the government of its importance and provided the entrepreneurs with an alternative to demolition tout court.[4] Some of those who inputted into this initiative were internationally renowned professionals such as Robert Venturi, Denise Scott Brown, Richard Rogers, Renzo Piano, and Zaha Hadid, as well as critics and historians including Alain de Botton and Kenneth Frampton, all prepared to point out that the RHG was not only the result of many years of research performed by the Smithsons on the topic of dwelling, but one of the most important modernist buildings in Great Britain.[5] The inhabitants were also able to tell their side of the story, helping to paint a more positive picture of the complex, in sharp contrast to the now stereotyped image of an unliveable, inhuman place fuelled by issues of isolation and anonymity.[6]

Since there was some discussion about the fact that several of the decision-makers had political interests at heart, Baillieu herself stressed how authoritative groups of experts in architecture and heritage disagreed so intensely about the building they had turned it into a battleground.[7] Despite the decision, the

---

4   A. Baillieu, "To the rescue of Robin Hood", *Building Design*, 22 February 2008, n. 1807, p. 2.
5   Cf. H. Crump, "Big names join BD's campaign to list Robin Hood Gardens", *Building Design*, 22 February 2008; "Venturi, Scott Brown and Hutton among over 500 supporting BD campaign", *Building Design*, 26 February 2008; W. Hurst and R. Olcayto, "Profession rallies to save threatened housing estate", *Building Design*, n. 1808, 29 February 2008, p. 1; D. Shariatmadari, "Prizewinners throw their weight behind Robin Hood Gardens campaign", *Building Design*, 4 March 2008, accessed (under submission only) on 21 January 2020.
6   R. Olcayto, "It's a great place to live, absolutely", *Building Design*, 29 February 2008, n. 1808, pp. 8–9.
7   A. Baillieu, "Putting politics over heritage", *Building Design*, 16 May 2008,

"A veritable history of housing since the 19th century is recorded in this area.
The Grosvenor Houses which have been demolished and Robin Gardens
which takes their place are separated by one hundred years."
(A. and P. Smithson, "Gentle Cultural Accommodation", in B.B. Taylor (ed.), "Team 10+20",
L'Architecture d'Aujourd'Hui, n. 177, January/February 1975, p. 6)

debate raged on, and in the summer of 2009, in order to keep the building in the limelight, an exhibition entitled "Robin Hood Gardens Re-vision" [8] was organised at the Royal Institute of British Architects. However, the arguments behind the diatribe were based on a deeper and more radical conflict that saw the RHG balanced between being considered an exemplary housing model, starting with its designers, and at the same time, a spectacular failure by contemporary critics.

The Robin Hood Gardens for Alison and Peter Smithson

In 1970 (while the construction of the RHG was in full swing), the Smithsons published one of their most famous books: *Ordinariness and Light*.[9] The book was a compendium of articles published between 1952 and 1960, followed by an appendix describing the housing complex still under construction. Their declared intent was unequivocally stated in the subtitle: *Urban theories 1952–60 and their application in a building project*. The RHG was presented to industry specialists as material proof of ten plus years of research on architecture and the city.

Three main issues emerge from the many theoretical questions that were raised. The first is identity and association, and the desire to re-identify man with his home, the community, and the city in which he lives. New architectures were intended to establish physical and symbolic clarity in contemporary Great Society, in a city that had eight million inhabitants and was experiencing another phase of extensive expansion after the post-war reconstruction years. The second spotlighted individual freedom and flexibility. The house—as a private, inviolable space—was a primary element considered by the Smithsons as

n. 1819, p. 2.

8   The curator, Alan Powers, was a point of reference in the battle engaged by the Twentieth Century Society; he collected the most important views that emerged during the discussion and published them in a book: A. Powers (ed.), *Robin Hood Gardens Re-vision*, The Twentieth Century Society: London, 2010.

9   A. and P. Smithson, *Ordinariness and Light. Urban theories 1952–1960 and their application in a building project 1963–1970*, Faber and Faber: London, 1970.

The streetside
(A. and P. Smithson, "Gentle Cultural Accommodation", in B.B. Taylor (ed.), "Team 10+20",
L'Architecture d'Aujourd'Hui, n. 177, January/February 1975, p. 8)

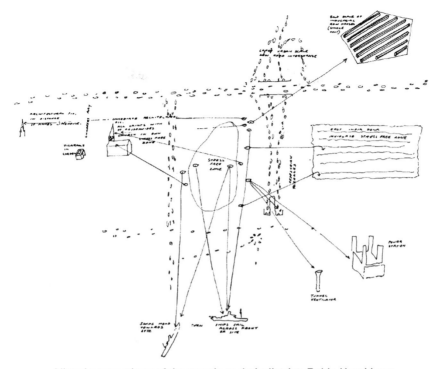

Visual connections of the people to their district, Robin Hood Lane
(A. and P. Smithson, *Ordinariness and Light*, Faber and Faber: London, 1970, p. 191)

having its own complexity, one that had to be taken into account. Automation and industrialisation were revolutionising the building industry, ignoring the unpredictability inherent in man and his needs. Finally, mobility. The Smithsons believed that the challenge launched by the changes and continuous growth of the twentieth-century city could be tackled by working on redistribution and regrouping. They thought of clusters with different densities, interspersed with big green areas, and joined by a diversified road infrastructure and a multilevel load-bearing skeleton to support the transformations.

In the Smithsons' introduction to the appendix, they explain how, due to the size and complexity of the site, their task was the first genuine opportunity to apply their ideas to a real case of residential housing. Although the project was considered to be the engine behind a radical renewal and relaunch of the whole neighbourhood, in actual fact, the brief text written and

"Space: it is a void which gives substance to the masses"
(A. and P. Smithson, "Gentle Cultural Accommodation", in B.B. Taylor (ed.), "Team 10+20",
L'Architecture d'Aujourd'Hui, n. 177, January/February 1975, p. 7)

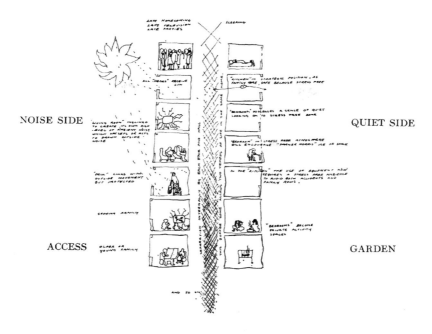

Reasoning behind the disposition of accommodation, Robin Hood Lane
(A. and P. Smithson, *Ordinariness and Light*, Faber and Faber: London, 1970, p. 199)

accompanied by tables and a few design sketches was chiefly intended to illustrate technical issues; it did not clarify how their aforementioned theories materialise in their compositional and design choices. Another opportunity—again in 1970—was the documentary produced by BBC Two, *The Smithsons on Housing,* in which the story about the RHG, presented by the authors as "a model, an example, and a new mode of urban organisation" focused entirely on describing their choices.[10]

The architects believed that the industrial site and its identification with the characteristic elements of the surroundings provided several opportunities: the coming and going of boats passing the bend in the Thames, the wharves of the old East India Docks, the chimneys of the power stations, the railway, but also the nearby Church of All Saints; these were all

10   B.S.W. Johnson, "The Smithsons on Housing", BBC Two Documentary, London. Broadcasted on 23 June 1970 (9.00 p.m.), 38', https://www.youtube.com/watch?v=UH5thwHTYNk, accessed on 4 May 2022.

territorial signs with which the layout and height of the two building blocks had to relate and establish an active dialogue. Flexibility is visible in the patterns of the spaces in the communal areas (the central green zone with different heights, materials, and equipment designed to satisfy the needs of children of different ages) and the decks[11] with their horizontal layout along the buildings, designed in such a way that their size created specific areas of fruition. This modulation also continued in the internal layout of each apartment where two separate areas were envisaged: the night areas for rest and silence facing the internal garden, and the relational spaces, the living room, towards the road. Finally, mobility. The high-traffic roads located on three sides of the RHG site were a feature that the two architects had to deal with immediately. Apart from the implementation of methods to reduce acoustic pollution, they separated vehicular and pedestrian traffic; the former was assigned a space intentionally lower than the road.

Unfortunately, this new and different attempt to explain to a non-specialist public, in the clearest and most direct manner possible, the choices and principles that inspired the shape of the complex did not elicit a positive response. The first reactions from the producer Bryan Stanley William Johnson and the director of BBC Two appear to confirm the difficulties the architects faced when they tried to explain the theoretical scope of their work. Several of Johnson's better known words reveal how effective communication was an obvious problem during the whole ideation and creation of the documentary, a problem which, despite all efforts, remained unsolved. "It's not what you say—but the way you say it, you are NOT talking to other architects but to a secular public—don't complain if they demolish your standpoint because you haven't explained things in a way they can understand".[12] Today, these words seem to herald a destiny that was to involve not only the documentary, but also the building itself.

---

11   The term *deck* in architecture can have multiple meanings and applications; as far as the RHG is concerned, it represents a horizontal circulation path outside the homes, used to access one's apartment.

12   J. Coe, *Like a Fiery Elephant. The Story of B. S. Johnson*, Bloomsbury USA Academic: New York, 2005, Italian trans. *Come un furioso elefante. La vita di B.S. Johnson in 160 frammenti*, Feltrinelli: Milan, 2011, p. 339.

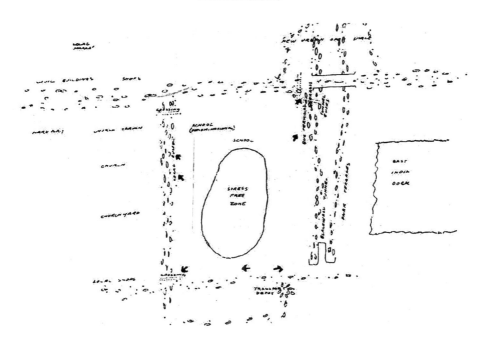

Traffic pattern. Desired routes of tenants district, Robin Hood Lane
(A. and P. Smithson, *Ordinariness and Light*, Faber and Faber: London, 1970, p. 189)

Defining a failure

In the years following the closure of the worksite, i.e., the early years of the building's life, the incommunicability of the project was to become one of the main arguments used by architectural critics and historians in their critical interpretation of the RHG. In his book *Crisis in architecture* (1974), Malcolm MacEwan—editor of *The Architect's Journal* and *RIBA Journal*—asked how the Smithsons' declared social and cultural goals had failed so miserably during the fifties (the episodes of vandalism and violence inside the complex were common knowledge). In answering the question, he talks about the authors' deep-rooted incomprehension vis-à-vis the public for whom they designed their works.[13] MacEwan believed that the

---

13   M. MacEwan, *Crisis in architecture*, RIBA Books: London, 1974; in particular, reference is made to the "Introduction", pp. 6–10, and to the chapter "Modern architecture", pp. 11–24.

Smithsons—typical exponents of the middle class living in the suburbs—talk about 'community' and 'association', but in actual fact were not part of any community except for their own social group and the intellectual circles to which they belonged; they were therefore estranged from the working class for whom they designed their architecture and the needs they wish to portray.

Two years later, in 1976, the opinion expressed by Manfredo Tafuri and Francesco Dal Co in *Architettura Contemporanea* was no less critical.[14] Their reflections on the spaces for relationships and meetings, as well as the originality of the suspended roads (the decks) intended to embrace and facilitate the casualness of urban life, were assumptions only partially achieved by the design experience of the RHG; these assumptions were better portrayed in the Park Hill complex in Sheffield designed by Lewis, Womersley, Lynn, and Smith.

Charles Jenck, in his *The Language of Post-Modern Architecture*, conclusively presented the RHG as the synthesis of several aspects believed to be behind the crisis of modern architecture.[15] The mistake made by the two British architects boils down to a more general tendency to decouple the symbology suggested by the architects, using the language of architecture, and the meanings—most of which are unpredictable—assigned by the public. In the case of the RHG, the Smithsons' commendable intentions to ensure identity and recognisability are negated by the built form which, on the contrary, suggests homogeneity and anonymity.

In the early eighties, Kenneth Frampton and William Curtis wrote, amongst other things, two authoritative and successful histories of modern architecture; they confirmed and conclusively crystallised an image of the RHG which, albeit emblematic of a specific and fertile season of reflections on architecture, remained a failed model.

14   M. Tafuri and F. Dal Co, *Architettura Contemporanea*, Electa: Milan, 1976; in particular the chapter "Il panorama internazionale degli anni '50 e '60", pp. 372–388.
15   C. Jencks, *The Language of Post-Modern Architecture*, Academy: London, 1977, in particular the chapter "The Death of Modern Architecture", pp. 9–37.

One of the last critiques, listing all the most important reasons why it should have been demolished, was the description of the RHG published in 1984 in the *Guide to London* edited by Peter Murray and Stephen Trombley. They used adjectives like "limited", "colourless", and "indefensible", ultimately implying that the problems of the RHG were vandalism and the negative feelings which, more in general—from the early seventies—had been the dominant sentiment towards high-density public housing.[16]

16   P. Murray and S. Trombley (eds.), *Modern British architecture since 1945*, F. Muller: London, 1984, p. 48. See also the books by O. Newman, *Defensible Space: Crime Prevention through Urban Design,* MacMillan: New York, 1972; and J.G. Ballard, *High Rise*, Flamingo: London, 1975.

Kim family house, still from the movie *Parasite*, director Bong Joon-ho, 2019

Luca Reale

Whatever Happened to People? Re-inhabiting the City

"First life, then spaces, then buildings. The other way around never works"[1], Jan Gehl

The debate on housing revolves around several main issues: diversification of family nuclei (singles, separated couples with children, non-resident students, immigrants, city workers, senior citizens living alone or with a care worker); predominance of conversions over newly built homes (densification or regeneration of the public city, repurposing of abandoned structures); multiplication of uses and requirements (house/work, cohousing, new lifestyles and ways of living). These issues increasingly prompt the creation of spaces and solutions that are flexible in time and space. Certain keywords of the past have become topical again: reconsideration of high-density housing, thanks to an awareness regarding limited terrain; differentiated supply of housing types, triggered by the atomisation of families and the fragmentation of users' needs; spatial and temporal flexibility of housing and the amount of associated outdoor space; quality and comfort juxtaposed against standards; greater graduality in passing from social sites to private and domestic spaces.

For years, we thought the problems of residential housing to be the undetermined nature of space "between houses" and the loss of a link between building and street. Projects and studies focused on interstitial spaces, on the in-between, on more or less surgical densifications. Is it possible that by focusing on morphology and space we ultimately neglected the simple issue of the underutilisation of existing heritage? We concentrated on urban density or, better still, on the lack of a sufficient

1   https://thedeveloper.live/podcasts/podcasts/first-life-then-spaces-then-buildings-the-other-way-around-never-works-, accessed on 12 February 2022.

minimum density, ignoring the fact that what is currently almost always lacking in public residential housing are the inhabitants, even when buildings are congruent and spaces are "resolved". Could it be that the crisis of the public city, rather than the shortage of urban density, is caused by the loss of "human" density? In the last few decades, there has been a drop in the number of inhabitants in big public residential complexes, in Rome for example, with an ensuing loss of vitality and the gradual disappearance of services and activities in the neighbourhood or district.

This is a two-headed argument about the European contemporary city: on the one hand, the demographic crisis (declining birth-rate, youth emigration, rather low incoming migratory flows) and, on the other, great inertia towards action. This can undoubtedly be due to regulatory issues or the lack of funds, but it also signals that these places are unattractive.

Space yet again

Let's review the past for a moment. In the late eighties, the phrase invented to publicise a car (Renault *Espace*) was: "What if real luxury was space?" This concept (space), so obvious and at the same time vaguely elusive, weathered the season of modernity—just think of Luigi Moretti's amazing magazine *Spazio*[2]—and was equally invoked by postmodern architects, and by the so-called architects of the *other modernity*[3] as well, by everyone who was, in other words, more or less critical towards functionalist orthodoxy.

Ever since the advent of modernity, the concept of space has ultimately played a privileged role in design, understandably so when compared, for example, to the concept of time. For architects involved in residential housing in the early decades of the twentieth century, space was the home, the environment

2   The editorials, including all the original drawings, have been republished in: L. Moretti, *Spazio. Gli editoriali e altri scritti*, Martinotti: Milan, 2019.

3   T. Avermaete, *Another Modern: The Post-War Architecture and Urbanism of Candilis-Josic-Woods*, NAi Publishers: Rotterdam, 2005.

in which inhabitants moved; it was defined by their movements and possible actions based on the extensive information in disciplinary handbooks focusing on the measurements of the human body (anthropometry, ergonomics), the minimum distance of the furnishings, and the layout of the rooms.

The architects who worked during that period concentrated not only on finding a solution for low-cost housing (specifically for blue-collar workers), i.e., a minimum-sized apartment at an affordable rent, but also a tangible way of revolutionising the structure of the city. So, on the one hand, the size of the home according to minimum standards was a spatial architectural issue, sometimes involving even the furnishings, e.g., the famous Frankfurt kitchen with its "U-shaped" layout designed by Grete Schütte-Lihotzky in 1926.[4] On the other, it was an experiment involving space in terms of the relationship between the home and the city, first at district level. In Italy, this was the season of the public housing through the double seven-year Ina-Casa period[5]—and then at city level in the sixties and seventies through its "formally completed parts", based on the principle of "standard size", if we consider the earlier season of the so called *167 Zones*[6], and the large public residential projects in general.

The two levels, the two design and research scales (housing and urban planning), veered in different directions. The free plan concept that was to become and remain so popular in the layout of houses up to the present day (e.g., lofts, flexibility, etc.), was on the contrary to become increasingly unsuccessful

4   Grete Schütte-Lihotzky's kitchen played an important role in the history of industrial products. After it was used in Ernst May's *Siedlungen* in Frankfurt, 5,000 units were produced each year. It became one of the most popular mass-produced pieces of furniture (its cost fell from 400 to 280 German marks thanks to the large number of manufactured units).

5   The INA (Istituto Nazionale per le Assicurazioni)-Casa interventions during the reconstruction in Italy were instituted by the Law n. 43, 24 February 1949, *Measures to increase workers' employment, facilitating the construction of houses for workers.* In the two seven-year periods (1949–1956, 1956–1963), about 2 million rooms and 355,000 flats were built.

6   These areas were the sites in which the Law n. 167, 18 April 1962, *Measures to foster the take-over of areas suitable for public housing construction* concentrated public housing after the INA-Casa periods. The areas were individuated by Public Housing Plans (PEEP, Piani per l'Edilizia Economica e Popolare), independently from the city master plans in force.

The so-called L-flat, Zeist, the Netherlands, 1960–1968

at the urban level. So, after a few years, we realised that the space between architectural organisms could not be left completely undefined; we also realised that the city was an efficient machine, but that proximity was necessary between houses, activities, and inhabitants. The problem lies in the indeterminacy of free space, so-called SLOAP (space left over after planning),[7] a "potential" space that all research on suburbs now considers crucial to their regeneration.

Space is, once again, the focal point of the discussion. For example, at the CIAM in Aix-en-Provence in 1953, Alison and Peter Smithson intercepted the signs of unease (and sometimes rejection) expressed by the inhabitants towards the new modern city; these signs prompted them to raise the issue of re-identification by proposing the famous Urban Re-identification Grid. After analysing the everyday life of a working-class neighbourhood in London, they used this grid to try and explain how people recognise themselves in their environment thanks to several "social practices" triggered by a concept of dwelling that was radically different compared to the "mechanical" concept of modern-functionalist architecture. The Smithsons replaced the four sections in the Athens Charter (housing, work, leisure, and circulation)—i.e., functional categories separate in space and time—with four genuinely "spatial" terms (house, road, neighbourhood, and city). These categories are linked to what Edward T. Hall proxemically called "social distance".[8] In actual fact, these categories were not at all new, but recalled the spaces of our old cities, based on what we could call a phenomenological interpretation of space. That kind of social distance had been dilated to the extreme in modern-functionalist architecture. It was the moment when in many places in Europe an attempt was made to gradually reduce/qualify the space "between houses". In this "organic" variant of modernism—linked more to the establishment of open spaces—spatial differences were decisively juxtaposed against the seriality of compositions in the twenties and thirties. Projects were designed chiefly at district level; their main

7   L. Ginsburg, "SLOAP—Space Left Over After Planning", *Architectural Review*, n. 920, 1973, pp. 201–266.

8   E.T. Hall, *The Hidden Dimension*, Doubleday: Garden City (NY), 1966.

Park family house, still from the movie *Parasite*, director Bong Joon-ho, 2019

objective was to create an urban space composed of a suitable mix of buildings in terms of size, type, and height. Similar but less "radical" versions of this approach also spread. In the Smithsons' project for the Nordweststadt district of Frankfurt (Germany), the principles of organic growth and relationship between the parts became the stated alternative to the concept of repetition of the optimal house (Raumstadt versus Zeilenbau).[9]

Today, at a historical moment in time, when architecture appears to have solved the problem of internal space, it is perhaps public space—forgotten in the generic individualist city—that is waiting for architects to propose a credible, civil solution. But all we have to do is extend our horizon to the whole world in order to understand that the battle for the space of the house, in terms of new *existenzminimum*, is still a key topic when defining dwelling in the contemporary city. In the film *Parasite* (2019),[10] the contrast between compressed and dilated space is the metaphor of an increasingly polarised society, both socially and economically. This conflict is visually represented by the domestic space of two families: the poky, cramped basement of the Kim family and the spacious house of the Park family swimming in a sea of vegetation and plants.

Is there no such thing as society?

In an interview in 1987, Margaret Thatcher stated that there are individual men and women and there are families, but there's no such thing as society.[11] This was a time when investment in

9   Built north of the Siedlung Römerstadt designed by E. May, the project (1961) won a competition; it embraced the principles of the *Spatial City (Raumstadt)* designed by Walter Schwagenscheidt (1949), by trying to recuperate the almost picturesque idea of the city.

10 The Korean film, directed by Bong Joon-ho, is set in Seoul and won the Golden Palm at the Cannes Film Festival (2019) and four Oscars (2020).

11 "They are casting their problems at society. And, you know, there's no such thing as society. There are individual men and women and there are families. And no government can do anything except through people, and people must look after themselves first. It is our duty to look after ourselves and then, also, to look after our neighbours." Interview in *"Women's Own"*, 1987, *Margaret Thatcher: a life in quotes,* https://www.theguardian.com/politics/2013/apr/08/margaret-thatcher-quotes, accessed on 14 February 2022.

Social housing, public facilities, and park in via Gallarate, Milan,
international competition, first prize, MAB Arquitectura (F. Marotta and M. Basile), 2009

public housing was at its lowest all over Europe; it was the end of a heroic parabola that had begun during post-WWII reconstruction and culminated in Italy with the so-called economic boom.[12] At the end of the eighties, there was a strong popular reaction, at times a decisive rejection towards big social housing projects. It marked the end of trust and consensus towards government-funded architecture and encouraged national disinvestment in council tenancy throughout Europe.

The period between the *Housing Reform Act* promulgated in 1971[13] and the complete implementation of the so-called Housing Plan ended in Italy in 1988 involved the construction of public housing for roughly 900,000 families; this was a huge number, almost three times the houses built by the INA-Casa Plans. But the approach was very different: the complexes built in the 167 zones had little in common with the neighbourhoods based on the Fanfani Plan[14]: the organicist and community-oriented concept—that considered neighbourhoods and the "human scale"[15] as a key issue—was replaced by a concept of self-sufficiency, but also of abstraction, a change in scale, and a break with the urban texture.

From that moment on, and for a couple of decades, Italy completely forgot—and almost eliminated—the social housing topic, convinced that the high percentage of Italian home owners (roughly 80%) could somehow compensate the demand for affordable housing. However, in the last few years, the demand for rent-controlled houses has gradually increased due to the 2007 economic-financial crisis that is still ongoing.

12   Conventionally, from 1958 to 1963, but in actual fact the period lasted from the fifties to the early seventies.

13   The Law n. 865, 22 October 1971, *Planning and co-ordination of public residential building; regulations on expropriation for public use,* also called *Housing Reform Act.*

14   The INA-Casa Law was promoted by the Minister of Labour and Social Welfare, Amintore Fanfani, one among the more remarkable Italian politicians of the leftist faction of the Democrazia Cristiana party in post-WWII Italy, and referred to the issues of the social Catholicism policies.

15   P. Di Biagi, *La grande ricostruzione. Il piano Ina-Casa e l'Italia degli anni cinquanta*, Donzelli: Rome, 2001.

Residential block EA2 in Bolzano, new CasaNova district, Bivio-Kaiserau area,
cdm architetti associati (E. Cappuccio, G. Donato, T. Macchi Cassia), 2012

The battle cry

Collective housing was for many centuries a marginal issue for architects; it suddenly took centre stage in the twentieth century, paving the way for a design research that considered the production of "parts of cities" (districts) rather than individual buildings as being the key to rationally solve the increasingly rapid and widespread expansion of urban centres. "Minimum dwelling has become the central problem of modern architecture and the battle cry of today's architectural avant-garde".[16] This is the incipit of *The Minimum Dwelling* by Karel Teige, a book that in 1932 tried to shed light on the urgent need for a radical reform of housing policies in Europe, starting with the need to modernise housing in order to achieve a form of collective living based on a new model of society. The model envisaged the gradual "disappearance" of the traditional family[17] in a "collectivist reconstruction of dwelling".

In the last few decades, different forms of social housing have become widespread, even in countries that have an overriding quota of housing stock for rent (Germany, France, Great Britain). Should investment in council housing in Italy become justifiably popular again (financial support for housing represents 0.1% of GDP, against 0.72% of the EU average), it will validate the right to housing enshrined in the Italian Constitution (art. 47); even so, it will be new forms of housing (not publicly funded) that will determine what happens in the future. There will, however, be two novelties: an increase in the weaker classes and public authorities that basically lack funds and available terrains. So it's not just a matter of redesigning social housing: the new "battle cry" should focus on assigning a clearer meaning to social housing, i.e., a new housing supply in which public and private players collaborate (coordinating and

16 K. Teige, *Nejmensi byt*, Vaclov Petr: Praha, 1932 (Engl. trans. *The Minimum Dwelling. The housing crisis, housing reform, the dwelling for the subsistence minimum, single family, rental and collective houses, regulatory plans for residential quarters, new forms of houses and apartments, the popular housing movement*, MIT Press: Cambridge (MA), 2002, p. 1).

17 Cf. L. Reale, *Abitare la città sovietica. Dal disurbanismo alla kommunalka: quartiere, casa e alloggio tra squilibri e illusioni*, in: R. Secchi and L. Spita (eds.), *Architettura tra due mari. Radici e trasformazioni nel Caucaso e nell'Asia Centrale*, Quodlibet: Macerata, 2018, pp. 187–217.

Urban Lake Housing in Pordenone, C+S (C. Cappai and M.A. Segantini), 2010

merging their interests) by not only launching participation in initiatives and marketing houses at affordable prices, but also by providing different supply types (rent, sale, reduced lease) located close to collective facilities capable of either reinventing a sense of community for the inhabitants or affirming a new identity for them.

Social housing and the transformation of the city

Housing should become part of the more general issue of dwelling, a concept that has continuously evolved in history: from the archetype concept of a roof/shelter, to the *existenz-minimum* standards representing the principle of social equality, and then on to the revival of the identity of the house (as a projection of self) and the flexibility/adaptability of contemporary houses. Strong ties still exist between housing policies, social cohesion, and the development of urban areas, but the conditions and scale of the projects have changed. Social housing[18] has often become a regeneration tool, the engine behind the sustainable transformation of the city (including moderate and paradigmatic projects) rather than a means to manage a growing city. More in general, in the last twenty years, low-cost housing is once again a field of research—as it was in the first decades of the twentieth century—involving architectural language and typological solutions. It is also an area in which to test new materials and innovative solutions involving energy and bioclimatics. The objective of social housing is not so much to find a quantitative solution to the demand for housing, but rather to provide services (integrated with the homes and often the result of long processes of participation) capable of producing inclusion and spaces that provide a better quality of life, while at the same time satisfying the complex needs of contemporary dwelling.

18   The Ministerial Decree of 22 April 2008 established social housing in Italy; it was envisaged for people who cannot afford to rent on the open market, or be granted a mortgage to buy a house, but nevertheless earn more than the sum specified in order to be eligible to be assigned a public housing unit (ERP).

Not many examples of social housing have been built in Italy, but the way forward is undoubtedly clear. The ongoing changes in the requirements of housing demand, coupled with increasingly widespread experimentation focusing on residency as the "reuse" of an abandoned existing structure, have increasingly nuanced the typological principles established for housing and have also turned flexibility into the key topic. The gap that architecture is currently trying to close is, on the one hand, the one that exists between the indefiniteness of the internal structure of the dwelling and, on the other, the uniqueness or the specificity of supply to the inhabitants. However, this clashes with rigid legislation, obviously in difficulties when faced with a housing demand that can no longer be standardised and is still based on expansion rather than transformation, on quantity rather than quality.

And what about people?

If we review the problem of the reduced number of inhabitants living in the public city in the last few decades, we realise that this is often the reason why these neighbourhoods have such poor vitality. The so-called housing emergency in Rome, for example, has always been attributed to insufficient maintenance, unsuccessful rent recovery, or the fact the buildings are very old (and now, finally, have very low density); this clearly demonstrates that underutilisation is the first issue we need to tackle. Where will we find the people we need to achieve an increase in the "intensity of use" in large areas of the city? How can we make these areas attractive again?

Several strategies have been theorised or undertaken, e.g., changes to the housing standards.[19] But we need to change our mental and cultural approach and ask ourselves whether concentrating the resident population in the same place is indeed a necessary added value in housing and the city in

19   In Italy, the standards regulating facilities connected to building interventions are still regulated by the Decree Law n. 1444, 2 April 1968. A group has been set up to review it; it was established by Decree n. 349, 31 July 2018 issued by the Ministry of Transport.

general. We must clearly be prepared for the opposite pressure of distancing between individuals which, since early 2020, is the main approach we must adopt in order to govern the global pandemic.[20]

A case study of the housing heritage belonging to the Municipality of Rome examined the issue of dividing or splitting up big apartments—a step that could represent a fundamental resource. Architecturally speaking, this initiative has immediate effects on the space of the city: urban density does not have to be either high or low in absolute terms—as maintained by Jacobs—but appropriate.[21] It is appropriate when it permits the initiation of activities indispensable to urban life, such as day nurseries, post offices, neighbourhood shops, pharmacies, etc. Urban (and especially housing) density in Rome is basically too low because many public housing neighbourhoods are sparsely populated. The research entitled *Roma cerca casa*[22] [Rome looks for home] developed a project for the regeneration of the public city based on the housing heritage of the Municipality of Rome. It is a pilot project focused on intensifying the use of this heritage, but with limited timescale and costs, to be achieved by dividing up the public housing units. One of the most widespread cliché about Rome is that it has very few social housing units: in actual fact, there are 74,000 public housing units of which 28,000 belong to the municipality and 36,000 to the public agency ATER. Apart from the problems

---

20   In this short article, I have tried, to the best of my ability, to gloss over the current health situation, well aware of the effects it has on domestic and urban living spaces, as well as its implications on the climate and environmental crisis and, more in general, the ensuing debate about the global capitalist model. Regarding these issues, please refer to the already extensive literature on this subject. See, for example: N. Chomsky and M. Waterstone, *The Precipice: Neoliberalism, the Pandemic and the Urgent Need for Radical Change*, Haymarket Books: Chicago, 2021. See also the Italian translation of a series of articles and interviews: N.C., *Crisi di civiltà. Pandemia e capitalismo*, Ponte alle Grazie: Milan, 2020 and S. Žižek, *Pandemic! Covid-19 Shakes the World*. Polity: New York, 2020; S. Z., *Pandemic! 2: Chronicles of a Time Lost*, Polity Press: New York, 2021.

21   "Densities are too low, or too high, when they frustrate city diversity instead of abetting it. This flaw in performance is why they are too low or too high". J. Jacobs, *The Death and Life of Great American Cities*, Random House: New York, 1961, p. 209.

22   F. De Matteis, M.R. Guarini, and L. Reale (eds.), *Roma cerca casa. La ridefinizione degli alloggi di edilizia residenziale pubblica come risposta alla domanda abitativa*, Maggioli: Santarcangelo di Romagna, 2016.

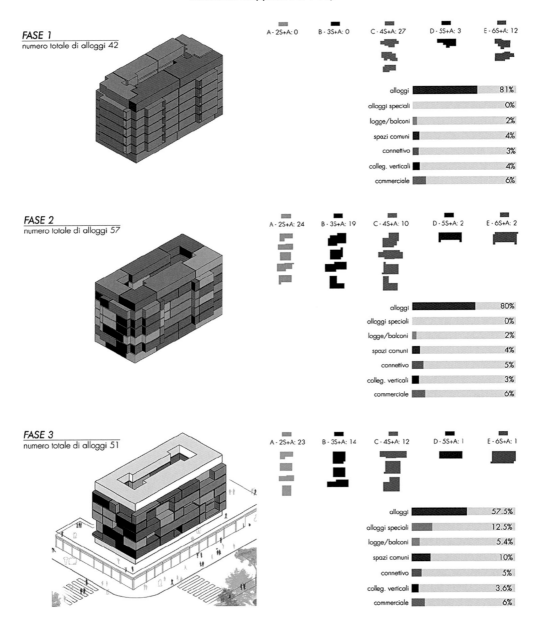

Phasing a building transformation, Rome, Balsamo Crivelli Square; 1: ordinary maintenance, 2: extraordinary maintenance and conservative sanitation, 3: renewal and conservative sanitation (F. De Matteis, M.R. Guarini, and L. Reale (eds.), *Roma cerca casa.
La ridefinizione degli alloggi di edilizia residenziale pubblica come risposta alla domanda
abitativa*, Maggioli: Santarcangelo di Romagna, 2016, p. 184)

linked to poor maintenance and the local budget deficit, this extensive heritage shows a very high level of underutilisation, in some cases almost 70%. In Corviale, for example, the complex is inhabited by only 4,000 of the 6,800 envisaged inhabitants.[23]

The division project expressed in the research *Roma cerca casa* was applied to a sample of 500 apartments based on a simple logic: the city has an extensive residential heritage; a large part of this stock are big apartments (roughly 40% are over 90 m^2); most of the families on the waiting list (16,000) are small (45.7% of households in Rome are made up of one person) who are not legally entitled to big houses. The simplest and most efficient way to solve this misalignment is to split up the apartments; this model has been applied in the private sector, especially in the last decade, i.e., since the economic-financial crisis in 2007. This sample of 500 apartments was screened using increasingly stricter criteria; the goal was to not only assess the feasibility and sustainability of the division projects in architectural, distributive, technical, and economic terms, but also theorise different transformation possibilities, more or less invasive and expensive.

Neither a nest nor a garage

We should, however, avoid making the same mistake again: in other words, we should not deal with the question of dwelling —in terms of space or people—only based on quantity, square metres, and technical-functional standards. Quite apart from the houses and the inhabitants, the kind of dwelling we have examined here is a much more meaningful and complex issue. "To dwell is human. Wild beasts have nests, cattle have stables, carriages fit into sheds, and there are garages for automobiles. Only humans can dwell."[24] In his essay entitled *Dwelling* (1984),

---

23   For example, 300 apartments in Corviale have a floor area of 118 m^2 where one elderly person lives alone (ATER Census, Rome 2016), in: E. Puccini, *Roma, la casa e l'emergenza abitativa che non c'è...*, April 2018, https://osservatoriocasaroma.com, accessed on 17 May 2022.

24   I. Illich, *Dwelling*, 1984, https://www.atlasofplaces.com/essays/dwelling/, accessed on 15 February 2022.

Ivan Illich links the concept of dwelling not only to a biological and instinctive co-action or the practical need for shelter ("A house is neither nest nor garage"), but to the "art of living". The philosopher's harsh critique of the capitalistic model (and subaltern, instrumental role of the architect's profession) induces him to state that the globally widespread dwelling model has produced "the same garage for the human—shelves to store the work-force overnight, handy for the means of its transportation".[25]

For centuries, the changeable nature of dwelling space has not been determined by instinct or genetics, but by culture, experience, and thought. In this sense, the critique of the ideology of the development of Modernity is even deeper. Even if we risk finding ourselves holding conservative positions vis-à-vis design culture, we must reflect on housing by trying to veer sharply towards the non-critical "progressive" tradition of Modernity. In a recent conference held at Sapienza University, Giorgio Agamben maintained that when faculties of architecture were established in universities, people seemed to lose their ability to build their own house as a natural activity practiced for centuries, and with it the possibility of feeling "at home". Recovering the freedom and ability to dwell means "to create, conserve and intensify customs and habits, in other words ways of being".[26] "[...] Man not only needs a den or nest but a house, in other words a place in which to 'dwell', where he can build, gather knowledge, and passionately practice his 'customs'. To build, i.e., the objective of architecture, presupposes or constitutively involves housing, the faculty of dwelling. For architecture, severing the link between construction and dwelling thus involves a radical crisis, one which those who seriously practice this art cannot but tackle".

Finally, it would be a mistake to limit the sense of dwelling to the internal space of the home. What lies outside our front door

25   "Shelves to store the work-force overnight, handy for the means of its transportation", I. Illich, *ibidem*.
26   G. Agamben, *Abitare e costruire*, conference held at the Faculty of Architecture, Sapienza University of Rome, 7 December 2018 (a short version is available at: https://www.quodlibet.it/giorgio-agamben-abitare-e-costruire, accessed on 15 February 2022).

is also shaped by dwelling, albeit in a different manner. Inhabited space exists on both sides of the threshold; Ivan Illich recalls that "the threshold is like the pivot of the space that dwelling creates".[27] On this side lies home, domestic space, and on the other lies the commons: a new meaning of dwelling should be sought in this threshold that shelters the community as the house shelters its members.

27   I. Illich, *op. cit.*

Houses by Danilo Trogu

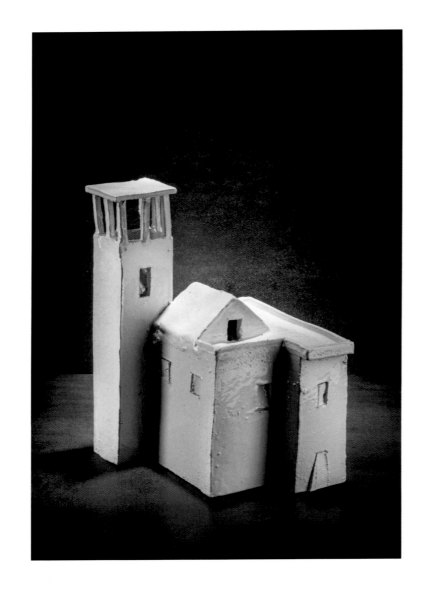

"As far as possible, the operation consists in subtracting, taking away one layer after another, down to the plastic substance"

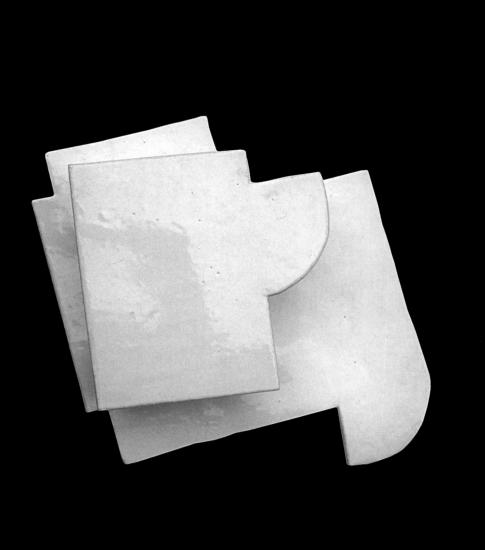

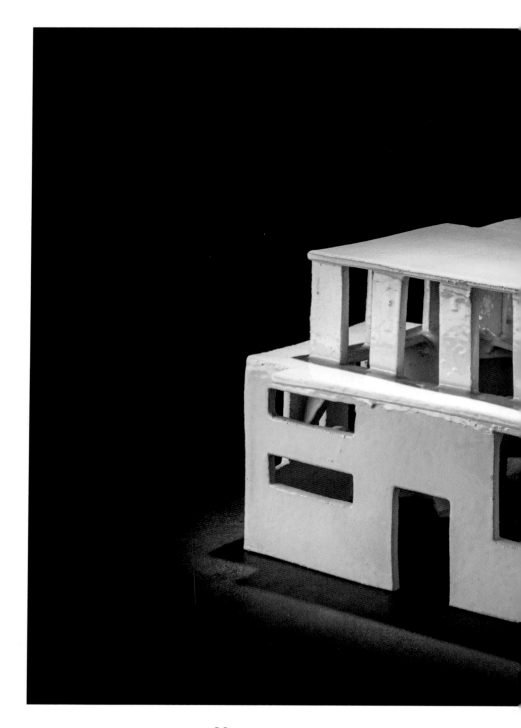

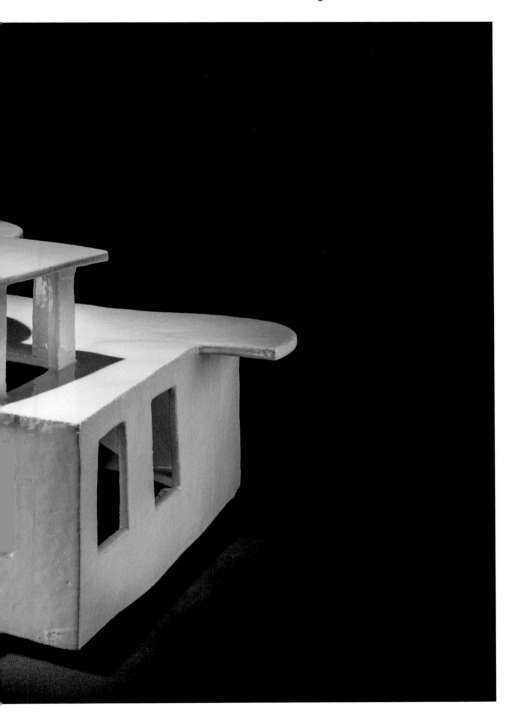

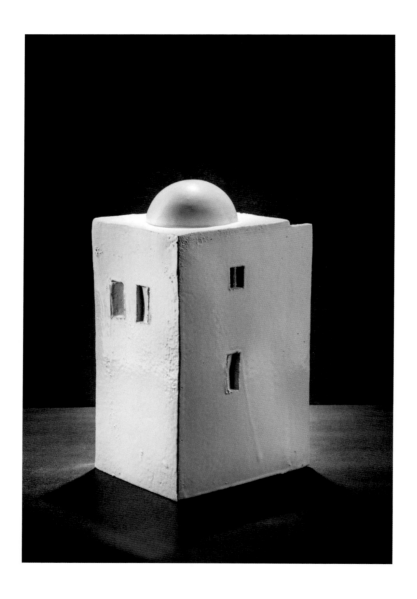

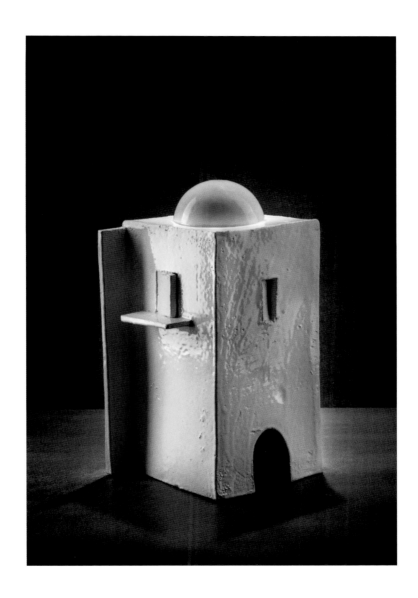

"To imagine geometry as an encounter between small neuroses, compulsions coupled point by point"

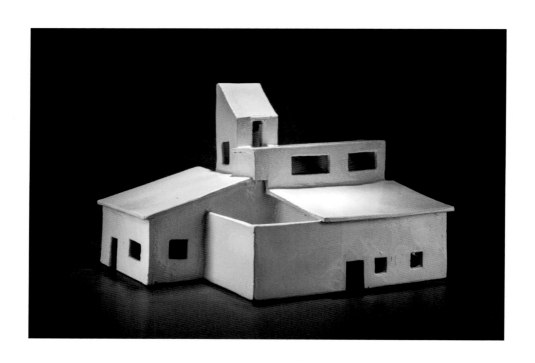

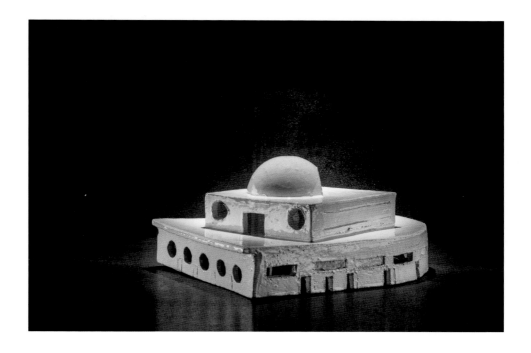

"The house as an introspective medium, house as pure form, house as a state of the soul"

The houses created by Danilo Trogu make up a series, beginning in 1980 and ending—perhaps temporarily—in 2016. Roughly thirty houses, assembled by one maker who works unaided with a primary material: clay.

The houses were created without any drawings, without the involvement of the *ratio* of measurement that architects, surveyors, and interior designers depend on so much. No scale is shown; the relationship with "reality" (reduction in size, reproduction of existing houses, customs of the disciplinary tradition of ceramic art) is not ignored, but interiorised.

The association between the house and its inhabitant is the "dedication". A person, idealised and reduced to a few basic traits, adjectivises a spatial configuration. Houses from which voices seem to emerge, and desires. The way in which the houses designed for Laurie Anderson, Gianluca Peluffo, Alfonso Femia, Alessandro Schiesaro, and others, see the light. The inhabitants emerge from the author's imagination and are arranged in an improbable Olympus. They generate sparks towards other houses.

Every gesture is impressed on the clay, either conforming it or cleaving it; every gesture harbours a memory. It is the traces of things that have been seen, loved, selected, and savoured with eyes shut. Memory is everything and, at the same time, something insidious, surplus information, and images, that makes the decanting of the experience and invention both laborious and labyrinthine.

So we come close to the fundamental flair in Trogu's work: a swinging back and forth between the wisdom of popular ceramics (created using the four basic colours that resist high-temperature fires, lit in many places of the African and European Mediterranean) and the contemporary research by artists like Asger Jorn and Pablo Picasso, two references which are present in Trogu's works. The action they share is not to apply a figurative text to a ceramic support, but to try to make "real" objects.

Inhab

itants

Inhabitants

With the advent of modernity in European housing, a legitimate authority became the entity that could identify and tax inhabitants, ask them to answer questions, and acknowledge their statuses, qualities, and rights. This legitimate authority is the constitutional state that scientifically measures and censuses the population and the houses. A scientific measurement of the power of societies has to be pursued through the dynamic correspondence between space and population. The investigation of the consistence and the disposition of the people in towns and countries leads to the concept of the inhabitant. In the same phase, a second group of subjects arises in order to explore new housing and living assets. It is composed by institutions, associations, groups, and enterprises—public as well as private, and devoted to housing in particular. An important role has been played by independent organisations, starting with several pioneering English societies such as the *Metropolitan Association for Improving the Dwellings of the Industrious Classes* (1841) and the *Society for Improving the Condition of the Labouring Classes* (1844). Institutions were established to develop and provide housing measures, often at municipal level. Due to the efforts of entrepreneurs, philanthropic organisations, charities, and cooperatives of employees and workers, a huge number of these tumultuous initiatives flourished and thrived. After the English *Artisans' and Labourers' Dwellings Improvement Act* (1868), the first housing laws were promulgated to try and introduce systematic measures capable of moving beyond local practices; their objective was to allocate greater economic resources compared to what could be provided at local level. Although in Europe circumstances in the twentieth century differed from country to country, they all acted in a similar manner in order to combine the measures implemented by specific bodies, national policies, and the credit system. Note that these actions were interdependent, characterised by the fact that these organisations were not financially autonomous. Complex social blocks developed convergent interests. This was one of the reasons why these institutions gradually began to try and orga- nise public action with bodies that had different kinds of territorial expertise: national, regional, provincial, municipal, or more recently, European or international.

In addition to the approach by the state or housing bodies, a third layer of definition of the identity of a resident existed. It was created by free thinkers: individual authors whose works produced a general theory of society that shaped the image of residents and their division (or union) in significant ensembles. The third group involved with residents was truly very different to the first two, which were established via a collective and contractual order. It was made up of writers, biologists, political scientists, and progressive engineers; to a certain extent, it could be created by anyone capable of producing significant and innovative statements about residents and their houses. Books ranging from *De Re Aedificatoria* by Leon Battista Alberti (in the 1450 version, or the *editio princeps* printed in 1485 by Nicolò di Lorenzo in Florence) to *Leviathan* by Thomas Hobbes (*Leviathan or the Matter, Form and Power of a Commonwealth Ecclesiastical and Civil*, Andrew Crook: London, 1651) affirmed the possibility of announcing a logical thin red line running between the individual, the state, and housing, based on the authority of reason and the logical consequences of its use. Certain ideas developed in the second half of the nineteenth century by the state engineer Ildefonso Cerdà Sunyer are no less interesting. He expressed them in his *Monografia estadistica de la clase obrera de Barcelona en 1856: Especimen de la vida urbana, con aplicación concreta en dicha clase* (later inserted as an appendix to vol. II of the *Teoria general de la urbanización y aplicación de sus principies y doctrinas a la reforma y ensanche de Barcelona,* Imprenta Espanola: Madrid, 1867). As the first radical explorer of urban modernity, Cerdà began by carefully studying existing or imaginary housing in order to design Barcelona as the prototype of the contemporary city. Theories of society sometimes influenced the definition of the resident by the states, and the rising of local housing experiments and associations. In rare and relevant moments, there are passages and exchanges in the definition of the resident among the three prototypic subjects we talked about.

In traditional societies, and in European societies before the XVII century, the religious ethics authority and the political civil authorities converge in a project concerning individuals. The early season of *Hôtels-Dieu (Hostels of God)* and *Alberghi dei Poveri* (literally *Hostels for the Poors*), starting with the Hôtel-Dieu in Paris (650), are evidence of this manner of considering the close-knit collaboration between powers, that gradually leave space to their programmatic separation. The season of Italian *Alberghi dei Poveri* (Genoa, yard started in 1652, Naples 1749) were the biggest housing machines ever attempted to achieve social inclusion before the advent of experiments with collective housing and *grand ensembles* in the twentieth century. Those who were interned there had to pass through a classification grid of the population: young women were divided from young men, children from adults, adults from the elderly. Purification of the social order could be attempted through spatial separation, the removal of a context harmful for the individual. Dividing the population into segments established classes of residents within which it was possible to create the concept of relative housing equality. In situations prior to modernity, political, ethical, and housing fields remained merged, or reciprocally unmeasured.

The advent of the Enlightenment saw the theory of society distance itself from the ideal-typical figure of *ancien régime* inhabitants. Equality and freedom made it possible to imagine a state of rights where all inhabitants are formally equal. One concept stands out: that of the individual, monad in society, bearer of minimum universal rights, declared free from cultural affiliation and from any status and identity. In its wake came the "house for all", the rational distribution of collectively produced wealth, and the destiny of surplus value. These issues have little to do with the events and achievements they are usually associated with in disciplinary fields and historiography, such as the collective rationalist housing so elegantly designed and built by non-profit cooperatives, for example the projects by Bruno Taut in Berlin and Ernst May in Frankfurt (Germany) during the Weimar Republic. They involved some of the middle classes, blue-collar workers and public employees, but not all classes of inhabitants, and much less the more underprivileged classes or ethnic and linguistic minorities. Only the so-called

Red Vienna housing experience was a notable exception, a sort of Austro-Marxist paroxysm suspended between the horrors of World War One and the abyss of annexation into National Socialist Germany. In other important movements that arose later (social democracies in Northern Europe, beginning in the thirties, especially in Sweden), reference is made to inhabitants who become part of a society with just one class of people. Gender was no longer separated, and working women were considered to play a key role in the evolution of space inside a house as well as in complementary public services.

After individuals gradually freed themselves from their social affiliation system, a crucial question remained: how does a person see himself as an inhabitant? In other words, what sparks the recognition process involving the degrees and forms of an inhabitant's membership compared to the way his identity is described by the state, housing organisations, and social theories? According to Marx and Engels, one way this can happen is through "class consciousness" capable of interven-ing with regard to the "housing issue" and modifying political behaviour. We can ideally place the biopolitical interventions of the maximalist state at the opposite end of the spectrum. No one asked those who were to be interned and redeemed whether they agreed with the housing measure to which they were subjected. Up to the present day, the projection of an imaginary identity onto individuals by those in power covertly passed the period of modernity, erupting very forcefully on the surface of the discourse in the seventies and eighties. The right of individuals and inhabitants to speak with their own voice, without legitimising mediation, became welded with the crisis of political forms of representation. When an anonymous resident of the brutalist grand ensemble of Rozzol Melara, Trieste, Italy (1968–1979) was faced with the undesirable features of the public housing unit he was assigned, he wrote to the Council House Institute: "Did anyone ask me if I wanted to live in a monument to utopia? All I wanted was a normal house." His simple words reflect the core issue: the difference between the way in which institutions see residents and the way in which residents see themselves.

The basic individual of modern life does not want to be super-imposed by external powers. Nevertheless, this is what happened during the twentieth and twenty-first centuries with mass-oriented communication and populisms. Profound flaws exist in a hypothetical direct relationship between an individual and political power; they lurk in the breakdown of democratic, representative, and participatory procedures, sometimes anticipating authoritarian management turns. The market configures the individual as a user of housing assets, the embodiment of socially constructed preferences, increasingly less referable to the satisfaction of elementary needs (i.e., linked to biological survival), and more and more to do either with the realm of desire and access to luxury goods, or capable of producing gratifying projections of identity. This individual struggles to be recognised as a fixed element, defined in universalistic declarations or even in more limited statements regarding rights to housing. He may discover he is malleable, not just haphazardly, but nonetheless subject to external influences and forces that can influence his behaviour, priorities, values, and propensity to purchase and consume. Alone in front of a political power aloof from everyday life, the individual meets the individual who is alone in front of our capitalist economy, which he can neither defeat nor change. Perhaps these are the reasons why we no longer postulate perfect coincidences between the individual, parts of the earth's crust, housing, and the city, as in the utopias of the twentieth century.

These general considerations about the inhabitants highlight the role of the intermediate social ties between the individual and society. The marital family is the reference for European modernity, the result of Reformation and Counter-Reformation in the Christian religion, but the extended family also acts as reference. The latter extends to other ways of acknowledging intermediate sociality, the neighbourhood unit, and the community. We could say the same for condominiums and cohousing. The social tie becomes closer, tangible, exhortative; it helps to recognise a lost bond of solidarity and living proximity. The reference can be extended to the corporations, confraternities, lobbies, municipalities, affective or interest-led cohabitations, stable or temporary forms of spaces and lifestyles that create the social worth with which the inhabitant identifies.

Starting in the sixties, and after the great rift in contemporary history (1973–1974), individuals increasingly saw their own status as relative to the achievement of freedom, also considered as the removal of ties from the past regarding gender, access to education, job, and mobility. The archetype of the tent was revived and became a caravan, Volkswagen minibus, motorcycle, sleeping bag, and Eskimo coat, icons of a journey that was no longer a return to real living but instead represented a will to go towards the outdoors. Real and apparent movements emerged; previous gender distinctions, high and low, cultured and popular, could no longer exist. The tent was therefore exploited by communities, as was the habitable chassis of a variety of vehicles, capable of moving one's own "small bubble" of life to new contexts, all over the world and beyond; this occurred thanks to the violent shock to housing imagery provided by the vision of a man on the moon and the sci-fi images launched by the media.

There was a shift from the ideal model of housing of Maupertuis by Claude-Nicolas Ledoux after the French Revolution to the caravan by Stewart Brand, the eponymous hero of counterculture who travelled around the United States with his caravan full of books and innovative products to teach the inhabitants about new ways of living freely. In 1968, the initiative became a book, *The Whole Earth Catalog*; it not only provided individuals with an informed access to everything that could boost their exploration of the faculty of living, but also allowed them to contribute with their own indications, comments, assessments, and proposals. The minority experiment was updated until it became a bestseller entitled *The Last Whole Earth Catalog* (1971) that sold two million copies. More "last editions" were published until in 1974 the paper version became a fanzine entitled *Co-Evolution Quarterly*; it was followed in 1985 by WELL, *Whole Earth 'Lectronic Link*, the prototype (created together with Larry Brilliant) of digital communities made up of informed, smart inhabitants. This last initiative, cited by Steve Jobs as the direct antecedent of the Google concept, emphasises a new condition of the individual, a cross between autonomous knowledge—such as artisanal skills and self-construction—and opportunities sparked by the production of digital infrastructures and market dynamics. This movement,

109

with its evolutions and contradictions, highlighted how much each inhabitant simultaneously belongs to multiple networks of relationships.

Acknowledging the differences between groups of inhabitants is crucial as regards contemporary housing, but it is not easily established in singular cities or local contexts. How is it possible to design a habitat that always consists of niches of different individuals living together without hierarchies, just like the communities that sporadically emerged in Europe after the year 1000? Slavoj Zizek has repeatedly observed that the horizon of human rights suspends the universalist visions of individuals and rights to which the "needs theories" and housing policies are linked. A resident, the recipient of a house, as well as the object of the stabilisation policies enacted by states and the target of building companies, is snuffed out in favour of the general figure of housing mobility, increasingly useful to allow individuals to take advantage of the opportunities provided by international production cycles. The beneficiary of the property market and policies of big investment funds is a relatively generic figure, distinguished by his purchasing power, temporary occupation of several houses, and penchant to appreciate the house in advance thanks to codified spatial representations, renders, plans, and images capable of conjuring up the overall aesthetics of a domestic environment. Bearing this in mind, the main answer currently provided to the residents' demand is diversification of what is offered by the property market and the inertial continuation of local housing dynamics. This answer is, at least in part, tautological: the market appreciates and promotes what, *hic et nunc*, is appreciated by the market, or exists and is available. The general project linking the resident's status to a role or a job, i.e., a permanent job in the secondary or tertiary sector, is now either dead or, at the very least, weak. What remains is the difficulty inherent in recognising and naming, in a stable and long-lasting manner, the new differences expressed by residents, and with them the new trends regarding the sharing of living spaces, both inside and outside the home.

Christopher McCandless in Alaska

Into the Wild.
How to Live Alone as a Student/Worker once Away from the Family Home

"Leave it to me as I find a way to be
consider me a satellite forever orbiting
i know all the rules but the rules did not know me
guaranteed", *Eddie Vedder*

From mom and dad into the wild: no, into the city

When you leave your parent's home to go and live alone, even Paris, Rome, London, Berlin, or Milan could be the most terrifying cities in the world if you have to pay the rent, the bills and provide food on your own. In other words, when you move to a new city, neighbourhood, or new house as a student/worker, and when what you possess is only your job and some adolescent savings, the most terrifying moment is when the landowner knocks on your door or starts sending annoying messages reminding you: "It is the end of the month, I haven't received the transfer yet" or "Please remember the electricity bills and condo taxes", or words to that effect. This continuous pressure, in addition to a standardised set of codes, languages, and habits, characterises a new contemporary individual, who can be considered as both a permanent worker and a nomad. On the one hand, a permanent worker to the extent that he/she possesses professional knowledge and skills that in contemporary capitalism can potentially produce value at any time. On the other, the nomads, who during the seventies would have been likened to hippies, are now dominating the world, as predicted by Gilles Deleuze. In *Difference and Repetition*, Deleuze observed what happened during the shift from Fordism to post-Fordism in the late seventies; he argues that the nomad, *nomos,* is someone "without property, enclosure or measure", a person whose habits are built and accumulated over a period of time in response to his needs, a mechanism that currently distinguishes a way of living which is almost identical everywhere in any metropolis or any village of the globe.[1]

Christopher McCandless (alias Alexander Supertramp) fired the first bullet of possible rebellion and disobedience against this way of living in modern society by trying to reject the generic way of life that the new generation of so-called "knowledge workers" must indistinguishably follow. His refusal to follow what his parents had envisaged for him—attending Harvard and afterwards a future career as a prestigious lawyer—demonstrates something that is more than a modern stereotype. The story narrated by Jon Krakauer in 1996 in his book *Into the Wild*—which became known to the public at large in 2007 thanks to the film with the same title directed by Sean Pean—depicts a young bachelor-graduate who gives up his parents' vision, money, and possessions and, apart for a few books, embarks on a radical journey into the American wilderness; his goal was to reach Alaska by himself. The film's scenes, made more evocative thanks to the music and words written by Eddie Vedder, abstracts all the complexities and contradictions of real life, and depicts the lonely boy every time he has to deal with a new situation, new friends, and affections, thus learning more and more of life's lessons and experiences; new people he takes care of (and who take care of him) until he experiences absolute loneliness in the iconic abandoned green bus where he lives the last days of his life.

From a contemporary point of view, this story is important because it helps us understand the relationship between the issue of family, studying-working-responsibility, and living, a crucial structure in the social composition of the "wilderness" of the city. And yet, as highlighted by Sergio Bologna[2], in recent decades, the crisis of the middle class that exploded with the economic crisis in 2008 coincided with the diffusion of an entire

1   G. Deleuze, *Différence et répétition*, Presses Universitaires de France: Paris, 1968, Engl. trans. *Difference and Repetition*, Columbia University Press: New York, 1994, pp. 462–463.

2   S. Bologna, *Ceti medi senza futuro? I risvolti della società della conoscenza*, DeriveApprodi: Rome, 2007.

generation of "knowledge workers", students, precarious employees, and many freelancers in different fields of labour. For them, terms like *precariousness, flexibility*, and *mobility* refer not only to working contracts, but also to their *modus vivendi*. According to Bologna[3], in order to understand the working conditions of this new generation of workers and then to suggest possible forms of coalition formation (like founding a workers' union or forming a collective), one must look at the bourgeois ideology of professionalism and intellectual labour, rather than at the old working class. It is in the ideology of the middle-class family that one can intercept the origins of intellectual labour, today reassembled in the modern middle class family and its educational programme.

More precisely, it is the discipline imposed by the family, as depicted by McCandless's story, that pushes sons and daughters toward higher education in the hope of a prestigious career; parents imagine their offspring as future professionals or respected figures (and still accept them at home if they fail or in times of precariousness). As part of a modern family, youngsters are supposed to try and finish their studies as soon as possible; they are pushed to their limits regarding hard work and competition, thus transforming their own lives, as well as their bedrooms, into a microcosm of self-realisation towards the ideology of the self-made man. In fact, if one considers the architecture and aesthetics of the room of a typical middle-class child, it is always imagined—by the architect, parents, and child—as a place of obligations and responsibilities, sometimes more similar to an office rather than a place of doing nothing, of pure imagination.

In today's world, for a typical 'alexsupertramp', his bedroom in mom and dad's house is both a place of retreat from family discipline and a refuge in times of financial problems[4]; it is also considered as a springboard towards a new life alone, *into the wild* of the aggressiveness of the city and the scenarios it offers to students, graduates, or non-EU immigrants entering

---

3   *Ivi*, pp. 56–63.
4   M. Fisher, *Capitalist Realism: Is there no Alternative?*, Zero Books: Winchester, UK, 2009, It. trans. *Realismo Capitalista*, Nero: Rome, 2018, p. 77.

the labour market. The appearance of these new individuals and their demand for shared apartments represents the key reason behind the return of minimum dwelling in the form of smaller and smaller living spaces accumulating everywhere and explicating the tangible production and social reproduction of the city.

The squalor and potential of minimum dwelling

In 1872, Friedrich Engels, in his famous pamphlet *The Housing Question*[5], posed, for the first time, the squalor of the minimum dwelling issue that was becoming the typical way people lived in the industrial city. For Engels, the housing shortage caused by the proletarianisation of huge masses of people, and the consequent increase of poor factory workers who moved to cities, was related to unaffordable housing and the deterioration of dwelling conditions, which also affected the middle classes. According to many contemporary reports and narratives, at the end of the century, overcrowded situations existed in certain neighbourhoods in London, Paris, Lyon, Prague, and Berlin. For example: multiple families in one apartment; people living in basements next to diseased cohabitants; others sharing the same bed or sleeping on the floor in rooms, hallways, or cellars without natural light or aeration.[6] The struggle for a place to sleep as a basic need, after a long day working in the factory, generated in the most populated areas of several European cities the following situation: it was possible to rent or sublet every single square metre of space at speculative prices, so much so that it wasn't just the room that was rented, but sometimes just the bed.

---

5   F. Engels, "Zur Wohnungsfrage", *Leipziger Zeitung Der Volksstaat*, June 1872–February 1873, (re-published as pamphlets, Leipzig, 1873; joint in a volume quoted as second edition, *Zur Wohnungsfrage*, Volksbuchhandlung: Göttingen/Zurich, 1887; Engl. trans. *The Housing Question*, International Publisher: New York, n.d. See also: "Zur Wohnungsfrage", in S. Schipper and L. Vollmer (eds.), *Wohnungsforschung: Ein Reader*, transcript Verlag: Bielefeld, 2021, pp. 197–214. https://doi.org/10.1515/9783839453513-010.
6   K. Teige, *Nejmensi Byt*, Vaclov Petr: Prague, 1932, Engl. trans. *The Minimum Dwelling,* MIT Press: Cambridge (MA), 2002, pp. 52–55.

Although the middle classes were better off (but were neverthe-less faced with the spectre of the 1929 economic crisis), it was due to these unhealthy conditions in horrifying and inhuman urban areas that minimum dwelling soon became the key architectural topic on the agenda of the Modern Movement at the II CIAM held in Frankfurt in 1929—and that of its critics.[7]

In his book *The Minimum Dwelling*, the Czechoslovakian poet and Marxist critic Karel Teige interpreted the discussions and outcomes of the II CIAM in Frankfurt and the search for new alternative forms of dwelling at-all-costs, highlighting the squalor and potential of minimum dwelling. Teige adopted Engels' political arguments that the housing issue is firstly a social question before being a spatial one and was convinced that a socialist revolution was possible; but he also was much more aware of the most problematic aspects of the II CIAM proposals. Teige's accusation was that in the twenties the architects of the Modern Movement were simply proposing to reduce the size of the *petit-bourgeois* house and adapt it to the working class. In an opposite direction, the brief focus on the squalor of minimum dwelling, namely on how the proletariat was already living, demonstrated how the minimised version of a middle-class apartment did not really correspond to the real *modus vivendi* of contemporary working-class factory workers, artists, students, intellectuals, and office workers: "Only by first passing through the hells of hovels, shacks, and hostels can the way eventually open up toward a higher form of dwelling in collective houses, devoid of family-based housekeeping".[8]

To a certain extent, the proposals launched at the II CIAM anticipated the ideology of mom and dad's home which, from the point of view of a generic *alexsupertramp* or a typical knowledge worker leaving his family, symbolises the micro-version of the welfare state; the family appears as the only anchor of salvation, providing a shelter, bed, meal, and minimum dwelling; the bedroom or the bed place in the same room with brothers or sisters depends entirely on someone's economy within the realm of the family. It is in fact curious to notice how,

7   G. Grassi, *Das Neue Frankfurt 1926-1931*, Dedalo: Bari, 2007.
8   K. Teige, *op. cit.*, 2002, p. 59.

at that particular moment in history, the bed place was used as a sort of unit of measure of the family apartment. This was strategically clarified by the arguments of many of those present at the CIAM in Frankfurt and by the graphical representations in the meeting's catalogues.[9]

While accepting and envisioning the bed place as an emancipatory potential, Teige's version of *existenzminimum* was exactly the opposite: instead of the micro-apartment, he proposed to reduce dwelling to the individual room plus the collectivisation of all the activities that could be socialised, such as domestic labour, dining, housekeeping, children's space, etc. His appeal to return to the private room embodies a condition already characteristic of the ways of living of the so-called "subject of subsistence minimum": the precarious workers of the twenties and thirties. The collectivisation of dwelling consisted precisely in replacing the mother's unpaid domestic labour with the mechanisation of domestic tasks such as laundry, cooking, and the socialisation of care labour and the raising of children thanks to a salaried staff of educators and care-workers.[10]

Living alone knowing there is someone else outside your room

Teige's book *The Minimum Dwelling* can be considered a theoretical project on communal dwelling argued through a selection of examples, ranging from the most embryonic German boarding houses, hotels for single women, and bachelor apartments to the most complex and emblematical examples such as American residential hotels and the Soviet Dom Kommuna, both presented in Teige's last chapter "Toward new forms of dwelling".[11] Precisely the topic and the structure of Teige's book was the main impetus for Dogma (Pier Vittorio

---

9   M. Korbi and A. Migotto, "Between Rationalization and Political Project: The Existenzminimum from Klein and Teige to Today", *Urban Planning, Housing Builds Cities*, vol. 4, n. 3, 2019, pp. 299–314; C. Aymonino, *L'abitazione razionale. Atti dei congressi CIAM, 1929–1930*, Marsilio: Padua, 1971.

10   P.V. Aureli and M. Tattara, *Loveless: The Minimum Dwelling and Its Discontents*, Black Square: Milan, 2019.

11   K. Teige, *op. cit.*, 2002, pp. 302–322.

Aureli and Martino Tattara) in 2019 for developing further
Teige's incomplete project through the book *Loveless,* as
research for the exhibition *Home Futures* at the Design Museum in London, a theoretical project tracing the contradictory
history of the minimum dwelling based on some of the, both
negative and positive, examples proposed by Karel Teige.
Dogma's book was published in a fundamental moment when
the minimum dwelling question has been strongly related with
the spread of a large amount of precarious knowledge workers.
In fact, Teige's last chapter may be seen in this light both as a
project on how should be the perfect organisational and
architectural form of collective dwelling, and as a panoramic
view of how the typical knowledge worker was living in countries like Germany, the USA, and the USSR during the 1920s.

The contemporary figure of the knowledge worker emerged
massively during the period of the Weimar Republic, in the
German-Austrian world, where he was defined with the term
Kopfarbeiter (brainworker), referring to a salaried worker
employed in the public or private tertiary sector.[12] Brainworkers
at the time were engaged in the tertiary sector, and, unlike
factory workers, as still less fundamental within the productive
cycle of capitalism, in Germany were granted worse welfare
and salary conditions. In the 1920s, clerks, engineers, commercial employees, as well as reporters, teachers, artists, etc. were
all starting to become precarious jobs with a very low income,
while workers were forced to migrate for better jobs from one
city to the other.

Considering the *ethos* of in-depth researches and sociological
studies on the social aspects of these new invisible lives,
architects like Walter Gropius, Hans Scharoun, Bernard
Hermkes, and Ludwig Hilberseimer tackled the situation of
these persons' ways of living in their projects of boarding
houses and hotel apartments. In the ten-storey boarding house
designed by Walter Gropius, a lower-middle income white-collar worker could live for either a long or short period in a very
flexible apartment that corresponded to his changeable
lifestyle. A typical room in the boarding house (also build as a

12   S. Bologna, *op. cit.,* pp. 111–117.

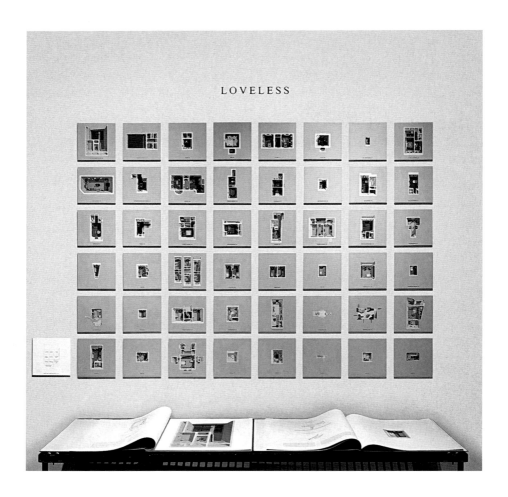

Loveless, Dogma, *Home Futures* exhibition, London 2019, The Design Museum

1:1 prototype for the Werkbund Exhibition in Paris in 1930[13]) had a generic layout with three bays, occupied by two single bedrooms and a central common living room, a shared bathroom, and a kitchenette. This solution was designed either for singles who did not know each other, or for couples who slept in separated rooms and benefited from the centralised facilities on the ground floor. Gropius' project had much in common with the projects by Ludwig Hilberseimer who already considered the metropolis as a place inhabited by nomads; in his designs, workers were extremely mobile and completely set apart from reproductive labour; he radicalised the idea of living in hotels by imagining his *Großstadtarchitektur* as a city with only hotels.[14]

In Hilberseimer's seminal book, the main reference for housing was the American residential hotel that had proliferated in metropolises like New York, Chicago, Seattle, or Los Angeles during the 1910s-20s. At that time, with the development of industrial capitalism in the twenties and thirties, the residential hotel offered accommodation for people living in the same hotel for more than a month; it provided kitchenless rooms and centralised collective services.[15] The city of New York had the highest concentration of intellectuals, white-collar employees, businessmen, graduate bachelors, and artists who came to town to make their fortune; they considered the hotel life as almost the only way they could live within the delirious wilderness of the Big Apple. Taylor's *Principles of Scientific Management* of labour radically changed capitalism and production, sparking a boom in skyscraper hotels all over Manhattan (residential hotels, grand hotels, and hotel clubs). Yet, for every single worker, there was always the possibility to find a cheap hotel room within walking distance to office districts, theatres, and the main train station. For example, the Biltmore Hotel and the Commodore, designed by the architectural firm Warren &

13 P. Overy, "Visions of the Future and the Immediate Past: The Werkbund Exhibition, Paris 1930", *Journal of Design History*, vol. 17, n. 4, 2004, pp. 337–357.

14 L. Hilberseimer, *Großstadtarchitektur*, Julius Hoffmann: Stuttgart, 1927; P.V. Aureli, "More and More About Less and Less: Notes Toward a History of Nonfigurative Architecture.", *Log*, n. 16, 2009, pp. 7–18.

15 P. Groth, *Living Downtown: The History of Residential Hotels in the United States*, University of California Press: Berkeley, 1994, pp. 5–7.

Collectivist reconstruction of dwelling

kitchen	dining	salon = club
house-keeping	bathing	children's space
services	physical culture	individual living cell

centralized and collectivized

Schema of a collective dwelling:

the centralization and collectivization of the economic, cultural, and social factors of the dwelling process;

the reduction of the "apartment" to an individual living cell. One room for each adult person,

whose content (function) is a living room and a bedroom;

the reproduction of a single space undifferentiated dwelling on a higher level;

material and organizational basis for socialist forms of life.

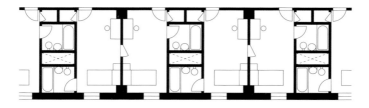

Karel Teige's 1932 diagram of the collectivisation of dwelling
Standardised hotel rooms, Geo. B. Post & Sons Architects for Statler Hotels, 1923

Wetmore between 1913 and 1919, were part of the Grand Central Terminal master plan, directly connected to the station's passages and underground platforms so passengers could easily walk to the hotel reception and lobby.

The generic hotel was a private enterprise managed exactly like a factory: centralised heating, standardised single rooms, factory-like kitchens with specialised sectors for food storage, assembly line dish-washers, and an army of specialised staff of cooks, waiters, service ladies, bellboys, and managers. In 1931, a person who lived in hotels like the Waldorf Astoria was not burdened with any individual form of repetitive work and familial responsibility—someone else took care of you, re-placed family life, and your mother's work; this left you free to live a life of pure hedonism and intellectual jobs. As a hotel guest, you could choose to stay alone in your private room on the upper floors of the skyscraper, or else be with other people in the main lobby, dine in the numerous restaurants, and join strangers in Turkish baths, gyms, oyster bars, or even libraries. Apart from those who lived alone in the hotel *for life*, collective life was always possible for non-guests: doctors, lawyers, architects, and freelance reporters used the lobbies as working places, while others, such as poetess Maya Angelou[16], paid for a room and used it to work during the day, without actually sleeping in the hotel.

This capitalistic model of living was, to a certain extent, used as reference by Soviet architects for the *Dom-Kommuna* project (Communal House) from 1925-30. Revolutionary politicians and intellectuals, such as Alexandra Kollontaj and Leon Trotsky, were familiar with Americanism and hotel life; they believed that the *new Soviet man* and his social emancipation could be reached only through abolition of the family and the collectivi-sation of domestic work including education, food preparation, care, and social life. Such an institutionalisation of collective life in the USSR, coupled with the abolition of private property and the nationalisation of the housing sector, explains the radical utopianism and rationality behind the reformation of

16   A. Fick, *New York Hotel Experience: Cultural and Societal Impacts of an American Invention*, transcript Verlag: Bielefeld, 2017, p. 37.

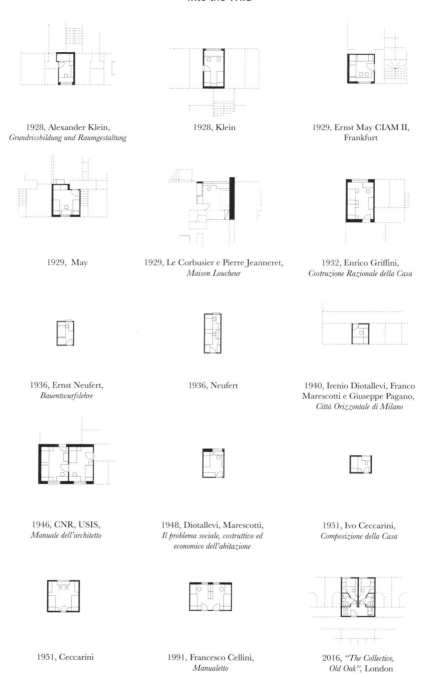

1928, Alexander Klein,
Grundrissbildung und Raumgestaltung

1928, Klein

1929, Ernst May CIAM II,
Frankfurt

1929, May

1929, Le Corbusier e Pierre Jeanneret,
Maison Loucheur

1932, Enrico Griffini,
Costruzione Razionale della Casa

1936, Ernst Neufert,
Bauentwurfslehre

1936, Neufert

1940, Irenio Diotallevi, Franco
Marescotti e Giuseppe Pagano,
Città Orizzontale di Milano

1946, CNR, USIS,
Manuale dell'architetto

1948, Diotallevi, Marescotti,
*Il problema sociale, costruttivo ed
economico dell'abitazione*

1951, Ivo Ceccarini,
Composizione della Casa

1951, Ceccarini

1991, Francesco Cellini,
Manualetto

2016, *"The Collective,
Old Oak"*, London

Camerette. Children's bedrooms in parents' home, from CIAM II to today

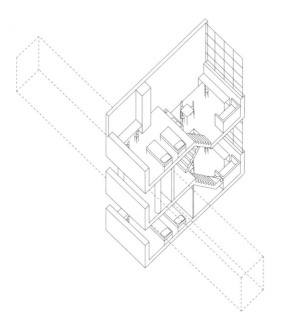

Narkomfin Cell-F, M. Ginzburg, 1930

dwelling and its reduction to a very private space: the room as a basic need for every worker, both factory worker and intellectual.

In the most radical experiments, the Dom-Kommuna (Communal House) was proposed as a city within a city, with private space reduced to a room of nine square metres and the collectivisation of all aspects of life, radically organised based on a factory regime of rules and a precise schedule of activities. Architects like Nikolai Kuzmin[17] proposed versions of Dom-Kommuna where family members were to be separated from each other: children slept in dormitories grouped by age, close to integrated schools and kindergarten; husbands and wives slept in separated dormitories or individual cells with adjoining doors next to their partner's cell.

17   N. Kuzmin, "Il problema dell'organizzazione scientifica del modo di vita", *SA* n. 3, 1930, Italian trans. in G. Canella and M. Meriggi (eds.), *SA Sovremennaja Arkhitektura,* Dedalo: Bari, 2007, pp. 528–534.

*Brother and sister's shared room in
parent's apartment*
students, Bari

"Posto-letto"
students, Bari

"Posto-letto"
students, Bari

"Posto-letto"
students, Brussels

Room in Airbnb
Brussels

Room in shared apartment
single worker, Brussels

Room in shared apartment
artist, Brussels

Room in shared apartment
intern, Coventry

Room in shared apartment
intern, Coventry

Room in shared apartment
student, Brussels

Room in shared apartment
single worker, Brussels

Room in shared apartment
single worker, Brussels

Room in shared apartment
single worker, Madrid

Studio-apartment
artist, Brussels

Studio-apartment
artist, Brussels

Studio-apartment
employee for EC, Brussels

Minimum dwellings of today: how precarious workers live

Studio-apartment
architect, Cologne

Studio-apartment
engineer, Tirana

Studio-apartment
couple, designers, Crema

Studio in Airbnb
Bari

Studio-apartment
researcher, Bari

Studio-apartment
freelance architect, Rome

Micro-appartament
The Collective, London

Micro-appartament
architect, Tokyo

Micro-apartment
architect, Tokyo

Micro-apartment
photographer, Milan

Studio-apartment
student, Paris

Studio-apartment
student, Paris

Studio-apartment
hotel worker, Paris

Apartament
single worker, Berlin

Home-office
freelance, Berlin

Home-office
freelance architect, Brussels

In total disagreement with these radicalisations, Moisej Ginzburg, co-founder of Group OSA, who had very well in mind the rational aspects of the American residential hotel, in his Dom-Narkomfin project of 1930 insisted that, for the rudimental cultural context of the USSR of the time, a gradual passage to collectivisation was needed. In the Dom-Narkomfin project (1930), he experimented with a gradual shift to collectivisation, from the lower floors to the rooftop: a mixed use of K-Cells, family apartments, minimal F-Cells for singles/couples, and sleeping cabins for nomads on the rooftop. The famous F-Cell apartment in the Narkomfin was basically a studio designed for the lifestyle of an intellectual or artist, a space with a double-height living room with a large window, a kitchenette, and a mezzanine bed place: the only collective functions in the building were a restaurant and a gym. The F-Cell, with its minimum, complex spatiality and its layout that allowed for a common *rue interieure*, represented and, arguably, still does represent the perfect balance between *staying alone forever* and the constant desire to explore what is outside.

Stop: co-living is no-living

While the term *minimum* referring to dwelling is currently confused with the idea of the capsule, with Ikea-like minimalism or with slogans like 'Less is enough', as regard real dwelling conditions, it refers to a more problematic situation. Once the new generation of workers are away from the financial realm of the family and without mom's care work, dwelling depends on the ability to have a stable job and income. Reviewing the current rental market of rooms and homes published on social network pages and websites for students and young knowledge workers, it is possible to argue that, paradoxically, the higher the income, the smaller the minimum dwelling they are able to afford. The city offers only two types of squalor spaces: the first, mostly for students and precarious workers, is the *posto-letto* (literally bed place) within a former family apartment shared by a collective of strangers. Paying for a *posto-letto* means adapting a collective form of life within a space that was formerly designed for a different way of living;

in many cases this generates conflict between cohabitants in the division of domestic work, irritation as regards inviting strangers, noise, etc.; the second refers to the micro-apartment or studio, generally for workers with a more stable income. Finally alone, living in a studio apartment means literally squeezing dwelling into one space where there is no longer a distinction between domestic work, studying or working.

While *petit-bourgeois* architects and academics are constantly focusing on commercial experiences of co-living such as *The Student Hotel* in Berlin, Paris, Barcelona, or Florence—where one can pay 500€ for just one week—or the Combo, ex-Crociferi, in Venice, proletarian students and knowledge workers live in the real world of low incomes and precariousness, and are parent-dependant. Reactionary positions like these have unfortunately an operative role in the real world: they open up and facilitate the terrain to speculators.

Past experiences of collective dwelling are not fetishist academic formalisms for *professori-di-composizione*, they reveal periods when domestic life and dwelling was radically questioned as a social problem, with real attempts to emancipate space and life itself. From an architectural point of view, the above examples demonstrate the possibilities that reduced private space offers to design: the less I possess, the bigger and more theatrical collective space could be, creating the perfect scenario for things and relationships that could not be designed or imagined, but at least always invented anew; a scenario where, at any moment, a typical *Into the Wild* story could take place. To do this, however, we (the designers, academics, and students) should perhaps stop designing forms for the sake of pure formalism, until our thoughts and criticism are mature enough so that we know how to destroy capitalism, its wilderness, and any traditional idea of the house, including our parents' bedroom.

How to Prepare your Home for Sale...so It Sells,
stills from Barb Schwarz promotional video, 1987

Federico Coricelli, Chiara Iacovone

Home Staging as a Practice Enabling Commodification

"I think that the idea of commodifying your environment or turning everything into a purchasable object seems likely to happen" [1]

Mark is a property manager based in Copenhagen. He entered the home-sharing business after a shocking and revealing episode. During his first experience as an Airbnb host, Mark realised that his guests used his and his wife's clothes to share videos on social media under the hashtag #weirdsex. Horrified, he installed spy cameras in the house to control his guests during their stays. After a while, he figured out that more and more guests were using his home to *act* and *perform*—literally —as characters in someone else's shoes. Mark reacted drastically. He deleted his real identity from all social media, quit his job, and created several fake host profiles to rent, on housing platforms, houses sublet by a real estate agency. From a specific website he bought photographic sets of daily life portraits made by professional actors. Then he set up the house as it if were lived in by the characters in the pictures: the fake hosts. In an interview he gave to Beka and Lemoine for their documentary *Selling Dreams*, Mark stated that he was fulfilling a precise market demand: "They wanted to have another life, another story, to be other characters for a few days. [...] It's not fake, it's true if you believe in it".[2] In 1967, Guy Debord wrote *The Society of Spectacle* about the dominance of the culture of images as a developing form of the concept of alienation, structuring a Marxist critique to life-pervasive

---

1   A. Bava, A. Branzi, R. Yu, and A.T. Harvey, *Everything that is solid melts into Airbnb*, Panel, Airbnb Pavilion, 2014, https://www.swissinstitute.net/event/panel-everything-that-is-solid-melts-into-airbnb-with-alessandro-bava-andrea-branzi-rachael-yu-and-aaron-taylor-harvey-of-airbnb-hosted-by-airbnb-pavilion-fabrizio-ballabio-alessandro-bava-luis/, accessed on 4 May 2022.
2   I. Beka and L. Lemoine, *Selling Dreams*, documentary, 2016, https://vimeo.com/ondemand/sellingdreams/189505421, accessed on 4 May 2022.

commodification.[3] During the last century, the power of images increased to the extent that they are now the medium used by profit chains to express and reproduce themselves. The production of imageries is behind the advertisement and consumption process. The rapid rise of new economies, mostly acting in digital space, has allowed a fast and capillary dissemination of the culture of images and, consequently, a pervasive process of commodification. In this article, we discuss the role of images as a commodifying tool implemented by digital platforms in the housing market. We question the way in which the tech-mediated market prompts a progressive dissolution of private domestic space into a *staged* commodity.

Residential property constitutes the first asset category globally in terms of value, representing 60% of the world's wealth, including stocks, bonds, and gold.[4] This is the result of a process that lasted fifty years, during which the real estate market mutually 'fed' on the neoliberal state ethos of a property -owning democracy, leading to what Samuel Stein defines the *Real Estate State*.[5] In this context, the residential function of housing is subject to its value as an asset. Nevertheless, this dual and contradictory condition is embedded in any commodity since Marx highlighted the coincidence of the use value and exchange value of commodities.[6] Therefore, house trading as a commodity is nothing new, while referring to the commodification of housing refers to the progressive growth of a large slice of the production and consumption of housing aimed only at speculation without even contemplating inhabitation. For example, Hellinikon, the massive development project in

3   G. Debord, *La Société du Spectacle*, Buchet-Chastel: Paris, 1967, Engl. trans. *The Society of the Spectacle*, Black and Red: Detroit, 1970.
4   The real estate market is worth about 217 trillion US dollars, almost "60 per cent of the value of all global assets or $217 trillion USD—with residential real estate comprising $163 trillion USD or 75 percent". (L. Farha, *Report of the special rapporteur on adequate housing as a component of the right to an adequate standard of living, and on the right to non-discrimination in this context*, United Nations Human Rights Council, https://www.ohchr.org/en/special-procedures/sr-housing/financialization-housing, accessed on 4 May 2022).
5   S. Stein, *Capital City: Gentrification and the Real Estate State*, Verso: New York, 2019.
6   As David Harvey critically analysed. See D. Harvey, *The Limits to Capital*, Verso: New York, 2018.

Athens, where the developers provided not even one square metre of social housing within a total of 260 hectares of development.[7]

The effects of hyper-commodification[8] are manifest in major western cities, such as New York or London, where the scale of investments is such that housing prices are unaffordable for the majority of the urban population.[9] Hyper-commodification of housing unfolds in terms of social exclusion and depopulation. In addition, commodification penetrates the multi-layered urban fabric beyond the real estate market. As already noted by Forrest and Williams in the 1980s, "in understanding the full implications of this commodification process, we must begin to comprehend the way these changes penetrate into the very fabric of daily life".[10] A similar argument is presented by Randy Martin in his book *Financialization of Daily Life* (2002), in which he highlights how the contemporary economic structure of self-entrepreneurship could extensively modify financial boundaries, letting them flood the private sphere.[11] Such dynamics are recognisable—amongst others—in the mecha-nism of the sharing economy, where companies make profits by financing everyday life activities or jobs formerly protected by corporations. UberEats monetised cycling; carpooling apps such as CarToGo converted motorists into taxi drivers; and TaskRabbit can now sell housekeeping services without any professional or insurance coverage. This marketplace also includes the domestic sphere, as companies involved in furniture design, property management, and renting complete the full spectrum of commodified aspects of domestic daily life.

7   http://thehellinikon.com/the-vision/, accessed on 4 May 2022.
8   D.J. Madden and P. Marcuse, *In Defense of Housing. The Politics of Crisis*, Verso: New York, 2016.
9   For New York, see S. Stein, *op. cit.* For London, see A. Minton, *Big Capital. Who Is London For?*, Penguin: London, 2017.
10   R. Forrest and P. Williams, "Commodification and Housing: Emerging Issues and Contradictions", *Environment and Planning*, vol. 16, n. 9, 1984, p. 1178.
11   R. Martin, *Financialization of Daily Life,* Temple University Press: Philadelphia, 2002.

Before and after home staging practice, HOME Philosophy Real Estate, 2020

"How to prepare your home for sale...so it sells!" [12]

Airbnb—the major short-term rental platform currently available—has revolutionised the hospitality and housing market since its inception in 2009. As for all the Silicon Valley tech companies, the funding and evaluation system of venture capital defines Airbnb's performance. Nevertheless, without considering market downturns, what Airbnb introduced was a concept potentially enabling the global commodification of any single housing unit around the world—including tree houses and boats.

It is important to note that in its early days, Airbnb was not even designed as a service for payment, following the example of websites like Craigslist or Couchsurfing, which based their profits on indirect revenue from advertisements and external funding. This highlights how the platform economy is even less attached to the value generated from the use of its products instead of the mass of data it generates. This interpretation, shared by Nick Srnicek in his book *Platform Capitalism,* [13] defines a taxonomy of the different typologies of platforms that currently exist. Airbnb falls into the "lean platform" category, as it generates revenue from housing rents without actually owning any of its listings.

The other disruptive innovation introduced by Airbnb—reputation—is one of the keys to the success of most platforms. [14] Any host and guest of an Airbnb home has to submit a detailed review, which automatically fits any single listing in a given market. In line with Srnicek's interpretation, the real asset that platforms produce is data. Reputation is built on a certain critical mass of stored data about the product, such as the number of reviews (and visits), the quality of its service, and its amenities. The greater the number, the better the reputation, the higher the price. A crucial aspect of this phenomenon is that a substantial part of the data used by Airbnb to sell its product involve pictures of the listings. Unlike the traditional hospitality sector that has a codified standard setting—for

---

12 https://www.youtube.com/watch?v=XVf6_rHnE2E, accessed on 4 May 2022.
13 N. Srnicek, *Platform Capitalism,* Polity Press: Cambridge (UK), 2016.
14 https://www.wired.co.uk/article/welcome-to-the-new-reputation-economy, accessed on 4 May 2022.

example, hotel stars—, Airbnb relies extensively on the effectiveness of its photographic material.[15] This fact significantly complicates a comparative evaluation of two "equivalent" market products, bypassing most of the traditional mantra of real estate: *location, location, location*.

On the other hand, this element of complexity justifies the company's massive initial effort to provide free photo shootings to hosts,[16] because once collected, the photos of interiors in the listings not only showed a certain quality, but sold a "genuine" product. If we take the sales and promotion process of ordinary real estate, we will find an enormous amount of renderings of interiors created by professional CGI companies to enable the developer to sell its buildings upfront, before completion. These interiors usually contain high-end design furniture present in 3D model libraries of the major digital companies in the real estate industry; this means that most of the time these objects are placeholder objects. In the case of Airbnb, the "reality" of images and their truthfulness is coupled with the quality of the pictures and the photo set in general. Unlike the mere descriptive aim of traditional real estate, an Airbnb photo set can include a still life of pottery on a table, a macro of some flowers in the garden, stock images of the neighbourhood, or landmarks in the surroundings.

These value extraction practices led to the creation of a parallel universe of new professionals and services. Many of the companies or businesses that use Airbnb manage a large number of properties, providing several services regarding the reservation process and the guests' sojourn. These range from the more practical automated check-in/check-out, luggage storage, and transfer from the airport to leisured experiences and catering services. Many services are also provided to the hosts, for example, complete management of the properties during the whole process, from online management to cleaning services, professional photographs, and consultancy. Indeed,

15   Further reputation systems introduced by the company are represented by the SuperHost awarding system and by the verified prime locations for which the company reserved the Airbnb Plus section in 2018.

16   L. Gallagher, *The Airbnb Story: How Three Guys Disrupted an Industry, Made Billions of Dollars ... and Plenty of Enemies*, Virgin Books: London, 2018.

some of these companies propose an advisory service involving renovation of the house in order to increase market appeal; the website of Dimorra Hospitality, a Neapolitan property manager company, states: "We turn your normal home into a safe source of income".[17]

This practice is called *home staging;* it is used to modernise or renovate housing units in order to gain higher profits during either a sale or rental. The very word, home staging, bespeaks a willingness to stage a scene for commercial purposes. Home staging does not only involve house renewal, but is more the emulation of new aesthetic standards and formal rules adapted to the tastes of the global market. According to an Italian association of home stagers (APHSI), after a home staging renewal, the time it takes to sell is reduced by roughly two thirds, while the sales price is reduced by just 4% compared with the 14% when traditional selling is involved. The cost of this service, again according to APHSI, is around 1,000 euros for an 80-square-metre apartment with minor renovations (painting, tidying, photo shoot, and advertisement).[18] The costs increase with significant adjustments, like greater renovation and the purchase of furniture.

Home staging first appeared in the United States during the seventies; it was intended to reduce sales time and avoid future discounts on the final price. Even then, this practice involved nothing more than a small renovation, however, the way in which it was both promoted and structured, reproduced existing practices in the ecology of housing commodification. Initially, home staging was chiefly used for North American middle-class family homes and was a kind of tutorial of how to present and set up the houses to possible buyers, without any structural changes. The real estate agent Barb Schwarz, who considers herself the first home stager,[19] describes in her promotional video shot more or less during the eighties and entitled *How to prepare your home for sale...so it sells!* how to

17 https://www.dimorra.it, accessed on 4 May 2022.
18 https://www.ilsole24ore.com/art/home-staging-cosi-casa-si--vende-piu-fretta-e-senza-sconti-AEKdp5eF, accessed on 4 May 2022.
19 Barb Schwarz holds roughly a dozen trademarks related to home staging, including The Creator of Home Staging®.

Zoom meeting using the background images provided by Sonder, 2019

set up the house for the buyers, because "the way you live in a home and the way you sell a home are two different things".[20]

Today, this practice is used in both the sales and rental market. In particular, this service quickly became more popular in the short-term rental sector due to the facilitated possibility of profit maximisation with minimal effort. Indeed, the recognisable success of home staging has been noted by Airbnb. Meridith Baer, one of the leading home stagers in the United States, wrote an article for the Airbnb blog in which she gives *ten simple tips* to improve the house set up and, as a result, "help to get more guests and keep them happy".[21] The list includes some functional elements ranging from the hotel-like equipped bathroom and the bedroom with a sitting area to the application of more ephemeral elements, such as flowers, painting walls or doors in colour, mirrors, and lights. Airbnb listings have a typical style; this has been highlighted by an AMO research project presented at the Oslo Architecture Triennale in 2016[22]; it included several examples from Airbnb listings around the world where this style is particularly obvious. Using a series of iconic photographs, they create a taxonomy where the living elements (parquet flooring, wooden tables, white light, and designer furnishings) became the standardised components of staged commodities.

Over the years, this practice has become more structured, and in the platform market, the actors have become more professional. Nowadays, the Airbnb market is in the hands of so-called multi-property hosts—hosts that manage multiple properties; they can be real companies, property managers, other platforms, real estate firms, and even construction firms. In Rome, in 2019, 18% of the hosts owned more than three properties, accounting for 53% of the stock.[23] These companies offer several additional services to the guests and house

20   https://www.youtube.com/watch?v=XVf6_rHnE2E, accessed on 4 May 2022.
21   https://blog.atairbnb.com/attract-guests-10-simple-tips-home-staging-expert-meridith-baer/, accessed on 4 May 2022.
22   L.A. Casanovas Blanco, I.G. Galan, C. Mínguez Carrasco, A. Navarrete Llopis, and M. Otero Verzier (eds.), *After Belonging: The Objects, Spaces, and Territories of the Ways We Stay in Transit*, Lars Müller Publishers: Zurich, 2016.
23   Data acquired by AirDNA.

owners (sometimes these societies are the owner themselves), including home staging. Across the globe, these companies manage and stage houses to make them profitable assets, letting them flow eventually into the vacation rental market. Some of them, such as Homm (that owns roughly 200 properties in Greece), offer anything from the renovation of the apartment, "use only top-quality products and high-end product brands",[24] to complete reconstruction from scratch; Homm owns two condo buildings in central Athens. They also offer advice regarding the Golden Visa resident permit program; this European programme involves obtaining a 5-year residence permit for non-EU citizens after investing a certain amount of money in several assets, including residential property.[25] Companies like Homm in Athens or Tamea International in Lisbon propose a full package ranging from the sale of the property to its management should owners want a return on their investment by renting out the property, possibly in the short-term rental market that provides flexibility and maximum profit; in these cases, the houses sold are already fully furnished, staged commodities ready to enter the rental market.

In its blog,[26] the Altido company (based in London, with around 2,000 properties in Europe) advises how to decorate a small flat in order to meet the demands of its clients and obtain as much value as possible from small spaces. While the new real estate unicorn Sonder (based in San Francisco, with around 8,500 properties across the globe) found its fortune by renting out fashionable designer apartments, home staging is not an option for this company, but a requirement. In a recent article in their blog, they present several images of staged houses created by Sonder interior designers, downloadable to be used as Zoom backgrounds.[27]

---

24   https://www.homm.gr/en/about/, accessed on 4 May 2022.
25   This programme is present in almost every European country; the investment in real estate can vary from €300,000 in Portugal, €250,000 in Greece, to €500,000 in Spain.
26   https://stayaltido.com/blog/stylingyourvacationrental, accessed on 4 May 2022.
27   https://blog.sonder.com/design/introducing-sonder-backgrounds-for-your-next-zoom-meeting/, accessed on 4 May 2022.

"A standard that the commodity has lived up to by turning the whole planet into a single world market" [28]

Airbnb's monopoly of the short-term rental market prompted an exponential growth of profitable investments on listings owned by larger economic enterprises rather than individuals or families. From a platform devoted to stimulate micro gains for households with a spare room to rent, in just a decade Airbnb became a marketplace for high-yield investments, involving more and more professionals from the real estate and the building industry. These changes happened across the full spectrum of the hospitality industry. In the post-war globalised world, hotel chains built a wide range of options for the growing middle classes, setting new standards for aesthetics, comfort, and ultimately for life—the ritual of the modern vacation. Airbnb introduced a revolutionary concept: that the main value of its product profits from the opposite of standardisation, since each listing is related to the host's identity. Nevertheless, as the Airbnb market was established with mass consumption in mind, some standards started to emerge globally. Striking similarities between the average two-bedroom flat listing occurred from Moscow to New York. Home staging found a mainstream "genre" for its plays, and Ikea contributed significantly as the set designer: "In some ways the generic Ikea home is almost invisible. It's repetition. It's predictability. Its sameness across the globe makes it immaterial. It becomes a predictable nexus from which you choose to explore the city. It, in itself, is not an experience. It's just the baseline allowing you to sleep. That's appealing to me because then it is sort of like – what is the minimum investment we can make to see the world? Or to facilitate other people seeing the world? Ikea definitely provides that."[29]

Hyggelig is the Danish word that describes the kind of aesthetic standard pursued by most Airbnb listings. The term refers to both the quality of a domestic space as *nice, pleasant, cosy,*

28   G. Debord, *op. cit.*, 1970, p. 19.
29   https://www.swissinstitute.net/event/panel-everything-that-is-solid-melts-into-airbnb-with-alessandro-bava-andrea-branzi-rachael-yu-and-aaron-taylor-harvey-of-airbnb-hosted-by-airbnb-pavilion-fabrizio-ballabio-alessandro-bava-luis/, accessed on 4 May 2022.

Details in Airbnb houses, 2019

and *comfortable*.[30] It's interesting to note how a word that initially referred to an atmosphere and experiential features was later used for physical objects, constructing images based on marketability and profitability. The domestic space of *hyggelig* could be related to the urban space of Airspace, a notion introduced by some urban geographers referring to the spatialisations of the sharing economy—including Airbnb—with its mix of comfort, hipsterish minimalism, and photogenic views, where human coexistence is efficiently regulated in time by algorithms.[31] To satisfy the demand for an authentic experience promoted by Airbnb's slogan "Belong Anywhere", home staging provides the tools to combine standardised comfort with signs of personalisation. Once viewed as a whole, the images of staged listings appear to have the twofold characteristic of being both generic and unique. The *hyggelig* of the white box with a minimal wooden furniture unit is coloured here and there by signs of local culture. The motto "Belong Anywhere" unfolds in the paradox of the simultaneous persistence of the comfort of commercial hospitality combined with the uniqueness of lived-in homes decorated with local *touches*.

Entering these staged interiors reveals how the typical rooms of the modern functional house are subject to slight changes in order to fulfil this double condition. As this may not be initially perceivable, a closer look unveils a slight myopia. A fully equipped kitchen, with a few freebies for coffee and tea making; a bathroom full of towels and some free shampoos, but with no sign of cleaning devices; or a living room without a TV, but filled with posters on the wall showing landmarks of the hosting location. These examples may represent a caricature of the staged home, but they reveal the quintessential aspect of home staging. The very empty space is filled with the bare minimum; necessary objects to provide comfort, while the decorative (low-cost) materials add value to the listing in its virtual marketing phase, but have a marginal role during the real experience.

30   The word is an extension of the Danish word *Hygge*. https://dictionary. cambridge.org/dictionary/english/hygge, accessed on 4 May 2022.

31   A. Pavoni and A.M. Brighenti, "Airspacing the City – Where Technophysics meets Atmoculture", *Azimuth*, V (2017), n. 10.

L'Aquila. A central street, 2010

Marina Ciampi, Anna Maria Paola Toti

Living in L'Aquila after the 2009 Earthquake. Forms and Practices of Space

Description of the research

This research can be considered the second phase of a study we began roughly ten years ago in the city of L'Aquila. Our objective was to record the dramatic physical, territorial, and social transformation caused by the terrible earthquake of 6 April 2009. In the wake of the intense emotions felt throughout the country—amplified by the mass media, institutions, and, often in functionalist terms, by contemporary political represen- tatives (both by members of government and the opposition)— my colleague Anna Maria Paola Toti and I decided to go to L'Aquila to sociologically document the event. Our aim was not to satisfy either an emotional or largely empathic impulse, or the natural need to narrate the reality of a devastated land; we wished to use a preliminary scientific approach based on visual sociology methods to counter the contemporary, ubiquitous, and at times sensational or prejudiced representations. We began our research a few months after the earthquake since we had to let some time pass in order to ensure a "certain detachment" and allow the community's pain and suffering to ease a little so that people were willing to talk to us. Without their input, the research would have been pointless.

The research was based on semi-structured interviews with privileged witnesses and ordinary people as well as on-site videos and photographs—all tools with which to document, analyse, gather data, and acquire an in-depth understanding of an event involving community structures, objects, spaces, memories, traditions, monuments, and the artistic and cultural heritage of a rather large territory. It is not easy to achieve a balance between shared empathy and non-involvement, between proximity and distance, i.e., what is required to ensure the *objectivation participante* proposed by Pierre Bourdieu[1]. Taking photographs of the disaster area and the ruins and rubble in the city and nearby municipalities means broadening one's viewpoint, delimiting the speculative horizon, and attributing value to the loss of lives and also to the loss of spatial indexes, domestic references, and historical stratifications. The images used in the sociological study also acted as a memory trigger; it made the persons and objects relevant and important and ontologically granted them the dignity of being worthy to be photographed.

As scholars we chose and selected the visual material for cognitive and heuristic purposes; the material was then incorporated in a documentary entitled *L'Aquila Reale*, which was presented at a number of national and international meetings. We selected several aggregating topics, both public and private, from amongst the socio-territorial contents to be studied and vast, *ground zero* desolation: dwelling (the individual *in* his habitat); the I-Thou relationships in terms of solidaristic forms and the construction of new neighbourhoods; the validity of the projects regarding material reconstruction and the reconstruction of imagery (both individual and collective). Like the work performed by the husband and wife duo, Helen and Robert Lynd, for their study entitled *Middletown*, we *returned* to L'Aquila after ten years to compare the status of the city just after the disaster with what it looked like ten years after reconstruction; we not only recorded the real changes that had taken place and proposed updated accounts about community life in the city, but we also focused on the revitalisation of "lost" places and the recovery of buildings crucial for the life of the community and socialisation (schools, markets, cinemas, meeting places, etc.).

The study is presently ongoing, but should be considered only as in progress, since the scenario still remains incomplete and *in fieri*. During our meetings with the interviewees, we discovered that the amount of funds allocated for reconstruction are

---

1   P. Bourdieu, "L'objectivation participante", *Actes de la Recherche en Sciences Sociales*, 2003, n. 150, pp. 43–57.

equivalent to a budget, but without a fixed programme or plan. The inhabitants of L'Aquila hope—and so should all Italians if it weren't for the fact that they tend to forget—that these funds be invested to achieve real urban and territorial recovery. Photographing and interviewing the inhabitants of L'Aquila is our way of telling them: "I care about you, I am with you, I am listening to your stories, I will be a witness of what you are experiencing".[2]

L'Aquila today: resilience and resistance

When sociologists return to study a place devastated by a catastrophic event such as the earthquake in L'Aquila, they already know they will observe conditions of *post res perditas*. The management of earlier, similar cases forces researchers to be realistic: they would be hard put to imagine that the capital of the Abruzzi region had been able to regain its former splendour. After such a devastating earthquake, the social fabric and morphology of the territory will still bear visible physical wounds and spatial changes which in some sites reflect a different image of the city.

It's ridiculous and ethically unfair to classify the disastrous effects of the earthquakes that have occurred in Italy in recent decades, but it is true that natural events, similar in magnitude and intensity, can cause very different damage to the community: the severity of the disaster is not related only to the event, but also to its effects on the social system involved. This is why L'Aquila and the fifty-six hamlets in the crater have become highly symbolic, as regards both the number of victims and the artistic importance of the ancient monuments and buildings that were destroyed, thus impoverishing the social and economic fabric of the city centre.[3] The tragedy triggered by any earthquake is that the natural destructive

2   P. Bourdieu, *Images d'Algérie: Une affinité élective*, Actes Sud, Camera Austria et la Fondation Liber: Paris, 2003, Italian trans. *In Algeria. Immagini dello sradicamento*, Carocci: Rome, 2012, p. 78.

3   M. Ciampi, "Ri-definizione del sociale e intervento pubblico nella ricostruzione de L'Aquila", *Rivista Trimestrale di Scienza dell'Amministrazione*, n. 3, Angeli: Milan, 2013.

Palazzo della Prefettura, 2010

event "impacts on a physically and socially produced vulnerable population"[4] that is therefore prevented from implementing collective countermeasures.

At each violent and unexpected shock, wherever it occurs, every individual is alone. His horizon of survival is limited to himself or a few of his neighbours; he is confused and overwhelmed by a primordial fear. Only afterwards, during so-called reconstruction, does *societas* gradually resurface; community ties are restored, as is the need to defend others and be defended by the social group. Sociologists focus on this phenomenology of restoration of normality and recovery of a community dimension; they wish to record the post-emergency phase and the level of reconstruction: recovery involves not only engineering and urban planning, but also the "structure of sentiment" animating these places[5], the cultural landscape, and the perspective horizon of the individual and the community.

As expert visual sociologists we retraced our steps during our return visit and reviewed the most important contents of our first visit. We compared the images gathered immediately after the earthquake with those illustrating the current situation. During the interviews held ten years ago, several problems had emerged as priority issues if real construction was to be achieved: resuming a personal and social life by no longer having to live in transitory or temporary housing (e.g., the houses in the New Towns or temporary housing modules) and thus be able to at least deceive oneself into thinking that the previous pre-earthquake life had begun again and hence alleviate the feeling of not belonging; finding friends and establishing non-opportunistic relationships, ones that are stable and profound, like those that had been lost; being able to access the city centre as the hub of everyday life and inter-subjective and cultural communication, not only for the locals, but also for tourists.

---

4   G. Ligi, *Antropologia dei disastri*, Laterza: Rome-Bari, 2009, p. 5.
5   E. De Martino, *La fine del mondo. Contributo alle analisi delle apocalissi culturali*, Einaudi: Turin, 1977.

After a decade, the mental state of the inhabitants living in the earthquake-hit area has obviously improved thanks to the strength and resilience of these lands. However, this lenitive effect appears to be linked to the passing of time, to less devastating personal circumstances, and to the ability to create associative networks focused on implementing primary projects for the community. Observant sociologists will link this general feeling, expressed by the new interviewees, to a second interpretation of the city for which they will use their eyes and ears: today, the city's skyline is rather unique due to the cumbersome and almost alien presence of numerous cranes—indefatigable arms working to reconstruct several city districts. Although L'Aquila no longer resembles the bombed-out city of Kabul, it does look like an open-air worksite: even the most distracted *flâneurs* walking along the streets of the city centre will suddenly be "jolted" out of their reverie by the sound of construction; their eyes will be captured by the long cables which, like hanging snakes, sway back and forth between elegantly restored buildings and others still shored up by retaining walls. Telltale signs of the destruction are still visible. In some places they reflect the image of a wounded city: desolate interiors behind broken windows, old placards of shops or private studios, and long canvases draped like shrouds around damaged churches. They tell of a life that no longer exists, a life that has begun again elsewhere.

In this incomplete scenario, L'Aquila looks like a tightrope walker suspended between a clear past and a present focused courageously on the future: there is evidence of a resumption of normal commercial activities (especially shops, bars, and restaurants) but this is accompanied—in the old city centre—by a stunted revival of the more crucial activities: schools, universities, theatres, cinemas, and markets. In the past, and also more recently, a hamlet without a market is an impoverished place lacking its most dynamic aspect of liveability. Anyone who has had this experience, like the inhabitants of L'Aquila, has felt an even greater loss, a feeling mentioned by all the interviewees. Not even the restored beauty of the city centre can allay this emotion unless it is accompanied by a social revitalisation and cultural stimulus project (L'Aquila is the sixth biggest city as regards the number of monuments in Italy and is therefore a tourist destination). To date, this kind of project cannot be considered as having been achieved completely.

Angelo De Nicola, a writer and journalist working at the newspaper Il Messaggero, has witnessed this second research phase. He provides valuable insight regarding perspective when he writes "We should distinguish between complete reconstruction—of the crater and the whole city—and that of the old city centre, an area around which the community has always clung; it represents a symbol both psychologically and economically, because before the earthquake 1,500 economic activities, shops, professional studios, etc. were located there (...)". He takes a positive view of the reconstruction, even if he points out certain problems, chiefly the delay in the reconstruction of public buildings compared to private ones since they are the real engine behind change: "Just think of the restoration and revival of the Basilica of San Bernardino (in the city centre) and the Basilica of Collemaggio which, even if located outside the city, is its symbol because it was founded by Pope Celestine V and houses his remains. The restoration of the Basilica of Collemaggio was a truly cyclopean undertaking and has been recognised as one of the best in Europe, but it was financed by ENI, a private company (...). Public investments are lagging behind: examples include the building symbol of the City Hall, constructed in a new location because the old one is still devastated, the Cathedral of San Massimo, where only the envelope still stands and the interior is now covered by dense vegetation, or the Church in Paganica. In this case, only the skeleton survived, while all its eighteenth-century artefacts were lost when the church collapsed. The inhabitants of L'Aquila are becoming world champions of resilience, successfully intervening in the public-private see-saw, while the fate of the old city centre is still unclear". From day one of the reconstruction, they fought to play a key role and obtain effective participation in the process. These are the words of Roberta Gargano, Communications and Marketing Director of the Teatro Stabile d'Abruzzo: "As citizens we rejected the idea of dividing the city into lots which would then be put up for public tender. Immediately after the earthquake, this solution had been approved by right-wing

Chiesa dei Gesuiti, 2020

politicians (the former Abruzzo Region) and left-wing politicians (the Municipality). Citizens would have played a marginal role; they would have been allowed to participate only when the project was completed. We strongly opposed this solution by acting forcefully and resisting so that we could personally implement reconstruction by creating consortia. This allowed us to present the first projects, thanks to the support and knowledge of experts and structuralists". By performing this accurate retrospective analysis, Roberta Gargano clarifies all the stages and procedures of the public-private relationship and notes how the allocated funds of the former Berlusconi Government were in fact sufficient, but were immediately blocked by bureaucratic procedures that slowed down the ensuing reconstruction. On the contrary, the decision to create consortia made it possible to access the funds and avoid the quicksand and red tape of bureaucracy; this led to the completion of roughly 80% of the works. According to the interviewee, problems arose when the consortia decided not to work with humanists and entrusted the projects exclusively to technicians; their projects were unhelpful, causing paralysis and disagreements and denying local citizens the possibility to cooperate with the other actors involved.

The several million euros already allocated have been blocked since 2009, while most public worksites are still waiting to be set up. In particular, a post on the Municipality's website states that—finally!—the notices of expression of interest in being assigned the design of three damaged schools were published on 24 June 2020. The schools are: the S. Barbara-San Sisto nursery school (5.1 million euros); the Celestino V primary school (2.4 million euros), and the first plot of the Pettino-Vetoio nursery school (2.075 million euros). Essential services such as primary schools have had to wait ten years before seeing the beginning of their revival. The same bureaucratic melting pot effect also applies to the recent "Decision to assign 2.1 million euros to start planning the allocation of the ReStart 2020 development programme funds, with which part of the resources for reconstruction are allotted to the development of cultural activities in the 2009 crater". These are all examples of the country's monstrous bureaucratic machine. Max Weber, the first sociologist to study its advantages and disadvantages, would have maintained that in L'Aquila bureaucracy was doing its best to reinforce its superior position, secreting information and objectives, while the State tried to stay in the shadows and avoid critical scrutiny.[6] This, however, is something that the citizens of L'Aquila did not support; they tried to fight the long public processes by cooperating directly in the overall reconstruction of the city.

All the interviewees wanted the procedures to be simplified since this would mean more rational procedures, but without losing control. Only a decisive intervention by the State can establish the fate of the old town centre, revitalise all the public offices, structures, and commercial and cultural activates, and make them once again available to the citizens of L'Aquila.

Part of the funds of the contract notice *Fare centro* is earmarked to be used to enhance and support public companies. Another important artistic-cultural event is the festival *I cantieri dell'immaginario*, sponsored by the Municipality and coordinated with the Teatro Stabile d'Abruzzo: these initiatives are an attempt to re-vitalise the regenerated spaces in the old city centre by attracting the crucial presence of the community. Roberta Gargano considers L'Aquila has always been a very core city, and the centre is where the city must look to the future. The earthquake destroyed the urban dimension and profoundly lacerated its socio-economic fabric, but it did not weaken the citizens' ability to reinvent themselves. Immediately after the quake, they reacted in a proactive manner to honour the loss of human lives and leave future generations a rebuilt, liveable city. Prior to the earthquake, the city's economy was based primarily on managerial and professional activities, rather than business. Today, many young people have jumpstarted a process of renewal, abandoning their traditional family professions, making new choices, investing in new projects, and ultimately changing the city's urban dynamics.

---

6   M. Weber, *Wirtschaft Und Gesellschaft*, Mohr: Tübingen, 1922.

A transparent programme is needed as regards timescale, resources, and objectives so that L'Aquila can regain its identity and have a future: this is the only way to reverse the dramatic seismic event and once again provide another opportunity for further growth and the reactivation of social relations in safe and non-dispersive places, for example those of the CASE project (Sustainable and Eco-compatible Anti-seismic Complexes).

We shouldn't forget that the city was nominated to become the Italian Capital of Culture 2021; due to the current pandemic, it will have to wait till 2022 for a possible, new allocation of resources, based on the provisions of the guidelines 2018–2020. This would constitute a very strong cultural attraction for the city (as it was recently for Matera) and boost its image. However, its candidacy doesn't seem to convince Gargano who proposes another much more appropriate and incisive brand name—the "city of reconstruction"—, one which would clearly be symbolically important. Her proposal would allow the city to also be acknowledged nationally. Despite all the delays, L'Aquila has been rebuilt from scratch, and its inhabitants have shown that they are worthy of the city, as human beings, citizens, and active witnesses of this transformation, in short as individuals well aware of the profound importance of human skills and abilities.

These considerations by Gargano recall Karl Marx's glorification of the "creative force of value", typical of human beings; its starting point is labour, in a form exclusive to man who not only changes the structure of natural materials, but also achieves a conscious goal that turns his action into law, a law to which he has to subordinate his will. This subjection is not temporary: working requires—for as long as it lasts—not only an effort by the entities involved, but also continuous attention which, however, is invisible except if willpower is in a state of constant tension.[7] We can say that the inhabitants of L'Aquila have worked hard to re-enhance their territory and give it back its renowned urban, economic, and social nature.

7   K. Marx, *Das Kapital. Kritik der politischen Oekonomie. Band I*, Meissner: Hamburg, 1867.

The cranes in the city centre seen from Ponte di Belvedere, 2019

Dynamics of the community, interstices, and non-places

The state of *atopia*—i.e., the "out of context" compared to the place limited by the *polis*—represents one of the forms we use to express the disorientation/estrangement of territoriality characterising the city of L'Aquila years after the earthquake on 6 April 2009. If *utopia* is a space without a real place, atopia, on the contrary, proclaims the breakdown of individuals—inhabitants who are defenceless against the degradation of spatiality due to the lack of their social-cultural environment (Turco, 2010). Atopia has complex social and territorial implications, insofar as the individual experiences a painful sense of loss, and dwelling takes the form of just being in a place to which one does not belong and simply experiences it as a location. It generates a sort of *topic negation* as well as an alteration of the temporal category, because the seismic event is a game changer, a *degré zero*, a sudden annihilation of a world that will never be the same. This traumatic event disrupted and reset the various microcosms, the daily routine that ensured a moment of ontological security[8], because it deprived the citizens of L'Aquila of a place— not only a physical place—where reproduction of the order regulating forms of social interaction takes place. A deep-rooted, radical upheaval between the "before" and "after"; a leap from one state to another; a social and urban metamorphosis.

The post-seismic scenario leaves a sense of suspension as regards both the city's artistic and architectural heritage and its urban, economic, historical, and social fabric. Heaps of rubble, crush barriers, and cranes have become a fixture in the panorama of this double disaster: on the one hand the tragic destruction, on the other the depressing reconstruction. Façades imprisoned by steel beams, wooden stanchions, nets, and crush barriers have been replaced by worksites that are turning the chaos of the cave-ins and rubble into other forms and views. Every demolition removes a painful patina of the city's history and creates a different configuration. Scaffolding still stands between the restored houses. The old city centre is

8   A. Giddens, *Modernity and Self-Identity. Self and Society in the Late Modern Age*, Polity Press: Cambridge (UK), 1991.

Via Paganica, 2020

still enveloped by an exasperating emptiness and deafening silence. Workmen and heavy vehicles fill the streets and alleys in the city centre and the air is always thick with the dust from the worksites. Everywhere there are *For sale* signs in front of uninhabited houses and shops. The economic flow is another dramatic litmus test. Due to the lack of services, public offices, and parking areas, very few commercial activities—chiefly wine shops and bars—have reopened in the old city centre. What L'Aquila lacks is a centre, a physical space for sociality, a hub around which everyday relationships revolve. The inhabitants continue to meet in "non-places", e.g., the *L'Aquilone* mall which was once a shopping centre and is now a "place" where they can spend their free time. These non-places are not territorial; they are anti-relational and anti-identity and do not create individual identities, symbolic relationships, and shared, joint heritage.[9] These other places represent suspended, neutral, meaningless contexts to which social actors have to adapt. The community has been scattered and fragmented throughout the territory, deprived of spatial and relational references, disrupted into forms of amorphous neighbourliness without a past; the inhabitants have been denied an urban planning project capable of reviving the social and material texture of the *polis*. Something is lacking: a feeling of sharing, the incorporated social knowledge inherent in all community members that enhances being and living together. Relationships with others and with a group are always closely linked to the place where we live. What emerges is that disorientation is now the basis of these relationships; as a result, reality itself tends to become a spatially uprooted reality. Citizens live in an undefined space; its functions are disseminated and distributed everywhere, despite every logic and urban plan. Space becomes foreign and no longer belongs to the inhabitants who wander aimlessly between the roads and streets because they lack the indications they need to find their way: "Where am I?", but also "Who am I compared to who?"[10].

9 M. Augé, *Non-Lieux. Introduction à une anthropologie de la surmodernité*, Seuil: Paris, 1992.

10 F. La Cecla, *Mente locale. Per un'antropologia dell'abitare*, Elèuthera: Milan, 1993.

Since the earthquake, everyday lives lack a relationship with the place that constitutes the life of every individual. For a community it is the place where things are positioned, happen, unfold, and define their quality, value, pertinence, and effectiveness in relation to the social ties the community has through the territory and its configurations.[11] Years later, L'Aquila is still experiencing temporariness, impermanence, transitoriness, increased mobility due to the fragmentation/dispersion of the population, and loss of the neighbourly relations and solidarity typical of everyday life, increasingly characterised by heterogeneous situations and complex contingent actions. The new symbolic, economic, and organisational dimension of the inhabitants' sociality has to deal with the redesign and reconfiguration of living spaces because the forms of things and interaction between individuals takes place in space.[12] The earthquake destroys the spaces used to socialise, the places of collective interaction and sharing that are crucial for every community. The *Gemeinschaft* represents a complex hub of relationships, of endless networks of stories and interactions between groups; it is here that each individual shares an ensemble of norms and values with everyone else. In fact, *praxis* and discourse create the space between individuals by virtue of a social relationship created by the existence of the city as a living space, as a space for discussion and free expression of thought.[13] One of the basic traits of the community is comprehension, *consensus*, i.e., common, reciprocal, associative feelings based on the intentions of a community; the latter represents the special force and social affection that binds individuals together as members of a whole. As a result, comprehension is based on intimate, reciprocal knowledge of each other.[14]

The erosion of spatial, relational references of shared sociality—caused by the destruction of the old city centre—coincides

11   A. Turco, *Configurazione della territorialità*, Angeli: Milan, 2010.
12   G. Simmel, *Soziologie. Untersuchungen über die Formen der Vergesellschaftung*, Duncker & Humblot: Berlin, 1908.
13   A.M.P. Toti, "L'Aquila, frammenti di comunità. Ri-costruzione e tras-mutazione sociale: un'esperienza sul campo", in A. Marata and R. Galdini (eds.), *DIVERSEcity*, (CNACCP). http://www.cittacreative.eu/wp-content/uploads/2019/07/toti_DIVERSEcity-2019.pdf, accessed on 4 May 2022.
14   F. Tönnies, *Gemeinschaft und Gesellschaft*, Reisland: Leipzig, 1887.

with the loss of the world or world alienation, i.e., with the disappearance of a shared world. The disintegration of this shared world leads to the loss of the stable structure on which we base our sense of reality and our identity as well as the background of practices and institutions where a possible public space for political action and deliberation emerges. The public sphere is the space where everything that appears can be seen and felt by all and is promoted in the broadest way possible. New ties and new forms of relationships have to be found in order to recreate the dialectical individual-space relationship.

Labyrinths of experience and space as a narrative

The study of social networks and the chrono-topical dimension of society in L'Aquila is crucial if we wish to understand the fragmentation of the city's urban, historical, and social fabric and the ensuing loss of the social uses of space. Everyday activities and relationships have deteriorated after the impover-ishment and loss of spaces where people can socialise. Space-time in L'Aquila has been transformed, and with it the topographic map, lifestyles, attitudes, and meeting places that create the individual as a social figure. Today, the city of L'Aquila is a social, economic, and urban planning laboratory after the earthquake completely devastated an entire urban area, depriving it of the territorial cohesion[15]—i.e. a centripetal social and urban action—that had, as its symbolic base, the city centre, the square that gave its citizens a sense of identity and affiliation. The role of memory—that produces images and stories—becomes a key element, because every meaningful experience structures the present regarding what-has-been and what could possibly be in the future; it is a weave merging individual experiences, collective experiences, and planning. Social actors see themselves as belonging to a community thanks to the narration of places. The *narratum* makes it possible to reconstruct the stratifications and interwoven

---

15   R. Dahrendorf, *Lebenschancen. Anläufe zur sozialen und politischen Theorie*, Suhrkamp: Frankfurt am Main, 1979.

Progetto CASE, 2013

events of the past and thus recompose the social fabric. Spaces become mnemonic footprints to be interpreted using the flow and interrelationships of the inhabitants, events, and objects. Georg Simmel's reflections about space are an unavoidable starting point in the study of everyday social interaction practices. The German sociologist thought that space played a crucial social role insofar as it is an activity of the soul, the method humans use to combine separate sensitive affections into unitary visions. The configurations of things, and the reciprocal action between individuals, become tangible in space; the latter is a model of human relations and "the possibility of being together"[16]. Space becomes the receptacle of memory and identity. The elaboration and transmission/ social representation of the past is extremely important, and so is the way in which its re-construction is not only re-introduced in collective and social interaction, but also shared by individuals. Complex conceptualisations facilitated by recollection and provided by memory allow researchers—thanks to random links of meanings—to analyse the paradigm of the subject's behaviour as a historical and social agent. The historicity of the biographies and interviews is a key topic since it highlights the configuration of the temporalised social constructions present in every narration. The historicity of an individual's experience cannot be considered only as a chronological series of events that occur along a timeline, but primarily as the arrangement of the infinite refractions of these events in every individual's life. These events are the warp and weft of every individual's life; they represent the multiform aspects of experience that allow social scientists to understand and explain the profound structure of social events.

Places are filled with meaning and symbolic importance, but they are also bearers of an indicative latent planning.[17] The interviews narrated their life experience after the earthquake and their attempt to reinstate order through an appropriation that was tactile and physical, and not simply visual. This points to the now illusive dimension of the *genius loci*, the unsuccessful recognition of one's territory, and the need to rebuild the

---

16   G. Simmel, *op. cit.*
17   C. Cellamare, *Fare città. Pratiche urbane e storie di luoghi*, Elèuthera: Milan, 2008.

city's history along the trajectory of urban identities: "The old city centre is reborn without the Town Hall (...), without the strong presence of offices, shops, and the market that historically, sociologically, and anthropologically has been one of the driving forces in the city. The daily market in Piazza Duomo that people are trying to re-establish in the square. Without these features the city centre plods along. Do we wish to create a historical city centre, a downtown for youngsters, with restaurants, clubs, and venues (to a certain extent this has already happened because there's a whole area where these activities have been reactivated) or do we wish the city to be suitable for the elderly? As you can see, the objective is very different, the programme is very different" (De Nicola). These places of aggregation, of collective services, of the life paths and urban practices of the inhabitants, are no longer full of people: "The old city centre had everything, all the public utilities offices, all the things that could make life pleasant for those who lived there and for the inhabitants of the suburbs. It has always been a centre-centric city. The destruction of the old city centre has created a situation of total estrangement" (Gargano). Although the old buildings have been reconstructed they lie empty, so much so they look like a film set: "The buildings are empty boxes; you feel like you're at the studios (Alessandro Ritoli, Colacchi bookshop). Sadly, one realises that the centre of L'Aquila "is balanced between life and death (...) there's no guarantee it will live... the disastrous hypothesis that the old city centre of L'Aquila could become a sort of Pompeii has yet to be averted" (De Nicola). The new Charter fragments and disintegrates the territory of L'Aquila, prompting the dissolution of the flow of interactions and intersubjectivity of everyday life. There has been no form of territorial planning, nor has the life prior to the earthquake been taken into consideration; the inhabitants find themselves in suspended, meaningless contexts. The residential structures built in new locations have uprooted the population, while the city centre has not been rebuilt. All this has impoverished social and community ties. The transitory nature of these situations, the "here" and also the "elsewhere" of these places create a feeling of suspended animation in the individual, forcing him to reflect on the evanescence of relationships. The dispersion processes involving the neighbourhood and usual centres of aggregation are sources of relentless depersonalisation; only the memory of "the way it was" before the earthquake somehow helps to overcome the hardship: "The new places where people meet and socialise are the restaurants, clubs, bars, and cafés where youngsters gather in the evening. In the past, the young inhabitants of L'Aquila used to take a stroll—with all its rituals—along the porticoes of Via del Corso; for centuries this represented its identity. Every column was occupied by a group with its own political penchant; every small street had its own identity. It was a sort of Facebook *ante litteram* where people got together to chat and gossip. We now regret everything we did not appreciate then, before the fateful date of April 6. Youngsters have different dynamics: they use Facebook, Instagram, and the many ubiquitous social networks that exist today; the identity of L'Aquila and its socialisation has almost slowed to a halt, not least because schools are no longer located in the centre, so the sort of osmosis they had with the city has been lost" (De Nicola). The destruction of the old city centre has led to upheavals regarding not only relational dynamics, but also labour because "Jobs were no longer a sure thing, and after the reconstruction many people diversified and migrated to other occupations. Even the city's dynamics have changed completely: entire generations have grown up without the city system, without the places of aggregation and casual meetings that used to characterise our lives" (Gargano).

It's been chiefly the youngsters who've reacted in a realistic manner, trying to re-aggregate this dispersion in the territory and recreate the community: "No plans have been made for young people, although they are our future. If this city wants to get back on its feet, it has to think of these youngsters who have managed to bring their parents back to the city centre. When many inhabitants of L'Aquila were relocated to the coast, it was the youngsters who wanted to come back to the city, undoubtedly a different city because it lacks its 'throbbing heart', but we hope that the centre will be reborn, because if L'Aquila is reborn without a city centre, then it will be another city" (De Nicola). The earthquake triggered huge changes: "We suddenly found ourselves uprooted and without a house. My strength and courage I owe to my daughters who decided to start over and opened a jewellery shop in the centre" (Ugo Mastropietro – President of the shopkeepers of the old city

Piazza del Duomo, 2020

centre). The desire to feel at home in the city, to walk its streets, and gather in old meeting places has often been a difficult choice: "Life in the city centre is hard for the few who have decided to come back; there're not many, but those who have come back are armed with great strength and courage, because there are no services or parking areas, it's still a worksite: mud, building works, workmen, noise, and dust" (De Nicola). The Covid-19 pandemic has once again obliged L'Aquila to undergo a metamorphosis; it is a real socio-anthropological shock forcing people to rethink the way we live in the world, view the world, and make policies. Suddenly the community has once again been thrown into the past: "This event has further paralysed the existing situation. The city is at a standstill, silent. Roads and streets are deserted, shops are closed due to the many antivirus restrictions decreed by law. Public and private worksites stand idle" (De Nicola). The epidemic has triggered changes in behaviour, practices, and the everyday dynamics of every individual, forced to live in a state of uncertainty caused by the permanent risk of infecting someone and being infected: "Although the tragedy of the earthquake has been overcome by people gathering in places that somehow transmitted a sense of normality, the normality we recovered by being together was lost when the lockdown started" (Gargano). Narrating and interpreting the places, fragments of urban life, and interstitial situations makes it possible to draw closer to the density of reality and penetrate the innermost depths of the social fabric, that *labyrinth of experience* typical of the life of both individuals and the community. Space is not just a physical, natural place, it is above all a space of life, of flows, of social networks that dissolve into multiple microspaces, intersections in which the individual lives and interacts: a network crossing points and weaving its skein. Thanks to the images of things, to the ability to seize things, it is possible to see the hidden pivots and hubs of the "gigantic mechanism of social life".[18]

---

18   W. Benjamin, *Einbahnstraße*, Suhrkamp Verlag, Frankfurt am Main, 1955.

Laurentino 38 public housing, Rome, 2019

Elena Bargelli

Squatting in Italian and European Law

Illegal occupation of buildings: Italian law

Illegal occupation of building is at the crossroad of conflicting rights and needs: private and public property rights, urban development, social security, and prevention of health and safety hazard on the one hand, the primary human need for shelter and the personal and societal consequences linked to eviction on the other hand. At first sight, it would appear to be an issue governed only by national law and falling under the heading "violation of property rights". It is, in fact, a behaviour reproved by law in liberal societies. The unauthorised occupation of buildings entitles a private owner to file claims to repossess his property (Art. 943 ff. Civ. Cod.) and ask for damages (Art. 2043 Civ. Cod.). As far as the unlawful occupation of public properties are concerned, the State may issue evacuation orders. The unauthorised occupation of immovables can be prosecuted as crime, as Art. 633 of the Italian Criminal Code makes clear. It states that "1. Whoever arbitrarily invades another's lands or buildings, public or private, with the intent to occupy them or profit from them, is punished, after a complaint by the offended party, with one to three years imprisonment and a fine varying from 103 euro to 1032 euro". This criminal provision protects property rights against any offender, regardless of whether the occupation is due to the need to find a shelter and no alternative accommodation is at disposal of the squatter. This quite harsh rule, however, is mitigated by the courts, which are prone to apply the general defence of the "state of necessity", according to Art. 54 of the Criminal Code ("A person shall not be punished if he was compelled to commit the criminal act by the necessity of saving himself or others from the current danger of a serious harm"). Accordingly, if the occupation is due to the need to save oneself from a danger or a serious harm caused by the lack of accommodation, no punishment should be ordered.[1] However, this defence has a quite strict field of application, because it excuses the squatter only if s/he is under a "current and transitory danger"; thus, it is not applicable if the occupation is not temporary, even where the prolonged stay is due to the occupant's poor health conditions[2] or financial distress.[3] The reason behind seems to be self-evident, as unauthorised occupation cannot be conceived as the ordinary means of tackling housing needs.

In addition to criminal law, other legal provisions are aimed to discourage squatting with different means. For example, Article 5 of the *Piano Casa (Housing Plan)* promulgated by the Renzi Government[4] prevents unauthorised persons to connect to public utilities and establish their residency in occupied buildings, although these measures are reported to be unable to discourage illegal occupations.[5] According to Law n. 48 of 18 April 2017, the prefect may avail himself of the police to enforce evictions ordered by the judicial authorities. The latest circular promulgated by the Minister of the Interior of 1 September 2018 clearly shows the predominant concern for the protection of property rights and considers unauthorised occupation a threat to the peaceful civil and social coexistence.[6] Nevertheless, even though the circular's general aim is to speed up evictions of illegally occupied premises, it recognises that certain compelling basic needs of vulnerable people must be taken into account and even (temporarily) prevail over the enforcement of property rights.

1 Court of Cassation, Criminal Chamber, 26-9-2007, n. 35580.
2 Court of Cassation, Criminal Chamber, 7-8-2012, n. 14222.
3 Court of Cassation, Criminal Chamber, 26-9-2020, n. 26225.
4 E. Ponzo, "Article 5 of the 'Piano Casa' promulgated by the Renzi Government. A dubious balance between the need for legality and the right to housing", 21 September 2014, https://www.costituzionalismo.it/larticolo-5-del-piano-casa-del-governo-renzi-un-dubbio-bilanciamento-tra-esigenze-di-legalita-e-diritto-alla-casa/?highlight=Ponzo, accessed on 19 February 2022.
5 https://www.filodiritto.com/occupazione-abusiva-di-alloggi-pubblici-e-privati, accessed on 19 February 2022.
6 https://www.interno.gov.it/it/amministrazione-trasparente/disposizioni-generali/atti-generali/atti-amministrativi-generali/circolari/circolare-1-settembre-2018-occupazione-arbitraria-immobili-indirizzi, accessed on 19 February 2022.

Of course, policymakers are in charge of enacting measures to prevent illegal squatting by tackling the underlying question of access to housing and affordability for lowest or no-income people, which lies at the very core of the unauthorised occupation of buildings. This is a quite complex question, as mortgages and rents are mostly unaffordable for the lowest income households, while public and social housing, being currently unable to meet the demand, requires the municipalities to commit to huge investments. Inadequate funds are allocated to support the income of households unable to pay the rent and at risk of eviction due to payments arrears as well as forced sales due to mortgage default, even though the emergency legislation following the COVID-19 pandemic has recently increased both the financial support of tenants being in arrears[7] and the allowances for low-income tenants.[8]

This contribution will not, however, assess the effectiveness of the public action; it is not intended to compare the different provisions and tools used to tackle squatting, or identify their most appropriate combination. The objective is to bring into focus the relevance and importance of the constitutional dimension of the "right to housing" vis-à-vis the illegal occupation of public or private properties. In fact, forced evictions evoke human rights standards to be respected in certain situations, including moratoria and measures to facilitate the quick rehousing of evicted people.[9]

The raised issue has huge practical implications, as illegal occupations of houses have increased in Italy, and an average of 6.4% of public dwellings are estimated to be squatted.[10]

---

7   The recent allocation is due to the Decree of the Ministry of Infrastructure and Sustainable Mobility of 30 July 2021.
8   The recent allocation is due to the Decree of the Ministry of Infrastructure and Sustainable Mobility of 18 August 2021.
9   For a general overview, see P. Kenna, S. Nassarre-Aznar, P. Sparkes, and C.U. Schmid (eds.), *Loss of Homes and Evictions across Europe. A Comparative Legal and Policy Examination*, Elgar Edgar Publishing: Cheltenham, 2018.
10   "Occupazioni abusive nell'ERP e ripristino della legalità", Federcasa, 6 July 2016, https://www.federcasa.it/occupazioni-abusive-nellerp-e-ripristino-della-legalita/, accessed on 19 February 2022.

Against this background, national and European courts play a key role, as they are called upon to strike a balance between the conflicting rights at stake and, possibly, to adjudicate the social right to housing. This paper will focus in particular on the case law of the European Court of Human Rights (ECtHR), which has repeatedly dealt with the right to protect one's home as (allegedly) protected by Art. 8 of the European Convention on Human Rights (ECHR).

The status of the right to housing as a human right was affirmed by the Italian Constitutional Court in 1988 when it stated: "the right to housing is one of the basic requisites of sociality the democratic State must comply with as laid down by the Constitution", and a "fundamental human right".[11] Notwithstanding this peremptory statement, the right to housing, one of the so-called "social rights", is considered not directly enforceable by individual citizens as it may be adjudicated only by means of regulatory choices and public policies. Arguments against the legitimacy of courts to adjudicate social rights like the right to housing are quite well-known.[12] It is widely believed that an individual who is lawfully excluded from public housing or housing benefit and who is unable to access the market is also unable to both challenge this adjudication, unless it is abusive or illegal, and demand to be allocated a dwelling that meets his/her housing needs. This idea is so uncontroversial that, in the Italian legal system, the issue has never been addressed by case law.

That said, the question remains as to whether the gap between the overarching status of the right to housing and its actual affordability might be reduced by a stronger "justiciability". This question is addressed by a series of rulings by the European Court of Human Rights.

11   Corte cost. 7-4-1988, n. 404, in Giust. civ., 1988, I, 1654.
12   J. King, *Judging Social Rights*, Cambridge University Press: Cambridge (UK), 2012.

Illegal occupation and the case law of the European Court of Human Rights

The legal basis for the protection of the right to housing within the European Convention on Human Rights is found in Article 8, which is entitled "Right to respect for private and family life". The European Court has adopted a wide interpretation of this article by arguing that "the loss of one's home is the most extreme form of interference with the respect for the home".[13] This argument lies at the core of the cases of eviction brought before the ECtHR. It is worth underlining that in most of such cases the eviction procedure is legitimate under national law. Two emblematic cases are given below as examples of the type of legal issues that the European Court has to deal with.

In Connors v. the United Kingdom (n. 66746/01 27.8.2004), the applicant complained that he and his family had been evicted from a gypsy caravan site run by a local authority, invoking Articles 6, 8, 13 and 14 of the Convention and Art. 1 Prot. 1. They claimed that they suffered so much from harassment and from being moved on with ever increasing frequency that they settled on the local authority's gypsy site at Cottingley Springs in Leeds (England), where they lived permanently for about 13 years. In February 1997, they moved on, complaining about, among other things, violence and disturbances preventing them from sleeping at night and the children from playing safely during the day. They moved into a rented house but were unable to adapt. In October 1998, the applicant and his wife returned to Cottingley Springs and were allowed to occupy a plot at the site provided that they, their family, and guests did not cause a "nuisance" to those living on the site or in its vicinity. On 29 March 1999, the applicant's adult daughter Margaret Connors was granted a licence to occupy the adjacent plot. However, on 31 January 2000, notice to quit was served on the family requiring them to vacate both plots. At this stage, the applicant and his wife lived with their four young children. On 1 August 2000, the eviction was enforced.

---

13   ECHR, 27-5-2004, ref. n. 66746/01, Connors v. the United Kingdom; ECHR, 24-4-2012, ref. n. 25446/06, Yordanova and others v. Bulgaria.

In Ivanova v. Bulgaria (no. 46577/15 21.4.2016), the applicant sought judicial review of the decision to demolish her house allegedly constructed in 2004–05 without a building permit, notwithstanding any arguments or evidence put forward to show otherwise. However, her claim was dismissed and, therefore, the applicant appealed. She submitted, inter alia, that the house was her only home and that its demolition would cause her considerable difficulties as she would be unable to secure another place to live. In a final judgment of 17 March 2015, the Supreme Administrative Court upheld the lower court's judgment. It agreed that the house was illegal and should be demolished. On 15 April 2015, the regional office of the National Building Control Directorate invited the first applicant to comply with the demolition order within fourteen days of receiving notice to do so. On 18 August 2015, the Burgas Municipal Ombudsman urged the Minister of Regional Development to stop the demolition on the basis that, although formally lawful, it would have a disproportionate impact on the applicants' lives. In response, on 25 September 2015, the Directorate's regional office reiterated its intention to proceed with the demolition. In October 2015, a social worker interviewed the first applicant and explained to her the possibilities to request social benefits. The first applicant stated that she was not interested in that because she preferred to remain in the house.

These two cases demonstrate that, as far as the ECtHR is concerned, it is irrelevant whether, according to the applicable national law, the person who is evicted is no longer allowed to stay in the dwelling or even whether the occupation was originally unlawful. The ECtHR's case law is based on the idea that a "home" is a factual concept, presupposing a household being settled in a place, which, consequently, becomes the centre of the family life, regardless of whether any occupant owes a property right or is otherwise entitled to use it.[14] Once a place is a "home", its loss is considered the hugest interference with one's private life according to Art. 8 ECHR.

This interpretation was initially triggered by cases of families belonging to ethnic minorities being evicted from a public site

---

14   ECHR, 25-9-1996, ref. n. 20348/92, Buckley v. the United Kingdom.

due to termination of a licence as in the cases quoted above.[15] Subsequently, this was extended to include squatting, the unauthorised demolition of buildings, and the renting of social housing units.[16]

The massive case law by the ECtHR provides a detailed procedural and substantive guidance for an eviction to be considered compliant with the "right to respect for the home" as recognised by Art. 8 ECHR. As to the procedural standards, the Court emphasises that eviction must be ordered by an independent court, as a consequence of a fair judicial proceeding where the right of the claimant to be heard is safeguarded. As the Court reiterates, "any person at risk of an interference with the right to home should in principle be able to have the proportionality and reasonableness of the measure determined by an independent tribunal". As emphasised by the ECtHR in the Bjedov v. Croatia case, summary proceedings[17] and enforcement procedures[18] do not fulfil this requirement.

As far as the substantial standards are concerned, the ECtHR emphasises that evictions must pass a proportionality test according to which the magnitude of the interference with the home must be balanced with the purpose they aim for; furthermore, they must also be considered "necessary in a democratic society" and correspond to an "urgent social need" (as reiterated in McKann v. the United Kingdom and Kay v. the United Kingdom cases). National courts and public administrations issuing eviction orders are primarily responsible for striking the balance between the conflicting interests at stake and appreciating these needs, whereas the ECtHR is entitled to verify whether the reasons given are sufficient, especially if the infringed right is an essential precondition to someone's life. The decisive circumstance of fact is whether the prolonged use of the premise as a place to live has been tolerated by the owner for a sufficiently long period of time ("The Court notes...

15 ECHR, 27-5-2004, ref. n. 66746/01, Connors v. the United Kingdom, *cit.*
16 ECHR, 11-10-2016, ref. n. 19841/06, Bagdonavicius v. Russia, *European Human Rights Law Review*, 2017, vol. 18, n. 3, September 2018, pp. 495–515, https://doi.org/10.1093/hrlr/ngy017.
17 ECHR, 27-9-1995, ref. n. 18984/91, McCann v. the United Kingdom, § 53.
18 ECHR, 29-5-2012, ref. n. 42150/09, Bjedov v. Croatia.

that for several decades the national authorities did not move to dislodge the applicants' families or ancestors and, therefore, *de facto* tolerated the unlawful Roma settlement... this fact is highly pertinent and should have been taken into consideration").[19] As far as public premises as concerned, this means that the prolonged factual possession of a "home", combined with the *inertia* of the owner, reinforces the occupant's expectation to its peaceful enjoyment, which is something the ECtHR is concerned for.

According to the above reported case law, the occupiers would be allowed to challenge forced evictions where procedural or substantial standards are not fulfilled. Individual or collective marginalization or vulnerability of those evicted (for example, the disadvantaged position of the social group they belong to, like Roma populations) are factual circumstances to be taken into account. The ECtHR is aware of the subversive potential of this defences in national law and specifies that it could only be applied in exceptional circumstances.[20] Nevertheless, the exemplary case in which the defence based on the social vulnerability of the evicted was applied (Bjedov v. Croatia, 2021)[21] seems to be anything but exceptional. In this case, an elderly and sick lady, holder of a specially protected tenancy of a socially owned flat, was evicted. This was allowed by national law, as she had not lived in the flat for more than six months. The lady complained that the eviction order violated her right to respect for her home according to Art. 8 ECHR. The court upheld the applicant's claim on the basis of the substantial standards reported above. In particular, it emphasised the need for the proportionality of the interference with rights protected by Art. 8 and its "necessity in a democratic society" (that is, its "pressing social need") to be assessed and concluded that the tenant would have suffered irreparable prejudice if she had been evicted. In addition, it stressed that the eviction would have imposed a greater economic burden on the society compared to letting her stay in the flat.

---

19 ECHR, Yordanova and others v. Bulgaria, *cit.*, § 121.
20 ECHR, McKann v. the United Kingdom, *cit.*, § 54.
21 ECHR, Bjedov v. Croatia, *cit.*

In addition, there are cases where the ECtHR's doctrine cannot be incorporated into pre-existing procedural safeguards. This occurs, for instance, where the public administration avails itself of the power to carry out a forced eviction without a previous judicial eviction order.[31] If this happens after a prolonged tolerance and a public property has become a "home" for the occupiers, the question arises whether the procedural safeguards recommended by the European Court may actually be respected. Indeed, even if those evicted are entitled to appeal to the administrative court and, therefore, the eviction is assessed by an "independent tribunal", any subsequent procedural guarantee would be ineffective against the immediate forced eviction.

"Right to respect for the home" and eviction from private buildings in Italy

Most cases of illegal occupation that have given rise to the ECtHR's doctrine examined in this contribution involve public buildings. The question arises as to whether this doctrine is applicable to illegal occupations of private properties. The argument of the opponents is that it is addressed only to public actors.[32] However, the decisive argument of the proponents is that the violation of the Convention occurs even where the relationships between private actors are involved, as stressed above. Nevertheless, according to a widespread opinion, the application of Art. 8 ECHR to private properties meets more limits.[33]

The case Casa di Cura Valle Fiorita v. Italy n. 67944/13 of 13 December 2018 shows that the ECtHR's doctrine is applicable even to private properties. Indeed, the building owned by a private company had been occupied by a group of activists

---

31   G.D. Falcon, "Esecutorietà ed esecuzione dell'atto amministrativo", *Dig Disc Pubbl.*, VI, 1991, p. 140.

32   UK Supreme Court, 15-6-2016, Mc Donald v. Mc Donald and others, https://www.supremecourt.uk/cases/uksc-2014-0234.html, accessed on 20 February 2022.

33   P. Kenna, "Introduction", in P. Kenna et al., *cit.*, p. 35.

belonging to the "fight for house movement". Notwithstanding the judicial eviction order, this had been never executed. As a consequence, the company submitted an application to the European Court for violation of the right of property (Art. 1 Prot. 1 ECHR) and the right to a fair and public hearing within a reasonable time (Art. 6). The Court ruled in favour of the owners. However, this judgment is not inconsistent with the previous ECtHR's case law. In fact, a huge difference compared to the cases cited earlier is that the company lodged a complaint since when the building had been occupied, and, therefore, had never tolerated the occupation. Furthermore, the Court positively assessed the arguments put forward by the Italian State to justify the prolonged non-execution of the eviction, that is the impossibility to find alternative accommodations for the occupiers due to the lack of public financial resources and the risk that the eviction might have disruptive social effects. However, the Court concluded that these arguments could justify a moratorium of the eviction only for the time required to find alternative accommodations. As a consequence, in ruling that the prolonged inertia of the police was unjustified, it did not contradict the doctrine proclaimed in cases of occupation of public buildings; instead it reiterated the need for the eviction to comply with certain standards in terms of timing and modalities, in order to take into account situations of vulnerability and social marginalisation.

This framework is confirmed by Decree-Law 14/2017 (as modified by Art. 31-*ter*, subs. 1, Decree-Law 113/2018), which imposes the public authority in charge of enforcing evictions the duty to choose the emergency measures most appropriate to protect occupiers, where situations of exceptional vulnerability exist and those evicted are unable to find alternative accommodation (Art. 11, subs. 3.1). This provision shows that the ECtHR's doctrine has become part of national law.

Justiciable housing rights

Illegal occupation for housing purposes takes a different shape if seen from the perspective of human rights. This dimension has been developed by the European Court of Human Rights much more than by domestic courts. The emerging concept of the "right to respect for the home" is independent from domestic classifications and embeds several social and human rights such as identity, self-determination, social inclusion, safety, access to services, child protection and development.[34] As a result of the analysis of the ECtHR's case law and its repercussions on domestic law, the conclusion can be drawn that a progress in the judicial protection of housing rights and, more generally, social rights has been pursued. The reported case law contributes to better shape the domestic doctrine of the vertical and horizontal effects of fundamental rights. Of course, it would be misleading to infer that justiciable housing rights might replace appropriate public policies. Nevertheless, the increase in unauthorised occupations due to housing needs, together with the lack of available alternatives, urges housing policies to cope with complex social issues. Against this background, courts may contribute to slowly advance "social justice", step by step, according to a method successfully defined as incremental.[35]

---

34 P. Kenna, "Introduction", in P. Kenna et al., *cit.*, p. 3.
35 J. King, *cit.*

Houses by Michele De Lucchi

"They are small, solid wooden houses, delicately crafted using a chainsaw, and then trimmed, shaping the surface with 'brushstrokes' of the blade"

Michele De Lucchi

"Sometimes I leave the houses for a while, so I can see the changes wrought by time, the cracks, the movement of the fibres, the ageing of the material"

Michele De Lucchi

"Mulling once again over very elementary shapes led me to envisage a world that still doesn't exist, but can exist, I just don't know where or how"

Michele De Lucchi

Michele De Lucchi has been making small wooden sculptures of architectures since 2004. First they were *Little Houses*, then *Condominiums*, *Towers and Skyscrapers*, *Palafittes*, *Verandas*, *Woodstacks*, *Sheds and Shacks*. The sculptures presented here are some of the first he produced between 2004 and 2008. They were made by assembling pieces of solid wood, cut or carved with a chainsaw: glued, interlocked, and fastened. They are not inspired by a drawing and are not made to scale; they neither follow linear geometries nor respect proportions that may make them look like producible architectural models. And yet, as each one of them appears, it affirms the presence—in a sort of motionless and timeless scene—of an inhabitable space.

Their appearance creates a world, thus continuing reflection on the construction of space based on the presence of the object that has always accompanied De Lucchi's research. Let's now radically shift our focus: from form to the system of relations that make up the object. Relations not limited to the many ways in which the different parts of an object can exist together, but more precisely the relations between technology and nature, between architecture and landscape, between the cultures and technical traditions involved in construction, between the many evocable timeframes of the wooden pieces, with their memories of the woods.

Little Houses construct the reality around them based on the intricate weave of their governing relations. Their figurative nature and their often enigmatic and austere, but also luminous and quiet features lie in the fact that they are made of ties and affinities, more than of matter. Each one can, in this sense, be interpreted as the exploration of a field of possibilities. A hospitable field, open to further technical and cultural contaminations; a field inviting us to reinterpret all of De Lucchi's works which, beyond their customarily attributed dichotomy, are split between artisanal instincts and industrial innovation, appeal to tradition and new age momentum, local and global aesthetics, brutalism next to sophisticated technological solutions. All this coexists and is not necessarily in contrast. What's important is that the bonds of coexistence are explicit, made evident, and thus exemplarily manifest in these small wooden architectures.

Hou

ses

Houses

In the second half of the nineteenth century, housing became a study topic and the subject matter of literature. Handbooks and repertoires hosted the classifications that emerged in relation to the imbalances in blue-collar housing, or the houses of the "dangerous and working" classes. For example, Edwin Chadwick, *Report to Her Majesty's Principal Secretary of State for the Home Department from the Poor Law Commissioners on an Inquiry into the sanitary condition of the labouring population of Great Britain: with Appendices*, printed by W. Clowes and sons for Her Majesty's Stationery Office: London, 1842; Alphonse Grun, *État de la question des habitations et logements insalubres*, Guillemin: Paris, 1849; Henry Roberts, *The Dwellings of the Labouring Classes, Their Arrangement and Construction*, The Society for Improving the Condition of the Labouring Classes by Seeleys, Misbet & Co.; J.W. Parker and Hatchard: London, 1850, Fr. trans., *Des Habitations des classes ouvrières*, Gide et J. Baudry: Paris, 1867 (sixth edition, revised and enlarged); Émile Muller, *Habitations ouvrières et agricoles, cités, bains et lavoirs, sociétés alimentaires, détails de construction, statuts, règlements et contrats, conseils hygiéniques...*, Dalmont: Paris, 1855–1856. The inquiries produced by parliamentary commissions regarding the condition of workers in big industrial agglomerates revealed the role played by nation states in introducing the housing issue. The systematic measurement of housing units shed light on the existence of long-term official lists, cadastral, and fiscal documents. It is interesting to bear in mind that these lists established links between heterogeneous data and practices (Michel Foucault would perhaps have called them a *dispositif*) combining planimetric representations, measurements of surfaces and volumes, technical equipments, and titles granting fruition of assets.

The first thing that stands out when leafing through these household cadastres and descriptions is the enormous difference between one house and another. Towards the end of the nineteenth century, census statistics preferred to use rooms as a uniform unit of measure; room size varied less compared to that of the whole house. There was a specific reason—usually taxation—for the introduction of criteria to classify the different social conditions embodied by the houses. The first method used to organise these differences was morphological; it involved assessing the action produced by the availability of materials, technical solutions, microclimatic conditions, and building culture. Regularity and repetitions refer to "building types", in which through collective authorial and anonymous advancement of knowledge, houses optimise their structure and room layout, becoming a recognisable element of civilisation. Today we have houses with a Greek, Roman, or Arab courtyard, close-knit tenements of Roman *insulae* and the *Mietskasernen* of real estate speculation, Chinese hutongs and wooden domestic architectures in Korea and Japan, underground houses in Mediterranean Africa and China, North-European urban row houses, huts in the Amazon and stilt river houses, Venetian palaces and Anglo-Saxon crescents: the list is destined to remain incongruous and open.

Taking into consideration the unequal layouts and quantity of houses, the incommensurable differences, and the impossibility to calculate, it is possible to develop several disciplinary approaches regarding houses. The first in-depth subject to be examined is the economy: how did the quantity and spatial distribution of houses become part of the reproduction process of capital? This was the weighty contribution provided by Engels, Marx, and Bourdieu, and more in general the initiatives in the nineteenth and twentieth centuries that within the framework of this endeavour focused on housing measures and solutions as well as facilities. Comprehensive visions of economic relations that structure society are proposed in authorial interpretations that sometimes evolved until they became general theories. The status quo, hypothetical interventions, and reforms are described within the frameworks that moved in this direction. They usually referred to the house as a patrimonial and financial asset (obviously the terms are not synonymous) and to the housing market, in a dialectic relationship with the role of the state and public intervention in general.

A second line of research on housing involves political thought. In this case, the house is important for the purposes of production, consensus, and the needs expressed by society or segments of society. In this context, the crucial question behind policies and projects is not an objective, natural, and quantitative term but is instead activated within theoretical constructs. The first and second line of thought are interlinked; there may be areas of superimposition which may even coincide in some cases. Housing policies and systematic projects of dwellings position the political role played in the field of housing centre stage.

A third line concerns the technical in-depth investigation of housing, as a field of reform made possible by applying tech-noscience, grafted onto the ways in which buildings are con-structed and maintained. A resident cannot directly control a well-designed project, something that instead has existed since time immemorial in the countryside thanks to customary laws and the collective solidarity practices used to build houses. The layout of the domestic environment becomes a job for technical professionals and corporations (surveyors, architects, engi-neers, suppliers, specialised technicians, public officials, and building companies) based on validation procedures governed by laws and regulations, and approved by bureaucracy. Towards the end of the nineteenth century, thanks to hygiene issues, it became an extremely important topic, allowing for solutions as well as descriptions and interpretations. Perhaps it is not incorrect to interpret the topics that emerged after the nine-teen-seventies—with a strong focus on the energy performance of houses, the eco-house, the passive house, and the regenera-tion of housing heritage—as a re-edition of the redeeming technical reform of the house. The third line of thought shows itself capable of infiltrating houses of every era, material configuration, and geographical location, and ultimately creat-ing something implicit in contemporary living.

Architectural and spatial innovation represent the fourth line in the development of modern thought regarding housing. Consid-ering the housing concept radically different from the past makes it possible to tackle the challenges of our age compared to previous eras. This appears to be the premise that emerged in the mid-nineteenth century and continued into the twenty-first century. There are times when innovation seemed within reach and involved the evolution of building techniques which, ranging from masonry structures and wooden ceilings to steel and reinforced concrete structures, facilitated the elimination of load-bearing vertical walls, the box-like closure of rooms, and their standard size, dictated by the recurrent length of common beams. At times, aesthetical principles triggered insurrection and reintroduce intimacy into houses in contact with a tumultuous, dangerous present, for example during the mythical De Stijl period. It's difficult to distinguish between the two-dimensional image of a painting by Mondrian or van Doesburg and the plan of a house by Gerrit Rietveld or Mies van der Rohe. Spatial innovation chose to experiment with two-dimensional images, which was considered a figurative text. Even more radical, the exclusion of the inhabitant and his humanity as a principle of individuation grants a 360° axonometric variation and the relativity of the architectural object, conceived and perceived from all points of view. Freedom and nihilism are interwoven: there is no going back to the previous situation. Moreover, renouncing the classical ornaments of architectural orders and their vegetal and floral variations pulls the meaning of decoration in a deeper human scope.

So, houses as goods, as factors in the production of capital, as part of the economic process; houses as the subject that is part of political thought, hypotheses of reform and revolution; houses as vectors of technologies and serial production; houses as a field for spatial invention. The four fields of innovation and experimentation of housing philosophy emerged in the nineteenth century and can be considered and used either in an innovative, rhetorical, or commercial manner.

Several phenomena facilitated the international sharing of solutions: the gradual increase in handbooks and magazines on housing, the first general histories about housing; and the fact that popular and economic housing became part of the discourse on hygiene; literature increased exponentially, and then abruptly stopped due to an event: World War One. Rhetoric was silenced by the horror of what was taking place. Houses and families became more feminine, were managed more by women, inaugurating a change in gender that was destined to become crucial in the social evolution of the house. This is evident in the studies by Dolores Heyden, notably in the book *The Grand Domestic Revolution* (The MIT Press: Cambridge (MA), 1981).

The great silence of the second half of the 1910s and early twenties was gradually overcome when housing became a topic in new functional, rational architecture. We can consider the new modern housing in architectural, urban, and sociological literature as the completion of nineteenth-century research on houses, despite the established conflict between bourgeois living and new aesthetics. Texts that appeared include: Deutscher Werkbund, *Bau und Wohnung*, Verlag Wedeking & Co: Stuttgart, 1927; Bruno Taut, *Bauen – der Neue Wohnbau*, Klinkhardt & Biermann: Berlin, 1927; Internationaler Kongress für Neues Bauen und Städtisches Hochbauamt in Frankfurt am Main (ed.), *Rationelle Bebauungsweisen*, Julius Hoffmann Verlag: Stuttgart, 1931. Immediately afterwards came the vast number of repertoires aimed at influencing building practices regarding the house and the city. We would like to recall: Enrico A. Griffini, *Costruzione razionale della casa. I nuovi materiali. Orientamenti attuali nella costruzione, la distribuzione, la organizzazione della casa*, Hoepli: Milan, 1931, new ed. *Costruzione razionale della casa. La teoria dell'abitazione. Nuovi sistemi costruttivi. Orientamenti attuali nella costruzione, la distribuzione, la organizzazione della casa*, Hoepli: Milan, 1933; new ed. in 2 vols. *Costruzione razionale della casa. Parte prima, Distribuzione. Organizzazione. Unificazione della casa. Nuovi orientamenti*, Hoepli: Milan, 1946; *Costruzione razionale della casa. Parte seconda, Nuovi sistemi costruttivi. Nuovi materiali. Opere di finitura*, Hoepli: Milan, 1947; Bruno Schwan, *Städtebau und Wohnungswesen der Welt | Town Planning and Housing through the World | L'Urbanisme et l'Habitation dans tous les Pays*, Wasmuth: Berlin, 1935; Werner Hegemann, *City Planning, Housing*, Architectural Publishing Company: New York, 1936–1938, 3 vols. (I. *Historical and Sociological;* II. *Political Ecomomy and Civic Art;* III. *A Graphic Review of Civic Art 1922–1937*). Other sections destined to become international were part of general modern architectural repertoires: reference is made here, in particular, to Alberto Sartoris,

Housing districts, Kilamba Klaxi, Angola, 2008

Dunia Mittner

Housing Datascape between European and African Urbanisation

A research programme

This essay lays the groundwork for a research programme on housing that will exploit several topical issues regarding contemporary urbanisation and civilisation to produce a productive and beneficial comparative international approach. It will initially focus on problems that are difficult to tackle from a disciplinary and political point of view: migrations; reception by and insertion in the population; a housing demand unmet by the market; demographic trends; informal and illegal settlements; energy transition; and the consequences of climate change on humans. In particular, it will concentrate on available aggregate data in three macroregions, and those who produce it: the European Union, especially the countries in Southern Europe,[1] North Africa,[2] and sub-Saharan West Africa.[3]

Several factors justify grouping these very large areas (tendentially big sub-continental regions): the large scale of these phenomena; the integration of economic, commercial, social, and media dynamics; and a reduced opportunity for single nation states to structurally intervene successfully due to the extent of the financial investments required to effectively influence this situation. These observations initially consider

1   The following countries are considered to be part of Southern Europe: Portugal, Spain, France, Italy, Slovenia, Croatia, Serbia, Bosnia, Albania, Montenegro, Greece, Cyprus, Malta, and Turkey.
2   The following countries are considered to be part of North Africa: Morocco, Western Sahara, Algeria, Tunisia, Libya, Egypt, and Sudan. Apart from Northern Sahara, Sudan is the only country in North Africa not to face the Mediterranean; as a result, certain organisations, and certain surveys, include it in North Africa, while others consider it to be part of East Africa.
3   The following countries are considered to be part of West Africa: Mauritania, Senegal, Cape Verde, Mali, Gambia, Guinea, Sierra Leone, Guinea Bissau, Liberia, Ivory Coast, Burkina Faso, Ghana, Niger, Benin, Togo, Niger, Nigeria, and Chad.

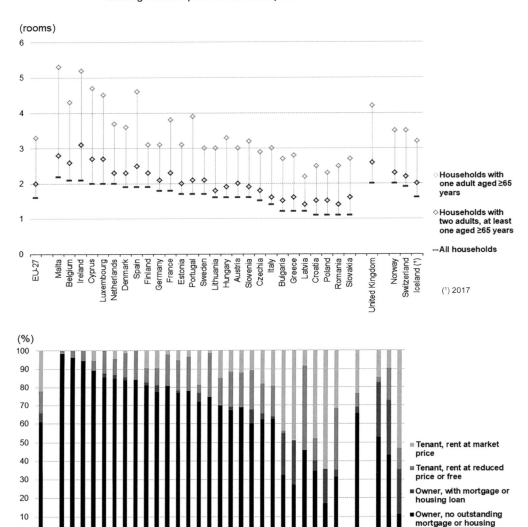

Note: the figure is ranked on the share of the population aged ≥65 years living alone and owning their dwelling (with or without a mortgage or housing loan).
(¹) 2017.

Average number of rooms per person, by type of household, 2018
People aged ≥65 years living alone, by tenure status, 2018
(source: Eurostat online data code ilc_lvho50a, ilc_lvho02)

the partial, inhomogeneous data available; the objective is to obtain a better, qualitative understanding of these trends in order to not only influence the housing policies primarily, but also assess the housing projects and strategies proposed by increasingly transnational financial clients.

Such a comprehensive and difficult research requires disciplinary skills, expertise, and know-how that go beyond the possibilities of an individual researcher.[4] However, I believe it helpful to describe and compare the main sources and highlight the different issues and problems they raise.

The data and the actors involved. Houses in European cities

Data regarding the number of houses in relation to individuals and families began to be collected in Europe after the advent of nation states and the application of a scientific method to a mobile, elusive entity such as human societies. Systematic censuses of the population and housing units[5] began in the nineteenth century when each country established a bureaucracy needed to gather data, thus giving rise to the discipline known as statistics. As my personal focus is on houses and urbanisation methods, I believe statistics produce quantitative data with an empirical origin and meaning; they provide a cognitive base on which to hang housing policies and projects.

Consolidated European data comes from national censuses and the processing performed by international research bodies

4   My point of view, consistent with my own education and training, is that of an architect-urban planner who believes that comprehension of several general movements of current civilisations is linked to the interpretation of urbanisation and housing. I was able to ascertain the scale of the issues and problems involved during a study of contemporary new towns (D. Mittner, *New Towns. An Investigation on Urbanism*, Jovis: Berlin, 2018) as well as during didactic experiences and studies performed as part of a cooperation between the Department ICEA (University of Padua) and the École Nationale Supérieure des Travaux Publics (ENSTP) in Yaoundé, Cameroon.

5   Censuses are normally carried out every ten years; the data began to be collected in the mid-nineteenth century, although each country started at a different moment in time.

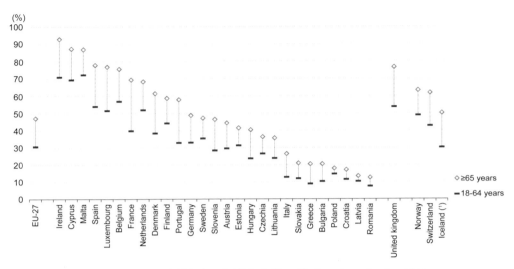

Note: a dwelling is defined as under-occupied if the household living in it has at its disposal more than the minimun number of rooms considered adequate, which is equal to: one room for the household; one room per couple in the household; one room for each single person aged 18 or more; one room per pair of single people of the same gender between 12 and 17 years of age; one room for each single person between 12 and 17 years of age and not included in the previous category; one room per pair of children under 12 years of age.
(¹) 2017

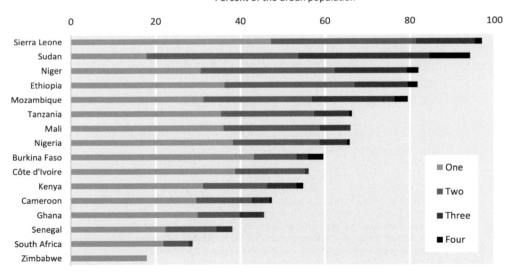

People living in under-occupied dwellings, by age class, 2018
Distribution of urban population by shelter deprivation
(The International Bank for Reconstruction and Development / The World Bank, 2015, p. 4, source: UN Habitat 2008)

that publish statistics, including *Eurostat*[6] (the statistical office of the EU) and the *OECD*.[7] These bodies either consider the regions in national states as spatial territorial elements or, in the case of the more in-depth data provided by the OECD, as 1 km² grid cells used as a basis to georeference data. The latter includes not only houses and urbanisation, but also, broadly speaking, demographic, economic, and social elements (e.g., services available to the population).

This data can be studied in many ways. Some data refer to the distribution of the population vis-à-vis different housing types, entitlement to the housing unit, distribution compared to property in urban areas, or the ratio between inhabitants and rooms, thus making it possible to calculate overcrowding. Data regarding the distribution of housing types and entitlement to housing units shows that: "in 2013, 41.1% of the EU population lived in flats, just over a third (34.0%) in detached houses, and 24.1% in semi-detached houses. (...) In 2013, over a quarter (27.3%) of the population in EU-28 lived in an owner-occupied home for which there was an outstanding loan or mortgage, while two fifths of the population (42.7%) lived in an owner-occupied home without a loan or mortgage. Seven out of ten people (70%) owned property in the EU-28, while a 19% share of the population lived as tenants with a market rent, and 11% as tenants in reduced-rent or free accommodation".[8]

---

6   For more information regarding housing data processed by Eurostat, cf. https://ec.europa.eu/eurostat/statistics-explained/index.php?title=Category:Housing, accessed on 23 September 2021; and Housing Europe, *The State of Housing in Europe 2021*, https://www.housingeurope.eu/resource-1535/features-governance-and-funding-of-the-european-affordable-housing-initiative-and-the-new-european-bauhaus, accessed on 10 October 2021.

7   The Organisation for Economic Co-operation and Development (OECD), "Better Policies for Better Lives", is an international organisation that produces quantitative data and studies regarding Europe and the so-called Western world, including North America and Australia, as well as several other states; https://www.oecd.org/. Regarding the case in question, the section entitled *Region and Cities Statistical Atlas* is particularly interesting, https://www.oecd.org/regional/, accessed on 30 September 2021.

8   EU Member States with the highest percentage of the population living in flats are Spain (65.4%), Latvia (65.3%), and Estonia (63.8%). The highest percentage of residents in detached houses are to be found in Croatia (70.9), Slovenia (66.5%), Hungary (64.0%), Norway (61.1%), Romania (60.1%), Serbia (60.5%), and Denmark (55.8%). The highest percentage of the population to live in semi-detached houses can be found in The Netherlands (60.7%), the United Kingdom (60.0%), and Ireland (58.3%). Cf. https://ec.europa.eu/eurostat/

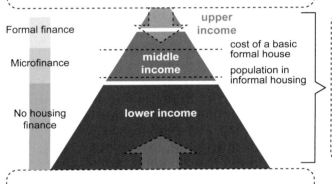

Harnessing Housing for Growth
Improve regulations and support for commercial and non-commercial lenders such as MFIs
Support bank access to liquidity and long term finance for mortages and developer finance

Formal finance

Microfinance

No housing finance

upper income

middle income

cost of a basic formal house

population in informal housing

lower income

Cross-Cutting
Improve city planning, building standards*
Enhance land administration practices and markets*
Strenghten domestic construction and building materials sectors
Support for rental markets*

Addressing Informality
Basic pro-poor infrastructure and slum upgrading*
Support for incremental, self-built housing
Leverage existing sources of savings and borrowing (e.g. savings groups and cooperatives)

*Entry point for local governments

Key activities for improving access to quality affordable housing
(The International Bank for Reconstruction and Development / The World Bank, 2015, p. 16)

Another important set of statistics focuses on international, national, and local real estate markets. These statistics are commissioned by financial or credit institutions, commercial organisations, non-profit organisations, and research offices involved in the field of construction and infrastructures that use them not only as statistics in support of economic actions, but also as reference to motivate and publicly justify action strategies. *Housing Europe*[9] is one of the bodies involved in affordable and social housing. The report entitled *The State of Housing in Europe 2021* highlights how rethinking and improving existing property represents the first action plan for European territories, due to the extensive stock of houses, most of which were built after the second half of the twentieth century during a period of widespread urbanisation.

Several features demonstrate how housing units are part of the single collaborating and biological mode governing human settlements. They include: attention to the energy behaviour of buildings; integration with mobility solutions; energy production and distribution systems; and the opportunity to contain the 'artificialisation' of horizontal surfaces. They are very general objectives, unanimously and openly shared by administrators, technicians, and opinion makers, but nevertheless opposed in practice by anonymous antagonists. These objectives include: the usefulness of producing low-cost housing in order to access the unsatisfied segment of those who demand housing; the intrinsic need to produce expansion by enterprise logic within the real estate market; and the inertial prosecution of expansion logic and continuous change.

Using the number of rooms as a unit of measure is linked to the number of stable residents in the house. It is an obvious effect of modernity linked to masonry construction systems and twentieth-century dwelling,[10] but it is sometimes less relevant

statistics-explained/index.php?title=Housing_statistics/it&oldid=265412, accessed on 4 July 2021.

9   Housing Europe, the European Federation of Public, Cooperative, and Social Housing providers, is a network of 43 national and regional federations in 25 countries, including 21 EU Member States. Together they manage around 25 million homes, roughly 11% of existing dwellings in Europe.

10   For example, G. Majorana-Calatabiano, *La statistica teorica e applicata*, Barbèra Editore: Florence, 1889, p. 101, emphasises how "The question of the

when considering different habitats with greater spatial fluidity and an interplay between the interior and exterior of houses. The ratio is used to calculate overcrowding; correspondences between demand and supply; scarcity of houses; and needs. It is fairly obvious that certain issues complicate the picture compared to previous categories and interpretation modes. They include: the elevated levels of individual mobility amongst European citizens; the projection of dwelling images on multiple housing types and places; and the fact people enjoy less work time (either imposed or actively pursued).

In Europe, the ratio between houses and the population reflects the ageing of the population; a demographic decline—not necessarily a negative factor—is not linked to the logic of nation states to boost their own power, the assertion of anthropisation, and the progressive increase in the Earth's population.

Settlement and demographic trends differ between regions in European countries; globalisation accentuates this difference. Southern Europe appears to be anthropologically characterised by a penchant for ownership; the latter represents a symbolic act and safe haven for the family's capitalisation. It also appears to be the area where there is an increase in the severity of the difficulties regarding integration in the economic and real estate dynamics of afflicted inner areas, mountainous areas, and foothill areas. "The global touristification of every-day life and the temporary use of houses are hardly sufficient to support the populations' activities during all the seasons of the year." The unequal distribution of the population compared to the censored houses reveals not only the problems associated with updating the census categories compared to

house in censuses has long been debated. An attempt was made to define the house; but to no avail. Neither the quality of a free-standing building, nor the division of ownership, nor that of doors along a road are suitable criteria. Houses can be very different in size; for a number of reasons, especially reasons to do with hygiene, it is important to know the amount of space available to every inhabitant. Since research on housing units was not suited to this purpose, the focus shifted to rooms; even though rooms still do not provide data regarding the space they occupy; however, the difference in their size, bearing in mind the way they are used in every house, is less than the difference between one house and another. Besides, it's much easier to get a good idea of the average size of rooms rather than that of houses".

contemporary customs, but also the difficulties intrinsic in housing mobility in these areas. In the past, entrepreneurial classes and political representatives considered the link between the home, real estate credit, and workplaces that applied permanent contracts in industry, agriculture, and services to be a factor that increased capital, projected future stability and economic prosperity, and acted to sedate social conflict. Starting in the eighties, different versions of neoliberalism became dominant. There was constant change not only in how to consider fundamental social ties, but also in how to assess the way in which economic behaviour influenced urbanisation.

This situation prompts several considerations, two in particular spring to mind: individuals who are at their best earning age are increasingly less inclined to ask for real estate credit and, secondly, the emergence of housing mobility is the best way to deal with an increasingly dynamic labour market.

The latter is not the only reason why relocation and migrations are so important. On this issue bear in mind the relationships that exist between EU Member States (and their extensive land and sea borders), the countries in Mediterranean Africa, and the countries in sub-Saharan Africa. This raises a fair and justifiable question: what housing initiatives are being adopted by legitimate national, international, and other authorities to produce effective policies and projects to address a widespread problematic situation?

The difficulty inherent in identifying stable housing over a period of time—housing considered to be satisfactory for the inhabitants, the State, and the main economic players (enterprises, land owners, credit institutes, and investment funds)—is more than reflected in the main adjectives used to describe the house. The latter has been defined "proletarian", "cheap", "economic", "working-class", "for all", "minimal", and "small" in order to establish total correspondence between territory and population, between residence and work, and thus render the objective of economic actions productive to the nth degree. The multiple shifts in these terms, backwards and forwards, prove how hard it is to establish a stable theory of society that

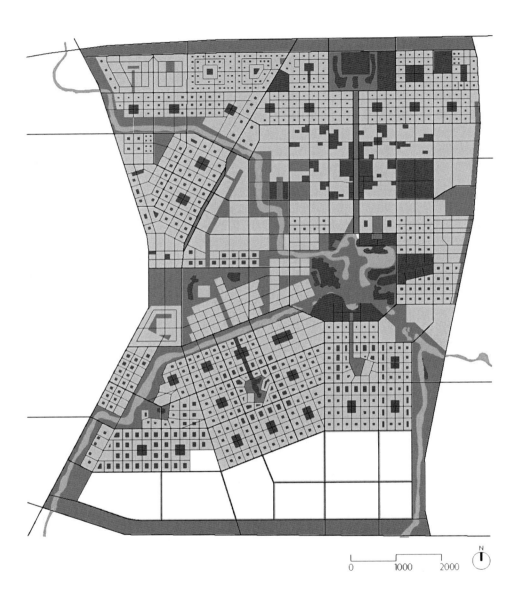

General plan, Kilamba Klaxi, Angola, 2008
(D. Mittner, *New Towns. An Investigation on Urbanism*, Jovis: Berlin, 2018, p. 266)

reflects a concept of what exactly is a house; it is a sort of effective mediacy of the term. The two currently active categories—*affordable* and *social*—are extremely variable; the term affordable is linked to the level of income and assets and varies enormously depending on the territory, but it can also vary even within the same context. As regards the latter term, assigning a "social" value to housing projects involves different elements: from the mix of housing surfaces to the type of assignees, from the presence of shared surfaces to the acknowledgement of new "types of inhabitants" to which the offer of suitable housing should correspond.

Data and players. Housing in cities in West Sub-Saharan and Mediterranean Africa

The problems created by the new poor due to regional differentiation in Europe[11] and the increased divide in income and assets between segments of the population are much worse in Mediterranean Africa, and even more so in Sub-Saharan Africa. These dramatic migrations, either caused by wars or the economy, have forced the European Union (especially in Southern Europe) to adjust its political agenda. Issues include: housing measures for first-line reception[12]; the processual dimension of the housing climax of migrants, ranging from first reception centres to recognition of citizenship; and the uncertain right to adequate housing. It's useful to remember how globalisation is not considered to have homologated the inequalities and imbalances inherited from the past, but instead has enabled systematic relations and an exchange of information, knowledge, assets, persons, and working skills—all elements capable of interacting and introducing innovation.

"Africa is undergoing rapid urbanisation that will result in almost 1.33 billion people living in cities by 2050, compared to

11 Cf. the entire study course by Antonio Tosi on this issue, and in particular his last book *Le case dei poveri. È ancora possibile pensare un welfare abitativo?*, Mimesis: Milan, 2017.

12 Cf. F. Paone and S. Scavino, "Housing and geopolitic Devices of Inclusion. Refugee Settlements", *BDC*, vol. 15, n. 2/2015, pp. 1–15.

Roads

Open Spaces

Buildings

Centralities

Basic urban layers: roads, open spaces, buildings, centralities, Kilamba Klaxi
(D. Mittner, *New Towns. An Investigation on Urbanism*, Jovis: Berlin, 2018, p. 267)

470 million at present. Around 2030, Africa's collective population will become 50 percent urban".[13] Since available aggregate
data regarding the population and housing on the African
continent[14] is inhomogeneous compared to that of the European continent, it's important to focus on macroscopic differences.[15] The way statistics are gathered in North African
countries is influenced by the administrative procedures
introduced by foreign countries during the colonial period, in
particular the French and British. Understandably, official sites
and sources focus on discontinuity with those practices (and
relative data) commonly used up to the sixties when African
states became politically independent. Individual states made
Herculean efforts to solve the demand for housing by making
huge public investments, while collaborating technologically
with western companies working in the area. Although these
efforts were certainly not uniformly implemented from one
country to another, they did mark the advent of a new and
better season compared to the previous period. Nevertheless,
these efforts did not structurally solve the problem.[16]

The season of neoliberalism, characterised by a significant lack
of confidence in the effectiveness of the actions of individual
nation states, was compounded by the quantitative increase in
urbanisation, an increment in the attraction of urban centres,
and globalisation. The ostensibly problematic result was
portrayed differently by available statistical sources. We can
justifiably state that the recent political and economic evolution
in North Africa shows how different the situation is in each

13 R. Keeton and M. Provoost (eds.), *To Build a City in Africa. A History and a
Manual*, International New Town Institute, nai010 publishers: Rotterdam, 2019,
p. 62.
14 The transformation currently underway on the African continent and all
associated opportunities were described in the catalogue of the exhibition
organised by the Milan Triennale in 2014. Cf. B. Albrecht (ed.), *Africa Big
Change Big Chance*, La Triennale di Milano/Editrice Compositori, Milan/
Bologna, 2014.
15 For a rapid comparison regarding the urban form of the 100 major cities on the
African continent, cf.: G. White, M. Pienaar, and B. Serfontein, *Africa Drawn -
One Hundred Cities*, Dom publishers: Berlin, 2015.
16 A summary of changes in dwelling and housing policies in Africa in the
decades after the sixties is documented in: UN-Habitat, *Affordable Land and
Housing in Africa*, chapter "A Brief Historical Snapshot of Housing Policy and
Practice Trends since the 1950s", United Nations Human Settlements
Programme, Nairobi (Kenya), 2011, pp. 4–10.

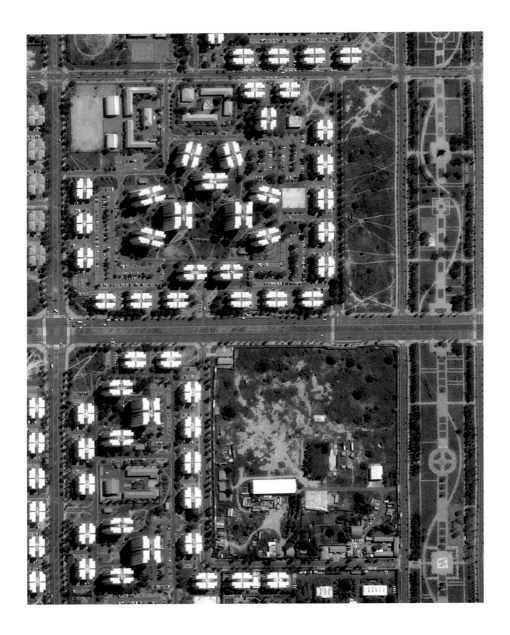

Urban organizational units, Kilamba Klaxi
(D. Mittner, New Towns. An Investigation on Urbanism, Jovis 2018, p. 269)

country, for example in Egypt, Libya, and Tunisia. The 9 million km^2 of desert between North and Sub-Saharan Africa[17] reveals the increasing influence of climate change, making it even more apparent and dramatic; it also modifies the mediating role played by Mediterranean Africa and the nearby Middle East vis-à-vis the movement of populations due to emergencies.

While the population in Europe is ageing rapidly and people's average lifespan is increasing, in Africa the population is still very young: the demographic decrease in Europe corresponds to an increase in Africa where, as in Europe, inhomogeneous regional measures are implemented. Coastal areas have become very attractive (since they are more integrated in international trade dynamics), and so have big urban agglomerations.

Many more data sources exist for Africa compared to Europe and the West, especially the ones provided by big international institutions, primarily the *World Bank* and the *UN Human Settlements Programme*.[18] Data is also provided by other international organisations (such as *SWAC*, with its *Africapolis project*[19]); these organisations focus on specific interests, fields

---

17   For a division of the African continent into geographical-climatic macro differences, cf.: P. Allison (ed.), *Adjaye Africa Architecture. A Photographic Survey of Metropolitan Architecture*, Thames and Hudson: London, 2011.

18   The UN-Habitat Human Settlements Programme, established in 1978, is a United Nations agency; it works in collaboration with local governments and partners in 90 countries to promote sustainable urbanisation and provide adequate shelter for all. Its many institutional activities and publications are online at www.unhabitat.org, accessed on 30 May 2021. One of the strongest mission statements of UN-Habitat is its coordinated, equitable, and international action regarding housing: "Everyone has a fundamental human right to housing, which ensures access to a safe, secure, habitable, and affordable home. UN-Habitat places affordability, sustainability, and inclusiveness of the housing sector at the core of the urbanisation process to ensure access to adequate housing for all. Housing is more than just a roof; it's the opportunity for better lives and a better future."

19   Africapolis.org and the 2021 Update is produced by the Sahel and West Africa Club (SWAC) in collaboration with e-geopolis.org. The Africapolis project started in 2008 with support from the French Development Agency (AFD). SWAC is an independent, international platform. Its Secretariat is hosted at the Organisation for Economic Co-operation and Development (OECD). Its mission is to promote regional policies that will improve the economic and social well-being of people in the Sahel and West Africa. The members are Austria, Belgium, Canada, CILSS, the ECOWAS Commission, the European Union, France, Luxembourg, Norway, the Netherlands, Switzerland, the UEMOA Commission, and the United States.

Housing districts, Kilamba Klaxi

of study, and ongoing actions that at times reciprocally overlap. Other more active players on the African continent, including the *Centre for Affordable Housing Finance in Africa (CAHF)*,[20] should also be included in this list.

For scholars who concentrate on the city and the territory, the neoliberal period provides access to sources where the settlement and housing phenomena, and the economic and financial manner in which they are studied, are so superimposed as to either seem or become synonymous. The framework of available data is enriched and complicated by the co-presence of the most important international financial and political players, as well as organisations that concurrently represent fields of study, the production of statistics, the promotion of investments, and commercial relations. Players also include authoritative urban environment research centres; one such centre is undoubtedly the *Urban Age Project*[21] at the *London School of Economics (LSE)* that is focusing primarily on comparing urban realities worldwide. The School should be credited for having reviewed available worldwide data and produced a visual summary of said data, thus highlighting contemporary global issues and problems.

In a world of new global relationships,[22] data shows (especially as regards West Africa) that the official number of houses that are built—albeit supported by international non-profit cooperatives—will not succeed in producing an increased, stable income among those who are meant to be the beneficiaries of these policies and projects. This scenario reinforces the importance of "microfinance" initiatives that can significantly broaden the project target and produce non-authoritative forms

20   The Centre for Affordable Housing Finance in Africa (CAHF) was established in 2014 in South Africa by a group of economic experts; its aim is to improve the workings of the housing finance markets throughout the African continent and bring information to the marketplace so that stakeholders in the public and private sector can make policy and investment decisions in favour of improved access to affordable housing.

21   One publication that should be mentioned is: R. Burdett and D. Sudjic, *The Endless City*, Phaidon: London/New York, 2007.

22   One of the most obvious changes that has taken place in the last ten years is the massive presence of big economic Chinese players and their ability to design and construct, including the foundation of the new administrative capital of Egypt, near Cairo, and general and railway infrastructures in Ethiopia.

of local development that the population can adopt and augment. This would undermine the juxtaposition between big projects by legitimate authorities (e.g., the foundation of new capitals such as Dodoma and Owerri after independence from major European states) and the enigma of the slums and informal and illegal houses that nevertheless proliferate and are replicated, perpetuating forms of exclusion and inequality. "In this context, I remember that the term informal sector, which inspired the term informal economy, first appeared in studies performed by the ILO in Africa in the seventies; it was used to define all small-scale productive activities which, for one reason or another, could not be linked to the modern sector. Although these activities were very widespread, if not prevalent, the fact they could not be included in the modern sector was enough to relegate them to a residual world: one where you have to struggle to survive. Upon closer examination, the informal settlements actually show that they are not separate realities or even places of exclusion when compared to the other parts of the city; indeed, one can observe forms of interdependence and even intermingling".[23]

It's not surprising that several small urban projects such as the ones proposed as part of the Elemental initiative developed by Alejandro Aravena[24] have achieved worldwide fame in the last decade as part of the imagery of architects, urban designers, and planners. The idea behind the project undermines the dichotomy between a project developed by an intellectual technician (responsible for the artistic shape of the buildings produced by the client's professional staff) and the changes, implementations, and assemblies produced by the inhabitants. This novel discourse involves a new anthropological pact

23 C. Diamantini, "La città nella tela del ragno", https://www.casadellacultura. it/1249/la-citt-agrave-nella-tela-del-ragno, 23 July 2021, accessed on 15 September 2021. Comments about the book by R. Keeton and M. Provoost (eds.), *To Build a City in Africa. A History and a Manual*, International New Town Institute, nai010 publishers: Rotterdam, 2019.
24 Elemental is the name of Alejandro Aravena's studio (with G. Arteaga, J. Cerda, V. Oddó, and D. Torres, Santiago de Chile, 2001) and several initiatives to improve the social conditions of underprivileged populations by implementing experimental projects, especially in the housing sector, and the design of low-cost housing, but also regarding urban planning initiatives or initiatives regarding public space.

between official projects and diffuse, anonymous, and intelligent changes regarding the city. This is certainly not a new topic for houses and the habitat in Africa after the crucial, controversial input by John Turner.[25] Unsurprisingly, he intervened in the early seventies at the start of a new phase in international economics and the advent of the collective awareness of the effects of growth. The specificities of sub-Saharan Africa have been revealed during the five decades when there was an increase in inequalities and illegal and informal habitats, and the five decades of policies and experiments in several continents and countries. In fact, compared to South American and Asian countries, sub-Saharan Africa is less willing to upgrade existing settlements. In the past, these actions and policies were considered to be forms of legitimisation of illegality and projections of these forms into the future, to the detriment of the collective efforts to produce a better, legalised habitat.[26]

A final remark

The most important topics appear to be, and currently are, the most difficult to tackle. In Europe, the Mediterranean, and sub-Saharan Africa, individual states share the same difficulties regarding the implementation of successful housing initiatives and the accentuation of regional differences in each state. In fact, there is no common description and interpretation of this issue. At this moment in time, an increase in the construction and modification of housing units undoubtedly goes a long way to allay the uncertainties regarding mobility and income that are experienced by individuals, families, and social and linguistic groups. There is also a strong, unwavering, and non-negotiable

25 J.C. Turner and R. Fichter (eds.), *Freedom to Build. Dweller Control of the Housing Process*, Macmillan: New York, 1972.

26 Among the main organisations active in this field, *Shelter Afrique* is the only pan-African finance institution to support the development of affordable housing. Established in 1982 with headquarters in Nairobi, Kenya, it is a partnership of 44 African governments, the African Development Bank (AfDB), and the Africa Reinsurance Corporation (Africa-Re). Shelter Afrique builds strategic partnerships and offers a host of products and related services to support affordable housing and commercial real estate. Cf. https://www.shelterafrique.org/en/, accessed on 26 January 2022.

Informal settlement, Yaoundé, 2019

234

focus on the conservation and enhancement of places, on the combination between acknowledgement of natural beauty sites and their biological function, and on anthropic modification, capable of enhancing their significance and fruition for man. This means we must relinquish the idea of immediately exploiting resources—a topic that was the leitmotif of past centuries and the warp and weft of international trade relations.

Having permanently defeated the opposition of other animal species and gained access to every corner of the Earth, the species to which we belong must now face a new and difficult challenge posed by self-containment and a virtuous decline in predatory behaviour and careless transformation of not only the medium- and long-term effects of urbanisation but, more in general, of the actions that affect the planet as a biological system. A new epochal approach would also involve giving up our low-cost logic in all fields, a logic that has contributed, and still contributes, to the worldwide democratisation of what were once oligarchic assets.

The goal is to combine the declared plan of sustainable and resilient development with tangible actions, capable of being systematically implemented in numerous places, and thus produce joint effects. An important step in this direction could be taken by harmonising tax criteria, statistical data, and records regarding the ownership of houses—first and foremost between states in the same macro-region, but above all internationally and globally. There has been one important signal in this direction; it took place recently in July 2020, when the G20 proposed the introduction of the Global Minimum Tax, a sort of minimum common denominator regarding the taxation of big mobile enterprises active across the globe. The fact that it is lower than the minimum tax envisaged in major countries is further proof of the difficulty to contain the big players of international development and growth within a framework of shared rights, capable of providing a constant rather than voluntary contribution to the redistribution of the profits and costs of economic activities.

Moore House entrance, C. Moore, New Haven, 1966

Manuel Carmona, Barbara Pierpaoli

New Haven 1966.
When Howard, Berengaria, and Ethel Blew up Moore House

Charles Moore's project for his house in New Haven belongs to a historical period known as "euphoric". In the field of architecture and design, the "explosive" atmosphere that existed in the sixties in America led to a sort of revolt, primarily at universities, against the serene elegance of the modern movement. A wide range of materials, techniques, and documentary sources began to be reviewed, and there was a rapprochement towards popular art, the vernacular, counterculture, and everyday life. Design tangibly embodied the social and political revolution that was underway: the world witnessed the advent of space missions, peace movements, and the struggle for minority rights.

Much has been written about the house in New Haven, and critics have, at every turn, emphasised its revolutionary, ironic, and intentionally transgressive nature. The facts revolving around the house are part of its history and include numerous ideas and important references for the theory and history of architecture.

The Lord of the Three Towers

In the mid-sixties, Moore moved to New Haven on the east coast of the United States where he bought a small dimly lit house built in the mid-nineteenth century. In 1965, he moved in and decided to restructure it by building three towers full of light and space inside the house. The towers rose through the floors of the house, floating freely in the old building and producing ambiguous effects between the old and the new. Moore was from California and he wasn't used to such cramped spaces, so his idea was to turn the interior into a spacious, light-filled area. In 1966, when restructuring was

J. Soane's House, London
Howard tower, Moore House

complete, the house's exterior remained practically unaltered and gave no indication of its fantastic inner universe. The house was like the geode Moore liked so much: "One image is dear to me, that of the geode, this object rough and awkward on the outside, sheltering a very different interior, welcoming, crystalline and brightly coloured."[1] These statements prompted him to compare it to the Alhambra or the house designed by John Soane, in that the outer surfaces were like a skin or shells which, when open, reveal an intricate, amazing interior.

The word "skin" is often used when referring to Moore's houses; in fact, the one in New Haven is part of a group of eight houses, "like eight successive skins."[2], that Moore built to live in during his prolific life. Moore taught at many universities in the United States, so wherever he went, he opened a new studio and built a new house. Although they were all different, they had a common denominator: part of the house was a strange pleasure area conveying messages. Although he had already experimented with his homes in Orinda (1962) and Sea Ranch (1964), the one in Connecticut is the most interesting, both spatially and conceptually. This is where he developed his theories more intensely and introduced more objects and devices that speak of a certain period and new ways of dwelling.

It's not surprising that his influence as a teacher was at its finest when he was at Yale from 1965 to 1970, a time when student activism was very powerful. The exhibition entitled *Architecture or Revolution: Charles Moore and Yale in the later 1960s* was held at the Yale School of Architecture Gallery in October 2001 in honour of his period as dean. These were subversive, euphoric years for the field of design; the new generation of students—who worked in Moore's or Venturi's studios—felt a sense of participation and commitment not only to the development of new aesthetics, but also to their prede-cessors' concern for rigid planning; they deemed the concep-tual to be sterile and limited. Young architects began to talk

1   C. Moore and G. Allen, *Dimensions. Space, Shape & Scale in Architecture*, Architectural Record Books: New York, 1976, p. 2.
2   C. Maniaque, "Charles Moore: une architecture des sensations", *L'Architecture d'Aujourd'hui*, n. 292, April 1994, p. 47.

Interior

about multisensory experiences and considered emotional and subjective aspects as being crucial to the design process. The spatial qualities began to change and portray meanings such as irony, mystery, ambiguity, contrast, conflict, perversion, or paradox. The three towers Moore built in New Haven—Howard, Berengaria and Ethel—caused an "internal explosion" because they contained all these ingredients. The house in New Haven is a compendium of all these ideas, merging the characteristic features of an age with the quality work of a great architect.

The house that wanted to be transparent

The house in New Haven was indeed transparent, but not like glass or crystal-clear water. Its transparency differed. Moore's effort to achieve visual spaciousness inside the house prompted him to use specific techniques and systems; his aim was to perceptively remove all possible obstacles, almost as if he wanted the house to be internally and ostensibly, even if not literally, transparent. To achieve his goal, Moore used certain techniques similar to the principles Colin Rowe presented in his article "Transparency: Literal and Phenomenal"—in collaboration with Robert Slutzky—published in 1963, a few years before Moore restructured his house.[3] Rowe was a historian and critic, and he was a contemporary of Moore; whenever they met, it was always in a university environment. After studying in London, Rowe won a grant to Yale, where Moore had also been a student. They both also had ties to the University of Architecture in Austin, Texas. Although they had their differences, this did not stop Moore from highlighting Rowe's importance and influence in the teaching of architecture; he considered that some of his books, e.g., *Collage City*[4], should be set books in American schools of architecture. It was in the abovementioned book that Rowe cites Moore as being one of the few whose architecture—spatial and constructive composition—can be defined as the end result of a process more or less equivalent

---

3   C. Rowe and R.Slutski, "Transparency: Literal and Phenomenal", *Perspecta*, vol. 8 (1963), pp. 45–54.
4   C. Rowe and F. Koetter, *Collage City,* MIT Press: Cambridge (MA)/London, 1978.

Berengaria tower, Moore House

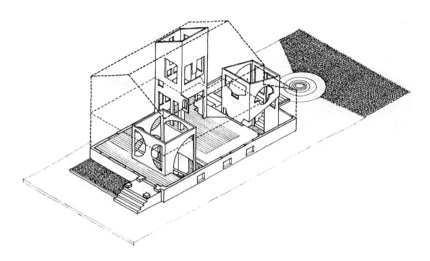

The three towers

to the collage technique: "heterogeneous objects combined with different tools: physical, optical, perceptive". These typical effects of Moore's architecture and, in particular, of the house in New Haven, reflected the ideas of several contemporary artistic movements that considered the individual as part of the creative spatial process. Amongst other things, the architect had been one of the first to introduce phenomenology into architecture in the United States. His explicit fondness for layering, i.e., superimposing several layers of materials and objects, is similar to the definition of Kepes' phenomenological transparency to which Rowe referred when he spoke about a quality inherent in spatial organisation: "Transparency however implies more than an optical characteristic; it implies a broader spatial order. Transparency means a simultaneous perception of different spatial locations. Space not only recedes but fluctuates in a continuous activity".[5]

Simultaneity, interpenetration, superimposition, ambivalence, and space-time are terms that connect the rooms in Moore's house to Rowe's idea of transparency. Apart from the

5   G. Kepes, *Language of Vision,* Paul Theobald and Co.: Chicago, 1969, p. 77.

243

Charles Moore at work in the Howard tower

stratification of the spaces in the house, other mechanisms increased its perceptive dimension: illusionistic effects based on the intentional lighting, or the incorporation of op art elements, supergraphics, trompe l'œil, anamorphisms, etc. Within an apparent "explosive" chaos, Howard, Berengaria, and Ethel created the required transparency thanks to a perfect, calculated organisational system that made it possible to look beyond the towers towards a seemingly endless space.

The towers were made of painted gypsum panels with empty spaces deliberately created in order to form fragments of geometric shapes that encouraged people to look at the recomposition. The arrangement of these shapes in repetitive strata created depth effects. Vertically, the towers visually connected all the floors. Howard, closest to the ground floor entrance, provided a view of the basement and increased the number of perspectives as one entered the house. Views were multiplied and superimposed thanks to the numerous geometric incisions in the walls, providing partial views; perception changed depending on the paths around the towers. Berengaria, the intermediate space, visually connected the other floors and let zenithal sunlight enter through the big skylight. Its walls had holes that looked like "windows"; these silver-painted surfaces resembled the façades of buildings. The fake outer façade effect was accentuated by the reflections created by a strobe light, encouraging one to imagine new perspectives and landscapes. Ethel, the tower closest to the courtyard, flooded the basement and dining room with light, connected the interior to the garden, and generated a constant visual flow from the interior to the exterior and vice versa. So, what could have been considered as a reduction of inhabitable space from the point of view of distribution and construction—because the towers occupied space—created a completely different result: expansion. In addition, the interstitial spaces created around the three towers produced the system which, using steps and corridors, joined the various floors and encouraged peripheral movements and paths. Like Piranesi's architectural fantasies, the ramps and stairs in the house in New Haven rose to dizzying heights.

Ethel tower, Moore House

"Animated" objects

"Objects considered incongruous a decade earlier jostled each other: stained-glass panels, Turkish carpets, Mexican pottery, and nineteenth-century family portraits mingled with industrial lighting equipment, exposed plumbing, a Wurlitzer jukebox, neon sculpture, negative-positive design motifs, mirror tricks, silver mylar, and a host of pop-mod-freak objects, co-existed in Moore's house."[6] His houses were full of all kinds of objects; in actual fact, we could say they were 'chock-a-block', and the house in New Haven was no exception. Howard, Berengaria, and Ethel were built using several layers of gypsum panels, cut to create geometric forms; this generated numerous cavities where Moore placed many of his decorative and personal tools. All the objects, in unison, as if they were on a stage, conveyed and narrated stories of the house, contemporary society, Moore, and space itself. Due to the different scales and contrasts, they provided the rooms with a new dimension, creating a new language—a language of objects, symbols, and meanings—that Moore mastered to perfection.

The entrance and back garden were not to be outdone and this initiated a dialogue between the house's interior and exterior. From the entrance—where the Georgian façade dialogues with a yellow tube sculpture—a path leads into the house and on to the rear courtyard, turned into a golf course with a shooting gallery, between the op art panels used to create the garden fence. "Surrounded on all sides by alien turf, the house develops vistas and dimensions internally. Photographs, drawings, statues, favored objects, and especially toys inhabit the recesses of its layered and interweaving walls at every available scale, peopling the house with recollection and fantasy to enlarge the illusion of the place".[7] As a result, the house reflects some of the principles Moore later established as the basis of his work "buildings should be free to talk"[8], i.e., the language they themselves promote to occupy space. The

6   C. R. Smith, *Supermannerism: New Attitudes in Post-Modern Architecture*, E.P. Dutton: New York, 1977, p. 53.
7   C. Moore, D. Lyndon, and G. Allen, *The Place of House,* University of California Press: Berkeley and Los Angeles, 2000, p. 64.
8   C. Moore, D. Lyndon, and G. Allen, *cit.*

architect created a certain atmosphere, something that corresponded to another of his principles: "The physical spaces that fill and surround the buildings should not be based on a series of abstractions (e.g., Cartesian coordinates) but on the human body and the senses – in the sense that we all have – of what things are".[9]

As mentioned earlier, Moore loved to organise and build space using superimposed layers. Several historians, for example C. Ray Smith, called this "supermannerist" rather than mannerist, because the elements colonising the house's internal spaces also gave the impression of an illusion. The objects created optical effects; these included Berengaria's strobe, Howard's paintings inside paintings, Ethel's brightly coloured circles, the classical columns salvaged from demolitions, baroque furniture, op art works, and neon lights. These objects and their relationships created a changeable system, considered as a mechanism prompting a shift from make-believe to reality, from two-dimensional to three-dimensional space, and from one architectural scale to another. This is where the concept of miniaturisation comes in—another characteristic of Moore's architecture. Miniaturisation is subject to several levels of configuration, in fact the reduction of scale of an object increases the dimension of the space around it. At the same time, the arrangement of small objects is meant to spark metaphorical connotations, similar to those of a miniature city—a resource that makes one reflect on the concept of place inside a house.

A city has entered the house!

Howard, Berengaria, and Ethel gave the house in New Haven a new dimension. The towers expanded the concept of inhabiting, allowing the house to escape its boundaries. The aforementioned perceptions encourage the mind to project one's imagination beyond the house's walls, unexpectedly revealing

9   C. Moore and G. Allen, *Dimensions. Space, Shape & Scale in Architecture,* Architectural Record Books: New York, 1976, p. 2.

other landscapes: "each shaft allows the body to follow the mind's eye (at least to the attic) plunging directly from the entry to the lower floor, twisting around Berengaria to the second-floor bedroom, bath, and sauna, or easing down broad steps toward the garden at the rear with its panoramic vista of the adjacent Holiday Inn, then doubling swiftly back beside Ethel to the protection of the kitchen".[10]

The words Moore uses to describe the paths and visuals available while moving around the house feel more like a description of an urban landscape than the layout of an internal space. It feels as if we are reading the map of a land we are moving in, a map of the dynamic qualities of the site, hence the shifting of the body and, as a result, the temporal dimension. In this case, the time factor is as important as the spatial qualities. The paths described by Moore may ostensibly appear only as functional movements, leading from one room to another, but they primarily convey a new way of conceiving movement as an aesthetic practice—that has nothing to do with the *promenade*. Spatial references are another aspect involving movement. Moore refers to this idea when he writes that "it is significant that a sense of centre is indispensable for the ordering of stimuli and an essential key to the psychic geography of our internal word".[11] In the house in New Haven, psycho-geography seems to fit this definition perfectly, because perceptions are linked to the effect and shape of the rooms and the way in which we move around them.

However, the house doesn't have just one centre, it has three—the towers—and another centre in the courtyard. The house is a space with multiple nuclei; their centres trigger a certain kind of movement between internal worlds full of juxtapositions and discontinuities. As a result, the house is not perceived as a continuous, linear, and orderly space, but rather the opposite: "Our own place, like our lives, is not bound up in one continuous space. Our order is not made in one discrete inside neatly separated from a hostile outside. We lead our lives, more

10   C. Moore, D. Lyndon, and G. Allen, *The Place of House,* University of California Press: Berkeley and Los Angeles, 2000, p. 62.
11   C. Moore, K. Bloomer, and J. Bloomer, *Body, Memory and Architecture,* Yale University Press: New Haven, 1977, p. 39.

Back garden

importantly, in disconnected, discontinuous space".[12] C. Ray Smith uses this citation about Moore in his book, referring to the architect's interest in intermediate places that provide this discontinuity.

A little later, in the seventies, the artist Gordon Matta-Clark also began to be interested in intermediate spaces and a certain ambiguity. After buying minuscule plots of land in New York State—unfit for construction—he stated that "a void exists in negative space that allows elements to be seen as mobile, in a dynamic manner".[13] The geometric incisions in the walls and floors that Matta-Clark made in houses and buildings for his artistic installations provided new experiences thanks to different perspectives and visual and physical paths that fragmented and expanded space, allowing for new interpretations of the context. The same thing happens in the enclosed space of the house in New Haven; the search for the expansion of space takes place thanks to fragmentation, voids, simultaneity, and movement. Agrest had this to say about this issue: "Through the windows of these towers it is possible to see fragments of space or objects, that only rarely appear as complete, thus obtaining visuals that always change based on different contextual relationships."[14] It's interesting to note that although these methods and objectives are present in different contexts—one in the city, the other inside a house—, they have generated images that could be interpreted as similar.

Normally, when we talk about intermediate spaces what springs to mind is an urban, industrial, or agricultural context, not a house's interior. But in Moore's discourse, the idea of the city in relation to a house's internal space is a metaphor that has always been present. The search for new experiences using the idea of place has been indicated by some critics, such as Norberg-Schulz or Jencks, as a modern way of considering domestic space. In houses designed by Moore

12   C. R. Smith, *op. cit.*, p. 235.
13   F. Careri, *Walkscapes. Camminare come pratica estetica*, Einaudi: Turin, 2006, p. 2.
14   D. Agrest, "Portrait d'un artiste. Form Diggers", *L'Architecture d'Aujourd'hui*, n. 184, March–April 1976, p. 56.

Conical Intersect, G. Matta-Clark, Les Halles, Paris, 1975

or MLTW[15], the concept of a house considered as a city—which in some cases they called an "aedicule village"—was always present.

Master of the Universe

Although the three towers were empty, something about them made them special. Not much happened inside, but they were the house's special spaces. Built with plywood and gypsum, they expressed richness and divided up space. For some authors, such as Caroline Maniaque, these tall, narrow structures were an elongated and distorted version of the ciborium, an element that remained part of Moore's architecture throughout his career. It embodied a special desire to generate order; it was a space imbued with meanings, and it created metaphors with other parts of his architecture. This explains why certain spaces in the house were considered more or less "sacred". The main physical and conceptual organisational resource used by Moore and by the MLTW studio in houses built in the sixties and seventies is said to have been inspired by the ciborium, with four columns and a roof, described in 1949 by John Summerson.[16] In this case, the ciborium is considered a symbolic element and metaphor of the centre of the universe enclosed within another space. Moore writes: "In our practice we have held to the belief that houses must be special place within place, separately the centre of the world for their inhabitants, yet carefully related to the larger place in which, they belong (...) the symbolic house, the aedicule, in which, for instance, pharaohs were crowned, and later still, altars or statues of saint were enshrined. In our own work, the aedicule provided a way of accommodating this general need for a symbolic centre in the midst of the specific demands of the household".[17] The central element was made up of four pilasters and a roof, thus gaining a special status and becoming a

---

15   MLTW was an office established in Berkeley, California in 1962 by Charles Moore, Donlyn Lyndon, Richard Whitaker, and William Turnbull.
16   J. Summerson, *Heavenly Mansion and Other Essays on Architecture*, Cresset Press: London, 1949.
17   C. Moore, D. Lyndon, and G. Allen, *op. cit.*, pp. 50–51.

symbolic almost cosmic space; it was so important that the rest of the house was subjugated to a system of levels of importance that went from the exterior to the interior, until it reached its highest level in the towers, emphasising its domesticity and protection. Although traditional ciboria are closed by a roof and open at the sides, and the towers in Moore's house in New Haven had no roof and partly closed sides, they embody the same symbolic function. This system of centres and subsequent stratifications recalls the mechanism of the matryoshka, a house in another house in which the act of inhabiting is preserved like a relic. Some authors consider Moore's ciborium as the architectural embodiment of the concept of spiritual evasion and physical confinement established by Gaston Bachelard in *La Poétique de l'espace*. In it he talks of the happiness of a character in Baudelaire's *Les Paradis artificiels* and equates it to the feeling of protection this person felt in his own home, in other words protected from the winter cold while he read Kant assisted by idealism and opium. This is how Bachelard conveys the idea of "the cottage inside the palace": "Nous avons chacun nos heures de chaumière et nos heures de palais".[18] Bachelard's sentence allows us to discern Moore's idea of inhabiting in the house in New Haven, where the three towers are the metaphor of the cottage and the palace.

Remarks

As mentioned earlier, if the ciborium is the symbolic centre of the house, in New Haven there are several centres. This multi-centrality boosts ambivalence and ambiguity which, unlike the spirit of the modern movement, makes this explosive advent of the Postmodern so extremely representative.[19] There isn't just one viewpoint, but many, an almost endless number of

---

18 "We all have our cottage moments and our palace moments." G. Bachelard, *La poétique de l'espace*, Presses Universitaires de France: Paris, 1961, p. 88.
19 Cf. R. Venturi, *Complexity and Contradiction in Architecture*, Museum of Modern Art: New York, 1966; C. Jencks, *The Language of Post Modern Architecture*, Rizzoli: New York, 1977; J. Otero-Pailos, *Architecture's Historical Turn: Phenomenology and the Rise of the Postmodern*, University of Minnesota Press: Minneapolis, 2010.

viewpoints, just like the experiences transmitted by the three towers; likewise, there is not just one story, but several, and none are definitive. The dichotomies such as centre-suburb, in-out, big-small, etc..., are diluted in New Haven; they are no longer antithetical and may possibly be able to co-exist in the same space-time. The form-function clarity and the univocity of space are concepts that are now no longer important; concepts such as stratification, fragment, disconnection, discontinuity, juxtaposition, make it possible to rediscover the meaning of space and time.[20] These concepts, like the stories revolving around Moore's house, demonstrate that it is a superlative example of a specific moment in the history of inhabiting, one that reflects a changing society. This autobiographical house not only provides several narratives about new ways of living and the search for the creation of feelings within domestic space—an environment which, more often than not, is confined to being functional—it also meticulously examines the trend that made it possible to introduce references and intellectual citations as a design method, a trend that began to be part of normal architectural practice at that time.

20   See also R. Martínez Martínez, "Arquitectura y empatía. Charles W. Moore (1925-1993)", *ZARCH. Journal of interdisciplinary studies in Architecture and Urbanism*, n. 2, 2014, pp. 146–157.

House for the year 2050, G. Rottier, 1965

Antonio di Campli

The Bushy Houses
by Guy Rottier

In a pamphlet printed in 1986 and entitled *L'architecture éphé-
mère et de récupération*[1], the French architect Guy Rottier[2]
described some of his design experiments regarding temporary
and emergency housing. He outlined a new urban planning of
the ephemeral focusing on topics such as recycling, energy
experiments, and the presence of specific urban materials, for
example 'non-reusable' holiday homes or villages to be disman-
tled at the end of the season.

In 1965, Rottier's project for a holiday village, to be burnt after
being used for just one summer, was selected for the *Grand
Prix International d'Urbanisme et Architecture* (1971). In 1966,
he imagined using Renault buses as temporary housing units in
Paris, and in 1967, he developed a hotel project involving buses
stripped of their engines and driver's cab. In 1968, he designed
a cardboard holiday home that was to last three months; its

1   See: J.-C. Daufresne, *Fêtes à Paris au XXe siècle, Architectures éphémères*,
     Pierre Mardaga: Sprimont, 2001, p. 264.
2   Willem Frederik Hendrik 'Guy' Rottier was born in 1922 in Tandjong Morawa in
     Indonesia to Dutch parents; he studied in The Hague where he graduated in
     Engineering, and then at the École des Beaux-Arts in Paris. He worked with Le
     Corbusier from 1947 to 1949, in particular on the design of the Unité
     d'habitation in Marseille. From 1950 to 1957, he collaborated with Jean Prouvé,
     Vladimir Bodiansky, Marcel Lods, and André Sive; in 1958, he opened his own
     office in Nice. In 1965, Rottier became a member of the GIAP (Groupe
     International d'Architecture Prospective, founded by Michel Ragon; the group
     included the architects Guy Rottier, Paul Maymont, Jean-Louis Chanéac, and
     Yona Friedman from France, Walter Jonas and Pascal Haussermann from
     Switzerland, Kenzo Tange and Akira Kurosawa from Japan, Archigram and
     Arthur Quarmby from Britain, Frei Otto from Germany, Mathias Goeritz from
     Mexico, and Manfredi Nicoletti from Italy). He was also a member of other
     groups—GEAM (Groupe d'Etudes de l'Architecture Mobile founded in 1957 by
     Yona Friedman) and COMPLES (Coopération Méditerranéenne pour l'Énergie
     Solaire)—and the international association "Habitat évolutif" together with
     Antti Lovag; from 1996, he was a member of the group of the "Conspiratifs"
     which he helped establish. As an architect and researcher, Rottier chiefly built
     single-family houses (Villa Cardi in Villefranche-sur-Mer in 1967, Arman House
     in Vence in 1968) but also taught at the Faculty of Architecture in Damascus
     (Syria) from 1970 to 1978, and later at the Faculty of Architecture in Rabat
     (Morocco) from 1978 to 1987. He died in 2013.

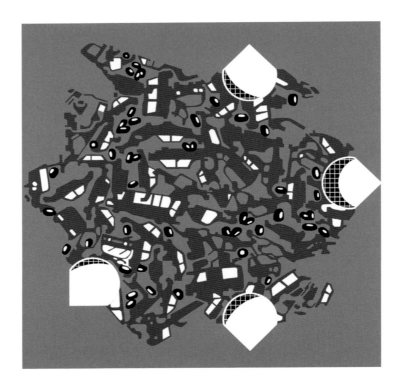

Buried house, car wrecks, G. Rottier, 1965

assembly using cardboard packing sheets (10m × 10m) and a PVC roof took three hours at most. During his research, he established an ensemble of links between the inventive design of new tourist facilities, the relationship between nomads and places, and recycling practices. His experiments on the design of leisure spaces can be regarded as anticipating a discourse on ecological dwelling, considered as an animistic and anarchic coexistence.

L'homme se défixera

In the fifties and sixties, after a period during which Rottier collaborated and exchanged ideas with outstanding scholars like Jean Prouvé and Le Corbusier, his studies focused on two research topics: the exploration of new nomad forms of dwelling, which were just emerging in western societies, and the evolutionary logics of urban space. In the sixties, urban populations in France found relocating had become easier than ever before thanks to new working hours and the fact that more and more people owned a car.[3] In particular, the architectural historian and critic Michel Ragon considered that the budding trend to buy weekend cottages[4] revealed not only a new desire for a nomad life, but also the growing importance of *loisir* that prevailed in western societies in the tertiary era.

3　The issues linked to this new freedom of movement recall several discourses on the relationship between leisure and technology debated in the thirties in France by the *Front Populaire*. For this movement, leisure was a key element in defining a model of life culturally more sophisticated for the middle and lower classes due to the fact they no longer had to do repetitive jobs. In the years that followed, the link between culture, leisure, and technology continued to characterise the discourse about the city. For example, the initiatives to build facilities and *Maisons de la culture* promoted by André Malraux during his time in the Ministry of Culture (1959–1969), for whom urban space was the centre of industrial labour but also of post-industrial leisure. On this issue, see: B. Rigby, *Popular Culture in Modern France,* Routledge: London, 1991.

4　According to Joffre Dumazedier, in the early seventies there were roughly 900,000 holiday homes in France (the figure would have been much higher if informal structures such as underutilised country houses or fishing huts had been included in the calculation). See: J. Dumazedier, *Sociologie empirique du loisir, Critique et contro-critique de la civilisation du loisir*, Éditions du Seuil: Paris, 1974, Engl. trans. *The Sociology of Leisure,* Elsevier: New York, 1974, p. 56.

At a time when expenditure for food was less than half that of consumer goods, the issue of *loisir*,[5] considered as recreation, entertainment, amusement, and cultivation of personal interests and body care, became part of the urban planning discourse in France as well as of the territorial policies that encouraged the construction of tourist facilities and holiday villages in the department of Landes and the Languedoc-Roussillon region, along the shores of the Mediterranean, and in Corsica.[6] As part of these processes, leisure became the key element characterising urban life, as did the increasingly widespread desire to "escape the city".[7] Several French architects enthusiastically observed this trend: they tried to satisfy this sense of spiralling displacement in their projects for new urban infrastructures by proposing very radical settlement solutions and new building types.[8] In post-war discourses on the city, discussions began to focus on the idea of space as movement and dislocation, characterised by concentration and dispersion phenomena.[9]

The words nomadic, labyrinthine, or polyvalent[10] became everyday adjectives to describe a concept of city which, as in

5   On this issue, see: J. Dumazedier, *Vers une civilisation du loisir?* Éditions du Seuil: Paris, 1962.

6   Examples include Jean Balladur's project for the new city of La Grande Motte in Languedoc, designed like a landscape of ziggurats, and the village of Port Grimaud on the Côte d'Azur, designed by François Spoerry, based on the redesign of traditional urban morphologies. All these initiatives, especially the studies by Paul Chemetov, Pierre Riboulet, and Candilis-Josic-Woods, considered housing a core issue. See: J. Dumazedier, "Logement et loisir en 1965", *Cahiers du centre paritaire du logement* n. 167, December 1964/January 1965, pp. 14–17.

7   A literary example of this issue can be found in Christiane Rochefort, *Les petits enfants du siècle,* Grasset: Paris, 1961, in which several families spend their holidays in the country in search of fresh air and pass the time talking about the quality of different models of cars, in particular the Citroen 4CV.

8   On this issue, see: E.B. Bernadac, *La maison de demain*, Robert Laffont: Paris, 1964; V. Willemin, *Maisons mobile*, Éditions alternatives: Paris, 2004.

9   Fascination for the issues regarding nomad dwelling became a key topic in French architectural research, not least thanks to scholars such as Deleuze and Guattari. See, on this issue: J. Berques, C.J.-P. Corbeau, J. Duvignaud, A. Guedez, et al., *Nomades et vagabonds,* Union générale d'éditions: Paris, 1975; G. Deleuze and F. Guattari, *A Thousand Plateaus: Capitalism and Schizophrenia*, University of Minnesota Press: Minneapolis, 1987.

10   In this context, the issue that obsessed the architectural avant-garde was whether or not this state was a condition or rather a remedy or reaction. Was it a process of freedom or mere dislocation? In 1963, Susan Sontag maintained: "Most serious thought in our time struggles with the feeling of homelessness.

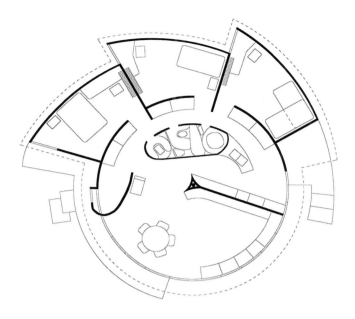

Plastic house, I. Schein, Y. Magnant, 1955

the prefigurations by Constant Nieuwenhuys or the Situationists, is increasingly represented as a ludic space. In these studies, the topic of the shell and the fascination for a concept of individualist, "nested" dwelling, became aesthetically and socially important. The augmented ability to shape materials such as plastic or reinforced concrete facilitated the ideation and production of shells designed using organic morphologies; this is why it was often considered a way to criticise the dominant language of right-angles and modernist orthodoxy. The shell suggests a sense of individual freedom and self-sufficiency; however, this introvert form of dwelling underpins the topic of the network. Although designed as single objects, the modular living devices were often considered part of a more complex, and spatially extended structure.

The felt unreliability of human experience brought about by the inhuman acceleration of historical change has led every sensitive modern mind to the recording of some kind of nausea, of intellectual vertigo. And the only way to cure this spiritual nausea seems to be, at least initially, to exacerbate it." See: S. Sontag, "The Anthropologist as Hero", in: *idem*, *Against Interpretation*, Anchor Books: New York, 1966, p. 69.

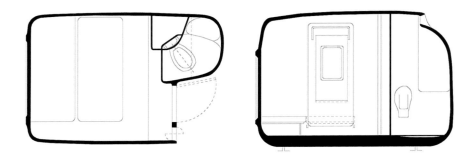

Mobile hotel cabin, I. Schein, Y. Magnant, 1955

Several of the projects by Ionel Schein—one of the first architects to design mobile leisure structures—are excellent examples. In 1955–1956, together with Yves Magnan and René André Coulon, he designed the first residential prototype made completely out of plastic: the *Maison tout en plastique* or *Cabine hôtelière mobile*. It was a cabin designed either as a holiday home or to be used for other purposes, e.g., as a travelling library; it could also be arranged and combined into complex formations. During that period, Paul Maymont worked on modular, transportable, prefab leisure structures with shapes recalling the geometries of crystals; these structures could be hooked onto reticular aerial structures to create houses suspended above the ground.

Three minor utopias

Within this particular operational context in which fascination for technological developments went hand in hand with the prefiguration of new spatial cities flying over existing cities, Guy Rottier[11] was indeed an architect who espoused the widespread counterculture spirit of the sixties; however, he

---

11   In the early fifties, Rottier began to develop several projects involving holiday homes and villages; he also tackled the issue of ecological design, for example in the *Nice Futur* project, developed with Yona Friedman, that was awarded the *Grand Prix d'Urbanisme et d'Architecture* in Cannes in 1970.

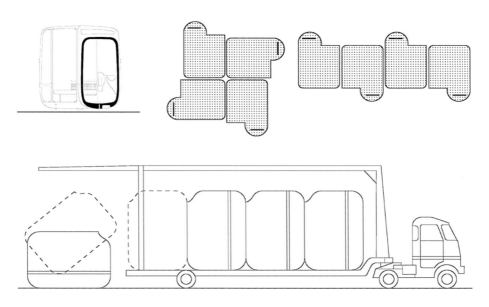

Mobile hotel cabin, I. Schein, Y. Magnant, 1955

stood out as having an ironic approach, primarily focusing on capturing changes in contemporary popular culture, in the media, and in the search for interlacement with artistic experiments.

After working with Le Corbusier in Marseille, Rottier called the research he continued from the fifties onwards an *architecture buissonnière*,[12] a "clandestine" architecture, antagonist of dogmas and the ossified discourses of modernism, marked by the presence of small utopias of waste, debris, inflatable elements, shaped landforms, rolling houses, and shells that move suspended on aerial infrastructures. Using these prefigurations, Rottier specifically tried to renew the imagery of the project of tourist space; he succeeded in configuring some parts of a theory of urban philosophy in which the precariousness of tourist dwelling is a considered, designed, and pursued condition. His efforts bespeak a special concept of mobile

12   The concept of *architecture buissonnière* was presented by Rottier together with that of *école buissonnière,* an expression which in French means "playing truant".

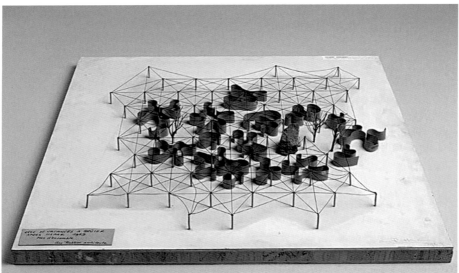

Cardboard holiday village, G. Rottier, 1969

dwelling, very different to that of the continuous movement present in the mobile urbanisations of Soviet disurbanists or the infrastructural fascinations behind Ludwig Hilberseimer's dispersed urban models.

The defining characteristic of Rottier's discourse is not his reference to traditional anti-modernist categories as local or traditional, but more his intention to define forms of inhabiting tourist space based on the construction of non-conflictual relations between temporary inhabitants and local society, rather than based on the passive contemplation or the desire to get the ownership of real estates.

This idea of tourist space could be called "minor", recalling Deleuze discussing Kafka,[13] insofar as it is defined by urban facilities and spaces that are constantly changing and lack fixed, manipulable, "foldable", disposable layouts. Although the habitat is designed according to very precise spatial images, it becomes an ephemeral, 'non-reusable' consumer object, where fascination for mobility does not correspond simply to the search for dislocation strategies, but the search for something that alters the sense of space in a house, turning it into some-thing that evolves.

The use of recycling techniques or ephemeral materials is often associated with situations such as *favelas*, poverty, or underde-velopment. Rottier thought that the architecture of recycling and the ephemeral was best used in the design of leisure spaces, places for temporary activities, or emergency housing. If new nomadism springs from the diffusion of leisure practices and holidays, it's useless to establish forms of tourist dwelling by replicating cheap traditional types in which to dwell for one month a year. Rottier thought it better to develop solutions that do not require fixed configurations or big economic invest-ments; places which, after being used, can return to their original state. This would preserve the importance of free spaces, make it possible to build relatively cheap infrastructure networks, and experiment with unusual materials. Instead of

13   G. Deleuze and F. Guattari, *Kafka. Pour une littérature mineure*, Les Éditions de Minuit: Paris, 1975.

Cardboard holiday village, G. Rottier, 1969

reiterating a lazy, conformist idea of comfort, a better plan is to provide structures that can be modelled; toy architectures which, for one summer season, could trigger new creative and relational skills in their occupants.[14]

Rottier's research on the design of tourist space branched out in three directions; the first explored the topic of the shell and network. His main aim was to define strategies of colonisation and the recovery of residual sites, or sites that were difficult to access. The second explored the recovery of discarded housing materials, for example solid waste and car bodies. In this case, Rottier tried to define design strategies for affordable housing. The third examined the reversibility of tourist sites as a priority issue. All three research fields represent an attempt to define new forms of interaction between tourists, places, and the local community.

His research on the shell and network is visible in two projects: *Maison de vacances volants*, presented at the *Salon des Arts Ménagers* in 1964, and *Maisons de vacances transportées par câbles*. The *Maison de vacances volants* is a plastic mono-coque helicopter that can make unauthorised landings on sites that are difficult to access. The fuel tank under the chassis allows the helicopter to fly up to a distance of 50 to 100 kilome-tres. This residential unit can accommodate two adults and two children; it contains a driver's cab, a double bed, bunk beds, a kitchen, and a shower room. The plastic chassis measures 4.90 m × 2.90 m. In 1965, Rottier proposed a project entitled *Mai-sons de vacances transportées par câbles* or *Cités sur fil*; this solution is well suited to mountainous sites where suspended houses made of canvas and plywood can be shifted using a system of cables arranged like the geometries of a spider's web; the access-parking system is located in the centre. Each cell is foldable and can move independently using a reactor. The spaces Rottier chose for these design experiments were sites where building was unmarketable, difficult, and therefore residual.

---

14   On Rottier's design experimentations see: A. Damani (ed.), *Guy Rottier. Roving Architecture*, Lienart: Paris, 2021. The volume presents an almost exhaustive collection of texts and projects matching the exhibition *Guy Rottier. Free Architecture* (Orléans, Frac Center, 15 October 2021/15 January 2023).

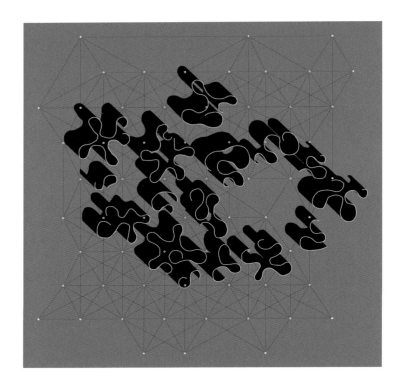

Cardboard holiday village, G. Rottier, 1969

The construction of tourist spaces as a way to recover dis-carded materials is also visible in the 1967 project for a *Village de vacances autobus*, a group of buses refurbished with beds and bathrooms joined by a distribution system. This recovery project involved the city buses sold by the Paris municipality; it was the result of a collaboration with the artist Arman, famous for his *Accumulations*, for whom Rottier designed a house.

From 1965 to 1978, Guy Rottier designed a series of *Maisons enterrées*, including the *Maison enterrée carcasses de voitures* in 1972. These projects were inspired by his study on traditional rammed earth architectures; they involve modelling the earth to create terraces or covering them with other recovered materials. The envelope's skeleton is made up of a concrete pipe system that thermally and acoustically insulates the rooms below.

The following projects illustrate the reversibility of tourist sites: *Maison de vacances en carton*, *Maison en carton à brûler après usage* in 1969, and *Village de vacances en carton*. The first two projects involve two residential facilities designed as a con-sumer product that can be discarded after use. The outer walls are made of folded cardboard to make them stiffer and more resistant. The PVC sheet roof is structurally independent and rests on a system of poles and cables. The burn-after-use cardboard house was designed to last just for the holidays; it was built in a way that allowed the occupants to modify the original structure.

This project evolved into the *Village de vacances en carton*. In this case, the cardboard shelters are freely arranged around the site, creating a compact space based on sharing and exchange in which the objective is to blur the boundary be-tween private and public spaces, a little like what happened in 1969 at Woodstock. The users can change the layout of the village created by a regular pattern of stakes and cables; the residential spaces are positioned inside this pattern based on curvilinear geometries. This particular urban space, without any amenities, lacks the traditional distinction between public and private and is characterised by a special community atmo-sphere in which the users are active players constantly inter-acting with other holidaymakers. The communal bathroom facilities are located next to the village. It is envisaged to last for three months.

Apart from issues linked to ecological problems and the observation of contemporary social phenomena or studies on traditional architectures in countries such as Yemen, Bali, or Morocco, these flying shell projects or projects involving houses made either of cardboard or an accumulated mass of discarded materials are in complete contrast with the formal approach and modernist conformism that was dominant at that time. Rottier was convinced that all materials had to be recovered and was anxious to provide the maximum number of people with cheap holiday homes; he defined a holiday home as a consumer asset to be destroyed after use, thrown away like an empty Coca-Cola bottle.

Tourists are one of the symbolic figures of modernity, but also one of the more opaque. They are both a resource and a problem compared not only to the places where they settle, but also to the inhabitants with whom they interact because they express a desire to appropriate and visually consume the spaces they cross, starting from an ostensibly marginal position. In the tourist space prefigured by Rottier, the tourist does appear to lose this conflictual trait. The unstable, recycled, and "non-reusable" habitat is ideally inhabited by a user for whom holidays do not involve the contemplation of the historical or environmental identity of the sites, but that of dwelling—the modelling of space that requires ongoing redefinition and a dense interaction with other social actors. In the new habitat, tourists actively interact on a predefined structure, modelling the surfaces, creating openings, altering the roofs with plastic sheets taken from the rubbish dump, and installing a system of aerial cables shaped like a spider's web. In this new dimension that does not involve the juxtaposition between insiders and outsiders, building holiday homes or entire settlements using ephemeral and easily manipulated materials becomes impor- tant from an urban and social point of view. It is therefore possible to understand the special radical nature of Rottier's cardboard utopias in which reused lightweight or discarded materials become the core elements of a seemingly ludic design approach, one which in actual fact aims at redefining the idea of tourist and social interactions within a holiday habitat.

Presentiment, prefiguration, nostalgia

In the sixties, many Marxist critics considered leisure spaces simply as places of mere consumption and alienation of the working classes. They did not take into account the transformation of society after Fordism and the ways in which urban spaces—including tourist sites—tended to replace factories as a place they could socialise, exploit, and struggle. Rottier's explicit critique of this approach was to explain how, compared to other sites, tourist spaces illustrate the antagonisms inside our modernity and are therefore a privileged field one can use to study the conflictual nature of the contemporary urban condition. In this respect, he considers leisure spaces similar to what continuous surfaces were for Archizoom in the No-Stop City or the Berlin Wall for Rem Koolhaas. Places that compress the most extraordinary promises of modernity and the most dangerous threats of alienation.

To defuse these threats, Rottier exasperated the bodily, kinaesthetic dimension present in practices involving dwelling in tourist spaces and its more ludic elements by prefiguring architectures that allow the materialisation of forms of full physical interaction with space. This process produces a *surplus*, a form of perception combining senses, images, bodies, and forms: an enjoyment that in the end self-destructs. To obtain this *surplus*, however, space must not be too structured; form, functions, and structure are no longer considered as significant elements of architecture; space must be multifunctional, polymorphous, and unfinished. Rather than pursuing spatial completeness, Rottier examines the value of the incomplete and of reuse since they contain feelings of anticipation, presentiment, prefiguration, and nostalgia.

This focus on precariousness, on what floats produces the dissolution of architecture in a temporary situation established by individuals and groups which are, in turn, ephemeral; once

271

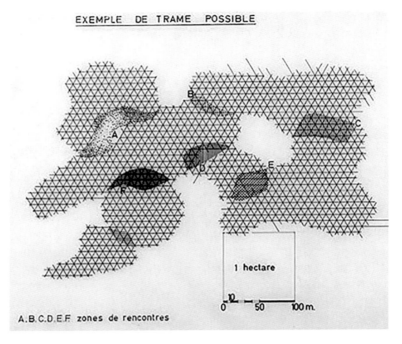

EXEMPLE DE TRAME POSSIBLE

1 hectare

A.B.C.D.E.F zones de rencontres

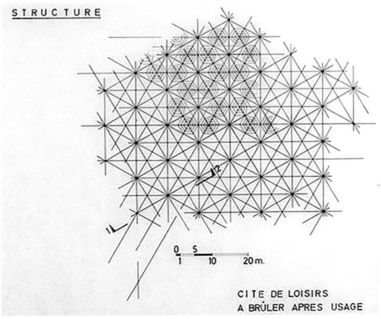

STRUCTURE

CITE DE LOISIRS
A BRÛLER APRES USAGE

Cardboard holiday village, G. Rottier, 1969

again, this topic recalls Constant Nieuwenhuys and his atmospheric *New Babylon*, or Richard Bofill who in the film *Esquizo* (1970) explores the production of space through transversal relationship between bodies, senses, emotions, and concepts.[15] These studies reveal how Rottier's clandestine process recovers not only modernity's discarded materials, but also its popularity, vulgarity, and hedonism. From this point of view, his cardboard houses and villages, his heaps of car bodies or shells suspended on spider's webs are architectures that do not lend themselves to being defined either according to compositional qualities or the respect for standards of equipment and services, but according to the possible interactions provided by the sites and the ways in which they can be transformed and ultimately destroyed.

15   The exasperation of the ludic element and forms of enjoyment of space also represent a criticism Rottier addresses towards the asceticism and minimalism that was rife in bourgeois morality and contemporary modernist aesthetics. This approach was common to numerous groups of French activists in the sixties, as was the students' condemnation of the poverty of everyday life, expressed within the Situationist movement. The critique of asceticism was characteristic primarily of the contemporary Marxist left and, in particular, French counterculture as well as the magazine *Actuel* that published projects by individuals such as Walter Jonas, Haus-Rucker-Co, Moshe Safdie, Hans Hollein, Buckminster Fuller, Ant Farm, and acted as a megaphone for protest groups such as the Dutch Provos and Kabouters, the North American Yippies and Weathermen, or members of the *Vive la révolution* movement who came from the Parisian suburb of La Courneuve and wanted to "enact a revolution in Europe to discover whether one can be happy in La Courneuve". See: VLR, "Peut-on être heureux a La Courneuve?", *Actuel* n. 7, April 1971; Internationale situationniste, Association fédérative générale des étudiants de Strasbourg, *De la misère en milieu étudiant considérée sous ses aspects èconomique, politique, psychologique, sexuel et notamment intellectuel et de quelques moyens pour y remédier,* impr. Weibel: Strasbourg, 1966.

273

Bijlmermeer, Amsterdam, F. Ottenhof with Inbo (A.C. Kromhout, J. Groet, K. Geerts), 1966–1982

Faut-il être (encore) absolument moderne?

There was a period coinciding more or less with the last quarter of the twentieth century when housing had become a marginal topic in the debate amongst architects, at least in countries where demographic dynamics had slowed enormously whilst other issues caught their attention. If you think about it, this is rather hard to believe at a time when the Covid-19 emergency has forced half of the world's population to stay at home[1] and when this domestic horizon is re-incorporating all the others: work—for those lucky enough to work from home—school, free time, virtual sociality, healthcare for the sick and, with hospitals off limits due to the impact of the epidemic, even the extreme moments of birth and death. Certain trends indicating a return to the domestic had already emerged;[2] even if we do not know what direction this current hegemony will take, and what effects it will have, it's reasonable to assume that the crisis will speed up the trend to place the house and its multiple manifestations at the heart of the debate.[3] As a result, its renewed centrality will probably continue to reinforce the attraction of modernist rhetoric, once again present in the conceptualisation of designs and their communication.[4] This revival is logical, because the different

1   A. Sandford, "Coronavirus: Half of humanity now on lockdown as 90 countries call for confinement", *Euronews*, https://www.euronews.com/2020/04/02/coronavirus-in-europe-spain-s-death-toll-hits-10-000-after-record-950-new-deaths-in-24-hou, accessed on 22 February 2022.
2   See, for example, the chapter "Design in 2 Seconds" in B. Colomina and M. Wigley, *Are We Human? Notes on an Archaeology of Design*, Lars Müller: Zurich, 2016, pp. 257 ff.
3   R. Haass, "The Pandemic Will Accelerate History Rather Than Reshape It. Not Every Crisis Is a Turning Point", https://www.foreignaffairs.com/articles/united-states/2020-04-07/pandemic-will-accelerate-history-rather-reshape-it, 7 April 2020, accessed on 22 February 2022.
4   "The more relevant precedent to consider may be not the period following World War II but the period following World War I, an era of declining American involvement and mounting international upheaval", *ibidem*. "Bauhaus is trendy today not only because of the recent anniversary of its founding, but also because of its commitment to style, accessibility and the integration of social thinking into urban design.", I. Klaus, "The Post-Pandemic Urban Future Is

A modified interior, DeFlat Kleiburg, Amsterdam, NL Architects + XVW architectuur, 2013–2016

configuration of the house were the main humus of the modern, i.e., the experimental field in which it developed and
tested its conceptual tools; however, it is also unexpected due
to the numerous, well-known fiascos that experience entailed,
all the more disastrous the more urgent the issues it promised
to answer.[5]

Therefore, Re-hab!

Apart from acknowledging the gradual return of this topic in
recent debate, both within the discipline and beyond its boundaries, the title of this research alludes to another topical issue
of modernism, sadly relevant once again: rehabilitation from a
pathological condition, the return to a previous situation of
"health" as the objective to be achieved.[6] The notion of treat-
ment comes out clear in the increasing prevalence of realist,
performative arguments over aesthetic or representative ones.
The Venice Biennale of Architecture 2020, prophetically
dedicated by curator Hashim Sarkis to a Barthesian *How will we
live together?*, indicates, amongst the issues to be addressed,
all the various dimensions of housing; the aim is to solicit the
imaginative talents of architects regarding "more diversified
and dignified" domestic spaces.[7] So, the "democratic" tension

Already Here", https://www.citylab.com/design/2020/04/coronavirus-urban-planning-cities-architecture-history/609262/, 6 April 2020, accessed on 22 April 2022.

5   A summary of the events surrounding housing and its new centrality is in my book *Housing is back in town. Breve guida all'abitazione collettiva*, LetteraVentidue: Siracusa, 2012. This essay is partly a continuation of its last chapter "Processi recenti", pp. 53 ff.

6   The revival of the modernist narrative and its "sanitary" mission would thus appear to implicate a conservative and consolatory view: "Traditional 'good vs. evil' stories follow a certain pattern: the world starts out as a good place, evil intrudes, good defeats evil, and the world goes back to being a good place. These stories are all about restoring the status quo, so they are implicitly conservative. Real science fiction stories follow a different pattern: the world starts out as a familiar place, a new discovery or invention disrupts everything, and the world is forever changed. These stories show the status quo being overturned, so they are implicitly progressive. (This observation is not original to me; it's something that scholars of science fiction have long noted.)", Halimah Marcus interviewed Ted Chiang, *Ted Chiang Explains the Disaster Novel We All Suddenly Live In*, https://electricliterature.com/ted-chiang-explains-the-disaster-novel-we-all-suddenly-live-in/, 31 March 2020, accessed on 22 February 2022.

7   For the programme of the Venice Biennale 2020, held in 2021 for the pandemic, see https://www.labiennale.org/it/architettura/2021/intervento-di-hashim-sarkis, accessed on 22 February 2022.

Interior

towards housing re-surfaces. The topic is probably the most characteristic and problematic legacy of the modern movement due to the large numbers involved, innovative experiments, political commitment, the enormity of the social issues that were tackled and, above all, the often unbridgeable distance between goals and results.

From the start, and throughout ensuing developments, these goals were often steered by metaphorically and operationally transposing bio-mental-medical-health principles into the architectural and urban field. In fact, when dealing with the living conditions of old cities, the buzz word was *rehabilitation*, achieved by working on the sewer system and applying housing hygiene regulations regarding distances, surfaces, lighting, and aeration on different scales. The elimination of ornamentation (believed to be receptacle of material and moral filth) and the "white" aesthetics associated with the modernist season are a by-product of the same hygienic drive, as was the reorganisation of spaces to embrace and determine new and healthier individual and social behaviour. As recently emphasised by Beatriz Colomina,[8] many avant-garde architectures built between the two world wars were in fact inspired by a hygiene-hospital concept. Rather than the Taylorist production system—called into question by the protagonists of the modern movement—, it was the positive mission of the institutionalisation of the health system and its salvific promise that provided their proposals with a powerful narrative, ambiguously suspended between the inauspicious diagnosis of the metropolitan modernisation disease and its acceleration as therapy. If Le Corbusier debuted by comparing cars, ships, and planes to Greek temples (thus implying the originality of the contemporary as a return to the origins), he very quickly began to refer to biological models: his *machines à habiter* were equipped with "exact respiration". The analytical approach of the "five points of architecture" used a perfect analogy with the human body, divided into skeleton, muscles, and organs.[9] The anthropomorphism of his *Ville Radieuse* (with the business centre in

---

8   B. Colomina, *X-ray Architecture*, Lars Müller Publishers: Zurich, 2019.
9   Le Corbusier, *Précisions sur un état présent de l'architecture et de l'urbanisme*, Crès: Paris, 1930, fig. 111–114.

Interior

the head and the industrial zone in the feet) extended the body-functional metaphor to the urban scale. Of course, the Swiss architect's ideas came after a long series of architectural *reflections* 'in the image and likeness' of man: from Vitruvius' considerations about the proportions of the human body to its interpretations during the Renaissance (Francesco di Giorgio, Vignola), from Villard de Honnecourt to the French manualists (Blondel). However, his anatomical symbology had a more organic and operational goal as regards the "machine" of the city, its social organisation, and its effects on health. In fact, sunlight, space, and green are the explicit protagonists cited on the cover of the book he dedicated to his ideal city[10]: these same parameters characterised the settlement rationale and healing premises of sanatoriums and were to determine the design solutions adopted in the construction of many modern neighbourhoods.

We all know to what extent the functionalist positivism adopted by Le Corbusier—and many of his colleagues—later clashed with reality. The proposed cure was in fact extremely radical ("Il faut tuer la rue corridor"[11]) and in many cases, the hygien-ic-social mechanisms designed by architects to tackle housing problems turned out to be paternalistic illusions, soon rejected by the intended inhabitants. The residual medical narratives, which had already shifted from the collective dimension of bodily hygiene to the fragmented dimension of the mind and individual well-being, were swept away by the hedonist and privacy-oriented wind of the eighties. The disciplinary debate retreated to its own independent field, engaging in an insistent study of its specific languages. Fifty years after the paradig-matic demolition of the Pruitt-Igoe housing project, what is it that induces us to set aside postmodern disenchantment and once again believe in architecture's ability to solve rather than represent problems, to cure ailments rather than ask brilliant questions? Obviously, the growing pressure of new "patholo-gies" is redirecting the debate towards functionalism. It's not

10 Le Corbusier, *La Ville Radieuse. Eléments d'une doctrine d'urbanisme pour l'équipement de la civilisation machiniste*, Éditions de l'Architecture d'Aujourd'hui: Boulogne-sur-Seine, 1935. *Soleil, espace, verdure* are mentioned in the title of the 1964 edition, Editions Vincent, Fréal & Cie: Paris.
11 Le Corbusier, *Précisions, cit.*, fig. 174–178.

only architecture—constitutionally sensitive to usefulness as the ultimate significance of its actions—but also the most diverse forms of art that are searching for extreme legitimisation by lending their voice to ethical and responsible requests directly involved in "repairing" reality or, at the very least, in denouncing the absurdities that create it.

A hundred years ago, the world had just survived a devastating pandemic. Europe had been decimated by a bloody war, and the industrialisation that had increased its destructive potential now focused its overpowering transformative energy on the entire spectrum of social interaction and its multifaceted presence in space and time. Terrible conditions, but only remotely comparable to the issues currently at stake, some of which, despite having been known for quite some time, have now reached a no longer negligible critical mass. The effects of a global population that has almost quadrupled are dramatically clear in the balance between the exploitation of resources and the ability to absorb emissions. The planet is literally feverish, and the globalisation of capitalism after the fall of the Berlin Wall has increased man's impact, fuelling consumption as well as much greater economic inequality. The middle class in affluent countries grows old as it watches its well-being wither inexorably and the social elevator remaining either blocked or inaccessible. Masses of desperate young people, uprooted by wars, economic processes, and climate change, press against Europe's borders. Computer technology and global interconnection have altered production methods, including cultural production, and superimposed the creation of tribal bubbles and increasingly sophisticated manipulative communication on the democratic promise of the dissemination of knowledge. Rather than enhancing an entropic levelling of different identities, the mirror effect sparked by the internet produces exacerbated juxtapositions, which boost today the political divide between city and countryside, between continually evolving individual subjectivity and the resistance associated with deep-rooted community traditions (and its inevitable consequences on housing).

In other words, if the gravity of the situation—in its contingent topicality and long-term perspective—induces us to again believe in the modernist promise of a linear relationship between the identification of needs and the possibility of satisfying them, the complex stratification of problems characterising that promise does nevertheless make the naivety of totalising narratives less exploitable than the ones once inspired by Fordist production or hospital institutionalisation. The latter, with all the possible distinctions concerning the power relations that fuelled them, were nonetheless the engines that drove the perspective of a better future. The prospect of sustainability—now dominant, even during the pandemic—appears instead to be technically conservative, not only in the "circulars" devices it leans on, but also in proposing survival as its main aim.[12] As a result, contemporary design experiments, and the way they are communicated, tend to focus on the pragmatic solution of partial and locally determined aspects, thereby giving up on grasping the big picture. So, although the resurgence of functionalist rhetoric is limited to providing an efficient means of conceptualisation and persuasion, with common ethical-performative components, it is often directed towards divergent objectives based on interpretations of reality that do not coincide and, above all, are more or less consciously unable to propose joint intervention strategies. Unlike the long season of modernity, in which substantial convergence towards generalised models was further corroborated by the quantitative pressure of the urban expansion that took place at that time, the panorama of the contemporary project of residence appears to be fragmented and episodic, especially when it tackles urgent issues. The trends that emerge are the result of reactions to similar conditions rather than actions determined by a common ideology.

The Kalkbreite complex, completed in Zurich in 2014 and designed by Müller Sigrist Architekten, is a particularly important example of this uncertainty and the issues that the residential project is facing in these early years of the new millennium. Its central urban location is heavily influenced by

12   "Sustainability [...] is quintessentially postmodern. And premodern too [...] today's notion of 'sustainability' mostly refers to, and derives from a strategy of survival: legitimate ambition for sure, even in post-historical times. But an ambition without drive, without impetus, and ultimately – by definition – without much of a future.", M. Carpo, "Sustainable?", *Log*, n. 10, 2007, p. 21.

The upper gallery
The former public road on the first floor

infrastructures— a railway link to the west and a tram depot inside the complex; the solution is a functional mix providing roughly 200 jobs (a little less than the number of inhabitants), stratified accessibility, and public and private spaces and uses. Compared to similar projects, its most evident feature are the very diverse living solutions as regards type, distribution, access points, and management. The choice ranges from single rooms (the complex has a sort of guesthouse for visitors) to 'cluster' apartments with several small dwellings located around communal spaces.[13] There are also more traditional apartments with two to five rooms for families of different sizes, some of which are in turn grouped in the Large Household, an association of apartments that share a professional kitchen where food is provided by a chef.[14] To satisfy the temporary requirements of families who are dealing with reunions or separations, the so-called Wohnjoker (relatively spacious rooms but without kitchens) are functionally linked to the apartment that requests them, even if they are not physically connected.[15]

13   "Cluster living is an important part of the overall Kalkbreite concept. It offers residents the possibility to live together and still be able to retire to an individual private room. Each small apartment with bath and kitchen is bigger and more spacious than a pure apartment room and offers sufficient possibilities to retreat. The kitchen-living room shared with nine other small flats is part of a concept that supports community life. The apartments are tailored to the needs of one person, thanks to their compact dimensions (26–45 m²).", https://www.kalkbreite.net/en/kalkbreite/habitation-kalkbreite/clusterapartments/, accessed on 22 February 2022.

14   "The Large Household is an association of apartments that offer an infrastructure for communal evening meals. At the heart of the building is a professional kitchen with paid chefs and equipped with a dining and recreation room. This space serves all connected apartments as an additional large living room and meeting point. From Monday to Friday in the evening a meal is offered to everyone at a moderate price. The residents themselves decide whether they want to join the communal meal (by appointment) or plan their meal individually. The common meal is ecologically advantageous, due food purchases of larger quantities and the shared infrastructure. The large household includes all apartments adjacent to the turquoise staircase (20 apartments), other residents of the house and some external members of the cooperative. The Large Household accounts for around one fifth of all Kalkbreite residents. Tenants of the Large Households have a say in choosing new renters.", https://www.kalkbreite.net/en/kalkbreite/habitation-kalkbreite/large-household/, accessed on 22 February 2022.

15   "A residential joker is a separate room that can be rented in addition to an apartment. The nine residential jokers at Kalkbreite are located at the Badenerstrasse part of the house on the third to the sixth floor accessible from the stairwells. They have built-in bathrooms with shower/WC, but no kitchen. At 27 to 29 m², the rooms are comparatively large. The residential jokers give residence spatial flexibility, allowing them more space on a temporary basis.

The Kalkbreite complex is a "bottom up" initiative promoted by a group of individuals who formed a cooperative and took advantage of the favourable conditions provided by Swiss legislation. The housing units are very different in terms of space and use because they are tailored to the client's specifications. The initiative was implemented thanks to the options provided by a participatory procedure and the socio-economic circumstances of one of the richest countries in the world. It was, however, a very sharp U-turn compared to the functionalist optimisation concept that had been pursued in the past, amongst others, by Alexander Klein, with some earlier experiments in both social housing and free market developments at the turn of the century. One example of the former is the Mirador, designed by MVRDV and Blanca Lleó in the Sanchinarro suburb of Madrid in 2005. For the Dutch office, this represents the realisation of an ongoing research about the typological proliferation of housing units considered part of its own design identity.[16] In fact, Winy Maas and partners debuted in 1991, winning the European competition with their Berlin Voids project—a sort of housing puzzle—that introduced the topic.[17] A similar Tetris-like solution characterises the VM houses by Plot (BIG + JDS), another extensively published project completed in Copenhagen, again in 2005.[18] In this case, it was a commercial initiative; the architects convinced the developer to discard homologation and instead offer a niche market of curious clients a range of solutions diversified as compared to average ones. Whether facilitated or speculative, the purpose of these projects was to explore mutation rather than establish a standard.

The residential jokers are always assigned to a "main flat", where the residents also eat. The residential jokers are rented out for a limited period; the period depends on individual needs and can last anywhere between six months and four years, depending on the situation. Families or flat-sharing communities in which the departure of a member—e.g. young adults—is foreseeable, can apply for a joker when they move in.", https://www.kalkbreite.net/en/kalkbreite/habitation-kalkbreite/residential-joker/, accessed on 22 February 2022.

16   MVRDV's website page introducing the topic of housing emphasises that "instead of creating a collective monoculture, we like to mix people and create buildings for many different inhabitants, being representatives for their city – vertical demo-graphics", https://www.mvrdv.nl/themes/2/housing, accessed on 22 February 2022.

17   https://www.mvrdv.nl/projects/165/berlin-voids, accessed 22 February 2022.

18   http://jdsa.eu/vm/, accessed on 22 February 2022.

The cooperative system, developed primarily in German-speaking countries, provided a favourable environment not only for legal and economic research on diversified types, but also for participation of the clients; this drove spatial experimentation towards unconventional forms of cohabitation that challenged the typical coincidence between family nucleus and housing unit. The goal of the cluster apartments recently explored by this kind of operation[19] is to achieve an efficient use of space, even with today's fragmented social conditions; the plan is to reduce the per capita area and combine the privacy of individual places with accessibility to shared services stratified in a complex topology. Undoubtedly, accommodation shared by individuals, couples, or families is not a new phenomenon. In the twentieth century, there were numerous examples (Soviet *kommunalka,* hippie communes in the American deserts, early twentieth-century reform communities, Warhol's Factory[20], etc.) where the reciprocal interaction of needs, ideologies, cultural trends, and new lifestyles marked the evolution of social interaction in living spaces. In recent years, there has been an increase in these signs, above all as regards numbers. According to a survey by the Pew Research Centre, cohabitation between adults in the United States has visibly increased in the

19   See, for example, the complex built along the Spree in Berlin by Silvia Carpaneto and others in 2013 (it is more than a cohousing project compared to Kalkbreite), https://www.archdaily.com/587590/coop-housing-project-at-the-river-spreefeld-carpaneto-architekten-fatkoehl-architekten-bararchitekten, accessed on 22 February 2022; and Haus A by Duplex Architekten, Zurich, 2015, https://duplex-architekten.swiss/en/projects/more-than-living/?tmpl=desktop, accessed on 22 February 2022.

20   I. Ábalos, "Warhol at the Factory: From Freudo-marxist Communes to the New York Loft", *The Good Life: A Guided Visit to the Houses of Modernity*, Park Books: Zurich, 2017 (2000), outlines the amazing links between the concepts of associated life, triggered in different ways by the ideas proposed by Marx, Freud, and Reich, and the loft of the New York artist. Ábalos highlights how, paradoxically, the most capitalist commune, in the city symbol of capitalism, inhabited by figures fascinated by capitalism, pushed to the limit this anarchic idea of dwelling, destined for an unforeseeable future depending on the instability of the family as an institution and the growing prestige of solitude as an alternative and voluntary style of life. J. Self and Hesselbrand, "Common Stock", in *Home Economics. Five new models for domestic life*, catalogue for Great Britain's pavilion at the Venice Biennale of Architecture, 2016, curated by S. Bose, J. Self, and F. Williams (The Spaces-Real: London, 2016), outlines the strange realisation of communist aspects in advanced capitalism: "The phrase 'sharing economy' neatly grafts communism directly onto capitalism, which is to say, it allows for the appropriation of solidarity and goodwill by neocapitalism", p. 79.

One of the new ground floor apartments

last decade[21] and similar situations are burgeoning in most advanced economies. They are mostly multigenerational families unequivocally driven by the recent subprime crisis, which nevertheless must be considered as part of the complex economic and existential situation at the "end of history". In fact, precariousness is now a long-term prospect that previous generations only experienced when passing from adolescence to adult life; this is due not only to the fact that market capital has become a single model, no longer challenged by the communist alternative, but also by the accelerated demand for digital technologies. Starting a family is increasingly inconceivable and materially impractical due to many factors: the stratospheric costs of accommodation in the metropolises of the financial and creative world; the dissolution of boundaries between work, leisure, and rest (caused by the space-time ubiquity of systems that manipulate and communicate information); and the loss of secure employment. The ensuing focus on the present means that personal identity is increasingly built on doing rather than having: enthusiastic urban professionals and marginal workers of the so-called gig economy are—either by choice or necessity—replacing possession with access to services for mobility, connection, jobs, and also housing.[22]

21 "American adults are increasingly sharing a home with other adults with whom they are not romantically involved. This arrangement, known as 'doubling up' or shared living, gained notice in the wake of the Great Recession, and nearly a decade later, the prevalence of shared living has continued to grow. [...] In 2017, nearly 79 million adults (31.9% of the adult population) lived in a shared household – that is, a household with at least one 'extra adult' who is not the household head, the spouse or unmarried partner of the head, or an 18 to 24-year-old student. In 1995, the earliest year with comparable data, 55 million adults (28.8%) lived in a shared household. In 2004, at the peak of home ownership and before the onset of the home foreclosure crisis, 27.4% of adults shared a household.", R. Fry, "More adults now share their living space, driven in part by parents living with their adult children", https://www.pewresearch.org/fact-tank/2018/01/31/more-adults-now-share-their-living-space-driven-in-part-by-parents-living-with-their-adult-children/, 31 January 2018, accessed on 22 February 2022.

22 "The collapse of work and leisure means our sense of self and identity is defined almost exclusively by what we do, and what others (LinkedIn, Twitter, etc.) say about what we do.", J. Self, "Work on, work on, but you'll always work alone", https://www.architectural-review.com/10002024.article, 1 February 2016, accessed on 22 February 2022. Adherence to this lifestyle by James Scott is less critical. Scott is chief operating officer at The Collective, a start-up dedicated to co-living founded by Reza Merchant. "As we decouple the function of living from the physical location [...], we will move to a model of subscription homes or providing living as a service. [...] I don't have

Co-working and co-living (but also commercial enterprises such as Starbucks or Tinder, the dating app) are just some of the ways in which the market has developed within this scenario. They seem to act as data compression protocols, intensifying use without significantly altering infrastructure: contemporary *Existenzminimum* does not, at least for now, appear to have produced specific expressive modes or important architectural and urban configurations. Capsular densification (often much higher than the generous standards of the Kalkbreite) is essentially adaptive, introvert, and based on a primary element: the bed, intensely individual and mass-produced.[23] Thus ends the modernist parabola of the bachelor, protagonist of Mies' more radical domestic projects, or mutant agent of Koolhaas' Manhattanism, ready to welcome female friends in a Playboy-style penthouse, and now reduced to living a neo-monastic life in individual cells[24]: it appears that the intuition of Le Corbusier, who saw in the Charterhouse of Ema the starting point of his exploration of collective modern living, has found its extreme realisation...

possessions anymore, I'm all about experiences and it's high time that our workspaces and living spaces caught up.", J. Mairs, 'In the future we will all be homeless' says co-living entrepreneur", https://www.dezeen.com/2016/07/15/in-the-future-we-will-all-be-homeless-says-co-living-entrepreneur-the-collective-james-scott-housing/, 15 July 2016, accessed on 22 February 2022.

23   "Young people [...] increasingly share homes built for families, converting all common spaces (living rooms, sometimes even bathrooms) into one-room cells. At such a large scale, this pressure to share spaces with strangers is driving individuals to spend more time alone in their rooms. For the first time ever, in 2014 the bed overtook the sofa as the most used piece of British household furniture, this is because we are watching less TV at the time when it is broadcast, and are spending more time at home watching our screens in bed rather than socialising.", J. Self, *op. cit.* See also B. Colomina, "Pyjama party: what we do in bed", *Architectural Review*, March 2019.

24   I. Ábalos, *op. cit.*, begins his book with a Nietzschean interpretation of Mies' patio house, indeed equipped with only one bed. The multifunctional metropolitan hotel, from the Waldorf Astoria to the Downtown Athletic Club, is the protagonist of the architectural mutation of the skyscraper described by R. Koolhaas, *Delirious New York. A Retroactive Manifesto for Manhattan*, The Monacelli Press: New York, 1978. B. Colomina, "Radical Interiority: Playboy Architecture 1953-1979", supplement to *Volume*, n. 33, 2012, pp. 2–5, outlines the lifestyle promoted by the famous magazine and its relationship with architecture. Jack Self, *op. cit.*, provides a snapshot of the current situation: "If we consider the statistics on how we live today, we seem to be returning to a monastic form of life: little or no sex, no children, one-room apartments in a closed complex, or little cells in a shared house. The architecture of the monastery is today reflected in every dwelling."

Although metropolitan nomadism is growing, it is, however, only one of the social segments of the housing market to which more traditionally stable and independent living situations turn to find solutions. Obviously, they are also faced with the same harsh economic conditions that fuelled shared accommodation. Naked House,[25] a not-for-profit developer located in London, is active in the thick of this crisis; its clients are median- to low-income buyers (in the capital roughly 35,000 pounds or 40,000 euros) who wish to maintain the cost of buying a house below a third of the household income. The main measures to achieve this are legal and economic; they introduce numerous expedients of the cooperative approach adopted in German -speaking countries into the British system, starting with the availability of public land that is rented out on long-term leases and a relationship between individual inhabitants and the other actors active in the process of a specifically established company. Downsizing the "house" to the bare necessities required to be considered as such—a climatised shell and a bathroom—is a crucial move to reduce general construction and financial costs as well as ensure its long-term value (guaranteed by a buyback agreement). These "shell houses" are on offer to buyers as spaces to be finished "cheaply" and adapted to the family's needs over time.

The open strategy used by Elemental in the regeneration of a Chilean shanty town and in other social housing projects thus reappears in one of the sanctuaries of advanced capitalism. Quinta Monroy,[26] built in Iquique in 2003, provided a sort of inhabitable sponge made up of basic units further enlarged by the owners. These self-built infills are permanent appropriations intended to add aesthetic, symbolic, and tangible value (of use and exchange), whereas in London everything takes place inside the envelope as a completely reversible intervention. Nevertheless, this is not only a question of "decorum", albeit unavoidable: the buildings must reflect the approved projects and ensure performance as regards hygiene, structure, energy, systems, acoustics, and safety, for which the

25   https://nakedhouse.org/, accessed on 22 February 2022.
26   https://www.archdaily.com/10775/quinta-monroy-elemental, accessed on 22 February 2022.

The corner entrance

technicians and professionals are personally responsible. Yet, although the margins for DIY in advanced countries are therefore much smaller, they can still provide interesting possibilities. One example is the recovery of one of the surviving sectors in the Bijlmermeer. This extensive district with its hexagonal layout south-west of Amsterdam, built by Dutch architect Fop Ottenhof and others between 1966 and 1982, was completed just as the ideological reasons for its construction were gradually weakening. The estate soon entered a period of rapid decline, with precocious campaigns of demolition and replacement by lower and more appealing building types. De Flat, the solution proposed by NL Architects and XVW architectuur, completed in 2016, ironically acknowledges the architectural and testimonial importance of this Brutalist architecture. After years of projects to bestow individuality on big prefab complexes in European suburbs, they relied on the sublime attractiveness of serial uniformity and fair-faced concrete ("Better than traver- tine!").[27] The project gave individuals ample initiative about how they wanted to complete the interiors (stripped and unfinished: "no kitchen, no shower, no heating, no rooms")[28] and instead focussed on carefully reorganising collective spaces and the interface between the latter and private spaces.

Retrofitting these popular blocks is undoubtedly urgent and able to free up the best architectural energies. Proof comes in the form of the prizes assigned by the EUmiesaward to De Flat in 2017, and, one year later, to Anne Lacaton and Jean-Philippe Vassal for their design in the Grand Parc district of Bordeaux[29] (built in the 1960s and renovated between 2014 and 2017). Unlike the Dutch example, residents were allowed to remain in their homes. A layer of new windows, envelopes, and big

---

27 http://www.nlarchitects.nl/slideshow/201/, slide 30. Regarding the appeal of uniformity: "By many, repetition was perceived as evil. Most attempts to renovate residential slabs in the Bijlmer had focused on differentiation, the objective, presumably, to get rid of the uniformity, to 'humanize' the architecture. But after two decades of individualization, fragmentation, atomization it seemed an attractive idea to actually strengthen unity: Revamp the Whole! It became time to embrace what is already there: to reveal and emphasize the intrinsic beauty, to Sublimize!", *ivi*, slide 27.

28 *Ivi*, slide 20.

29 https://www.lacatonvassal.com/index.php?idp=80, accessed on 22 February 2022.

seamless verandas were added to the rather poor-quality buildings, improving their energy performance and providing the flats with additional spaces. Here, the subtractive solution pursued in Amsterdam turns into an additive approach nevertheless based on an extreme version of modernist seriality, greater availability of space, and in the functional uncertainty that allows appropriation, as a peripheral answer to shared hyper-density and the typological and formal individualisation of metropolitan centres.

Using building optimisation to combine cost management and improved performance once again produces convincing narratives as well as expressive reasons and identity. Topics and theories from the 1960s were successfully re-introduced in new constructions. Superlofts is one example; the initiative by architect Marc Koehler in several Dutch cities began in 2012 and has now been adopted in other European countries. It was intended to update the personalised approach to industrialised building explored by N.J. Habraken[30] when individual freedom and trust in technique not only fuelled structuralist experiments, but also the libertarian utopias of Archigram, Constant, Friedman, and many others. The common trait of those studies was interaction between the continuous transformation of individual life space and long-lasting, generic infrastructure, now reinterpreted in a prefabrication system organised in space and time; the objective is to provide flexible solutions and manage the replacement of building parts depending on their lifespan. This means combining productive control over general costs and quality of the elements; it also and above all involves environmental sustainability and the possibility of taking advantage of subsequent opportunities for performance enhancement and functional adaptation. Rather than envisaging a specific outcome, Koehler's project is like an evolutionary assembly kit that translated neo-modernist pragmatism into a hyper-elastic version and is sold together with a consultancy service about the integrated processes between uses of space and physical conformations. In so doing, the Superlofts system

---

30   See N.J. Habraken, *Supports. An Alternative to Mass Housing*, The Architectural Press: London, 1972. The studies by the Open Building group are based on his theories, https://www.openbuilding.co, accessed on 22 February 2022.

combines several of the contemporary strategies that had emerged up to that point. It began as a cooperative of individuals who joined forces after the subprime crisis and now offers its expertise to both this kind of initiatives and commercial developments. The co-op is also ready to implement participatory bottom-up design processes for both private and collective spaces, and to integrate self-building. It offers different forms of ownership and sharing, and also embraces services and activities not associated with community-managed housing. It uses a "core and shell" approach that provides flexible interior layouts. It proposes apartments ranging from 30 to 200 square metres (also organised in duplexes), embedded in a three-dimensional Tetris. It is ready to include the broadest range of overlap between work, leisure, and the home.

What sort of concept of the city emerges from this albeit partial scenario of contemporary housing? When Marc Koehler proposed his Superlofts, he used the metaphor of the village,[31] offering a sort of representation of the urban in sociological and functional terms, rather than physical and spatial. The built versions and, above all, the way in which the project is promoted, reflect an open system able to adopt different configurations. At the same time, it is introvert, autonomous, adjusted to the local conditions that define its size and general conformation, but also basically uninfluenced by them. Something similar happened in the Kalkbreite, albeit characterised by the specificity of a difficult site. Müller Sigrist's design accepted the block configuration of this part of the city, but reproduced an intensified version of its functional and social complexity and dwelling types. The communal garden in the courtyard on the third floor, above the tram depot, is part of this fractal trend, sucking public space back into the block. If in Zurich the garden rises towards the apartments, in Amsterdam the apartments move towards the green area that physically and ideologically separates the big blocks of the Bijlmermeer. In this case, the elimination of the pedestrian walkway on the first floor—an

---

31   "Having built ten award-winning Superlofts across The Netherlands, we know how to create new kinds of urban communities that act as villages within a city. We understand that creating these communities requires access to shared spaces and resources", https://superlofts.co/our-offer/#home-maker, accessed on 22 February 2022.

The regenerated sector of the elevated subway

outcome of the modernist dogma of separation from the automobile—made it possible to insert bigger and more efficient connections between the two sides of the building and to fill the ground floor (previously occupied by storage) with residences and different activities. This minimum but strategic U-turn nevertheless represents the concept of continuity with the traditional relationship that exists between a building and public space. Something similar is also visible in the much more muscular solution of the Mirador, where the block typology imposed by Sanchinarro's master plan is vertically rotated, turning the inner courtyard into a huge hole half way up the building. Around this empty space, we can again recognise the additive attitude of the village, whose different "buildings" are grouped together and connected by an annular system of pathways. The "urban" nature of these projects— whether pursued operationally or only as a metaphor—is linked to an equivalent and contrary trend towards interiority and self-sufficiency, boosted by research on sustainability. Control over the flows of materials, energy, emissions, and behaviour, common to most sustainable tactics, has gradually extended the isolation between interior and exterior from the scale of the building type to that of its aggregations, from thermo-acoustic aspects to the notion of ensembles organised by concentric topologies, each virtually independent at all levels.

Is this what the pandemic and its consequences will cause to prevail? In the midst of this emergency, we know that shared housing makes social distancing[32] very difficult; it's also natural to assume that lesser urban density could be determined by an

32   "More American adults now share living spaces, but not necessarily the same understandings of orders to stay at home. In late March, a text message appeared on Twitter from a student at Brigham Young University in Salt Lake City. She asked her flatmate not to invite guests to their shared space during the coronavirus epidemic, since her immune system was compromised. 'I'm glad that you are seeking to stay safe,' came the reply, 'however, you can't prevent me from having people over. So you can expect to see Brett over often, and if that's an issue for you, you can stay in your room.' Not surprisingly, this was retweeted everywhere, the Salt Lake City health department weighed in ('Brett could do his part in flattening the curve by visiting virtually,' it scolded) and by the next day #StayHomeBrett was one of the top ten trending hashtags nationally", *Please shower on entry: House-sharers find covid-19 restrictions especially hard to deal with*, https://www.economist.com/united-states/2020/04/11/house-sharers-find-covid-19-restrictions-especially-hard-to-deal-with, 11 April 2020, accessed on 24 February 2022.

acceleration in virtual presence. Then again, human dispersion is particularly expensive in economic and environmental terms; it is also impractical in the short term and potentially damaging in terms of healthcare due to the subsequent and increased reduction of the natural ecosystem (that many indicate as the ultimate cause of the spillover of viruses that are dangerous to our health). What happened during the pandemic—with outbreaks in small towns and several metropolitan areas that unexpectedly but successfully managed the spreading of the contagion—requires that we critically assess the topic of density. Looking back at similar catastrophic events reveals a similarly controversial picture, with important, long-lasting urban alterations (when it was clear how to intervene in order to avoid, for example, the spreading of cholera) and the understandable inertia of rigid, heavy machines, incapable of adjusting with the necessary speed.

According to Colomina, the biggest boost to modernist innovation wasn't the Spanish flu—which was over relatively quickly, despite its devastating impact—but tuberculosis, with its array of diagnostic instruments and therapies. Alvar Aalto, for example, debuted with a historicist style, but changed his approach by designing sanatoriums; he initially participated in a competition for a tuberculosis sanatorium in Kinkomaa[33] and then designed his masterpiece in Paimio. The horizontality of contemporary avant-garde architecture could have been an outcome of a hill condition, both addressed by design and personally experienced.[34] The widespread use of X-rays

33 "Tuberculosis helped make modern architecture modern. It is not that modern architects made modern sanatoriums. Rather, sanatoriums modernized architects. Aalto was a neoclassical architect before his 'conversion to functionalism' in the 1927 competition entry for a tuberculosis sanatorium at Kinkomaa, Finland, an unrealized project of horizontal lines and wide terraces for the cure that anticipates Paimio", B. Colomina, *op. cit.* p. 65.

34 "Aalto himself had been sick at the time of the competition for the building and claimed that having to lie in bed for an extended period of time had been crucial to his understanding of the problem. Architecture always had been conceived for the vertical person, but here was a client permanently in the horizontal", *ibidem.* "Giedion's passing comment that the therapeutic horizontality designed for the convalescents will soon shape all future cities suggests a completely new explanation for the relentless horizontal framing of modern architecture. Could it in fact be related to the horizontality of the occupant, the tuberculosis convalescent lying on the chaise and the psychoanalytic patient on the couch, the paradigmatic clients of modern architecture? As Erich Mendelsohn put it:

(together with the abolition of privacy in hospitals and the therapeutic importance of sunlight) acted as a catalyst for the architecture designed by Mies and many others who explored the topic of transparency. The maestro from Aachen published X-rays in the magazine *G*, and his projects for skyscrapers along Friedrichstrasse, Berlin—from their overall conception to their representation—owe much to the visual trend unlocked by Roentgen's discovery.[35]

We all know now that medical-modernist building strategies (air, light, vegetation, smooth white surfaces...) were totally ineffective to heal tuberculosis, which was ultimately cured by antibiotics. Nevertheless, the medical paranoia produced powerful architectural imagery capable of extending its influence beyond the salvific premises that had inspired it. The spatial measures we are currently discussing to prevent contagion are once again raising the more obsolete and determinist part of modernist medical narrative; it appears that the latter's standards can be updated by simply adding the offset of a metre to the size of the human body on the first pages of the *Neufert*[36] (or by introducing transparent screens...). A cure is more necessary than ever in order to save us in the short term, but also the quality of our social relations—a key aspect in contemporary housing experiments. Even if it were not effective, it would nonetheless be important to trigger experimentation—something that is unavoidable in a discipline that uses the suspension of incredulity as the ultimate tool to design the future.

'Modern man, amidst the flurry of his fast moving life, can find equilibrium only in the free horizontal.' The horizontal itself becomes emblematic of health. Both the horizontal view from the inside and the view of horizontals from the outside induce health. The sanatorium aesthetic was itself medicinal, able to transform any building into a form of therapy", *ivi*, p. 113.

35   "Mies van der Rohe wrote about his work as 'skin and bones' architecture and rendered his project for the Friedrichstrasse Skyscraper of 1919 and his Glass Skyscraper of 1922 as if seen through an X-ray machine. Mies was deeply interested in X-ray images and used them as illustrations in his articles, as in the April 1926 issue of *G*, where the silhouette of the head of a woman appears next to the X-ray of the same head. He even put an image of a bone alongside his glass skyscraper in an issue of the magazine *Merz* to drive the point home", *ivi*, p. 137.

36   The Vitruvian image of the *Homo ad circulum* drawn by Leonardo da Vinci decorates several international editions of the book (originally E. Neufert, *Bauentwurfslehre*, Bauwelt: Berlin, 1938), also known as "the Neufert", still the standard reference for spatial requirements in building design and site planning.

Authors

Elena Bargelli, Full Professor of Private Law at the Department of Political Sciences, University of Pisa.

Manuel Carmona, PhD in Architecture at Polytechnic University of Madrid

Marina Ciampi, Associate Professor of Sociology at the Department of Social Sciences and Economics, Sapienza University of Rome.

Giovanni Corbellini, Full Professor of Architectural Design at the Department of Architecture and Design, Polytechnic of Turin.

Federico Coricelli, PhD in Architecture, History and Project, Polytechnic of Turin, currently teaching at KIT Karlsruhe.

Michele De Lucchi, Full Professor at the Design Faculty of the Polytechnic of Milan and member of the National Academy of San Luca in Rome, has designed architectures all over the world and objects for the most famous European companies.

Antonio di Campli, Assistant Professor of Urban Planning at the Interuniversity Department of Regional and Urban Studies and Planning, Polytechnic of Turin.

Marson Korbi, Postdoc in Architecture, History and Theory at the École Polytechnique Fédérale de Lausanne (EPFL).

Chiara Iacovone, Postdoc Research Fellow at the Interuniversity Department of Regional and Urban Studies and Planning, Polytechnic of Turin.

Dunia Mittner, Associate Professor of Urban Planning at the Department of Civil, Environmental and Architectural Engineering, University of Padua.

Fabrizio Paone, Associate Professor of Urban Planning at the Interuniversity Department of Regional and Urban Studies and Planning, Polytechnic of Turin.

Barbara Pierpaoli, PhD in Architecture, Polytechnic University of Madrid.

Luca Reale, Associate Professor of Architecture at the Department of Architecture and Design, Sapienza University of Rome.

Andrea Ronzino, PhD in Architecture, History and Project, Polytechnic of Turin.

Michela Rosso, Associate Professor of History of Architecture at the Department of Architecture and Design, Polytechnic of Turin.

Sebastiano Roveroni, PhD in Architecture and Urban Design, University of Trieste.

Angelo Sampieri, Associate Professor of Urban Planning at the Interuniversity Department of Regional and Urban Studies and Planning, Polytechnic of Turin.

Anna Maria Paola Toti, Assistant Professor of Sociology at the Department of Social Sciences and Economics, Sapienza University of Rome.

Danilo Trogu, ceramist, diplomate at the Art Institute in Savona, owner of "La casa dell'Arte" in Albisola Capo, Italy, a futurist lab postponed in present time. Among his works are the installations in Euroméditerranée, Marseille, France, and the large abstract compositions in the Italian Space Agency, Rome.

ReHab was possible thanks to the support of the Interuniversity Department of Regional and Urban Studies and Planning (DIST) of the Polytechnic of Turin. The study was launched during the International Seminar *ReHab Housing Strategies* held at the Castle of Valentino (Turin) in December 2019. It has led to the creation of a website, two master degree seminars, numerous essays, and now a book. The authors owe a great deal to what they learned during the international discussions, including the meetings of the European Network for Housing Research (ENHR) held in Uppsala on the topic of *More together, more apart: Migration, densification, segregation* (June 2018), in Athens on the topic of *Housing for the next European social model* (Harokopio University, August 2019), and in Granada, entitled *The House. Domestic Spaces, Forms of Inhabitations* (Congreso Internacional Cultura y Ciudad, organised by Escuela Tecnica Superior de Arquitectura of the University of Granada, January 2019).

We would like to extend our special thanks to those who collaborated in the study, events, and in the publication of this book. In particular the large group of researchers who launched the research programme: Cristina Bianchetti, Grazia Brunetta, Silvia Crivello, Antonio di Campli, Giulia Sonetti, Ianira Vassallo, Elisabetta Bello, Matteo D'Ambros, Sebastiano Roveroni, Quirino Spinelli (Polytechnic of Turin, DIST), Giovanni Corbellini, Michela Rosso, Jacopo Gresleri, Andrea Ronzino (Polytechnic of Turin, DAD), Elena Bargelli (University of Pisa, Department of Political Sciences), Laura Fregolent (IUAV University, Department of Design and Planning in Complex Environments), Luca Reale (Sapienza University of Rome, Department of Architectural and Design). A great thankfulness is due to Bruno Bruchi, who photographed the houses by Danilo Trogu especially for the ReHab project. Our special thanks go to Quirino Spinelli who developed the website and worked with us to organise the seminar; Beatrice Agulli and Maria Pizzorni Altes who helped coordinate the event; Sebastiano Roveroni who contributed to the publication of this book.

Lares and Penates exist in our house, too. The Scientific Committee invoked them when we launched the study and we would very much like to name and thank them. The first is Carlo Olmo; our generation owes so much to him and his teachings—midway between a historical method and philology—regarding architecture and the city. The second is Cristina Bianchetti whose research on the body, space, and housing sparked reflections that led to an uneasy rethink of the spatial fundamentals of modern houses. Finally, Antonio Tosi, the scholar who for five decades paved a truly unique research path focusing on living, inhabitants, and houses; his research contributions are crucial for anyone interested in this subject, not only in Italy.

We would like to dedicate this book to Antonio Tosi

Amsterdam Stadsarchief: 274; Bello A., Casonato L.: 74; Brakkee S. (courtesy of): 278, 280, 284, 292; Cangani D.: 168; Casonato L., Bello A.: 74; Charles Moore Foundation: 243; Ciampi M.: 144, 148, 152, 158; CJ Entertainment, Barunson E&A (movie production), Academy Two (original 2019 distribution): 64, 70; Coricelli F. and Iacovone C.: 130, 138, 142; Daily Mail: 28, 29; Di Campli A.: 261, 262, 263; Dogma: 120; Eurostat: 214, 216; frac-centre.fr: 256, 258, 264, 266, 268, 272; Gardner G.: 238; Hellman L.: 36; Hill J.: 236, 238, 242, 244; HOME Philosophy Real Estate: 134; Iacovone C. and Coricelli F: 130, 138, 142; International Bank for Reconstruction and Development / The World Bank: 218, 220; Jones T. R.: 42; Korbi M.: 122, 124, 125, 126; Martha S.: 230; Martiradonna A.: 76; McCandless C.: 112; McGrath N.: 240, 246, 250; Mittner D.: 224, 226, 228, 234; Petitjean M.: 252; Poelstra S. (courtesy of): 284, 296; RIBA: 28, 32, 34; Riolzi P.: 72; Roveroni S.: 20; Toti A.M.P.: 156, 162, 166; UN Habitat: 218; Van der Burg M. (courtesy of): 288; Van Grunsven J. (courtesy of): 276; Whitechapel Gallery: 18, 24.

The editors have made every effort to secure permission to reproduce the listed illustrations and photographs. We apologize for any inadvert errors or omissions and kindly ask to be notified of any corrections that should be incorporated in any future reprints or editions of this publication.

The general texts "Living", "Inhabitants" and "Houses" that introduce the sections of the book were written by Fabrizio Paone and Angelo Sampieri.
The statements accompanying the two visual essays were taken from the writings of Danilo Trogu, and Michele de Lucchi, and were selected together with the authors.
The text on page 101 about the houses by Danilo Trogu was written by Fabrizio Paone; the one on page 201 about the houses by Michele De Lucchi was written by Angelo Sampieri.
The first and second sections of the chapter "Living in L'Aquila after the 2009 Earthquake. Forms and Practices of Space" were written by Marina Ciampi; the third and fourth sections were written by Anna Maria Paola Toti.

Imprint

© 2022 by jovis Verlag GmbH
Texts by kind permission of the authors.
Pictures by kind permission of the photographers/holders of the picture rights.

Cover image: *The Dream of St. Ursula* by Vittore Carpaccio, 1495,
Gallerie dell'Accademia di Venezia

Translation: Erika Geraldine Young
Copy editing: Bianca Murphy
Layout and setting: Sebastiano Roveroni
Lithography: Bild1Druck, Berlin
Printed in the European Union.

Bibliographic information published by the Deutsche Nationalbibliothek
The Deutsche Nationalbibliothek lists this publication in the Deutsche National-
bibliografie; detailed bibliographic data are available on the Internet at http://
dnb.d-nb.de

jovis Verlag GmbH
Lützowstraße 33
10785 Berlin

www.jovis.de

jovis books are available worldwide in select bookstores. Please contact your
nearest bookseller or visit www.jovis.de for information concerning your local
distribution.

ISBN 978-3-86859-716-5 (Softcover)

ISBN 978-3-86859-789-9 (PDF)